*Henry James and the
Suspense of Masculinity*

Henry James and the Suspense of Masculinity

LELAND S. PERSON

PENN

University of Pennsylvania Press

Philadelphia

Copyright © 2003 University of Pennsylvania Press
All rights reserved
Printed in the United States of America on acid-free paper

10 9 8 7 6 5 4 3 2 1

Published by
University of Pennsylvania Press
Philadelphia, Pennsylvania 19104-4011

Library of Congress Cataloging-in-Publication Data

Person, Leland, S.
  Henry James and the suspense of masculinity / Leland S. Person.
    p. cm.
  ISBN 0-8122-3725-0 (cloth : alk. paper)
  Includes bibliographical references and index.
  1. James, Henry, 1843–1916—Knowledge—Psychology. 2. James, Henry, 1843–1916—
Characters—Men. 3. Psychological fiction, American—History and criticism.
4. Homosexuality and literature—United States. 5. Masculinity in literature. 6. Sex role in
literature. 6. Men in literature. 8. Sex in literature. I. Title.
PS2127.P8 P47   2003
813'.4 21   2003040218

For Pam and Spencer

Contents

Introduction: Henry James and the Plural Terms of Masculinity   1

1. Configuring Male Desire and Identity in *Roderick Hudson*   39

2. Nursing the Thunderbolt of Manhood in *The American*   65

3. Sheathing the Sword of Gentle Manhood in *The Portrait of a Lady*   86

4. Reconstructing Masculinity in *The Bostonians*   105

5. Deploying Homo-Aesthetic Desire in the Tales of Writers and Artists   124

6. The Paradox of Masochistic Manhood in *The Golden Bowl*   149

Notes   175

Works Cited   193

Index   203

Acknowledgments   207

Introduction: Henry James and the Plural Terms of Masculinity

> *Here I sit: impatient to work: only wanting to concentrate myself, to keep at it: full of ideas, full of ambition, full of capacity—as I believe. Sometimes the discouragements, however, seem greater than anything else—the delays, the interruptions, the* éparpillement, *etc. But courage, courage, and forward, forward. If one must generalize, that is the only generalization. There is an immensity to be done, and, without vain presumption—I shall at the worst do a part of it. But all one's manhood must be at one's side.*
>
> —James, Complete Notebooks 44

In the unfinished story "Hugh Merrow," Henry James recounts a conversation between the eponymous artist and a young couple, the Archdeans, who want him to paint the portrait of a child. A surrogate rather than a replica, the portrait would serve as the child the husband and wife have been unable to conceive. Although in his first note for the story James had imagined the couple requesting that the child be a girl (*Complete Notebooks* 192), in the version James eventually wrote they ask the artist to make the decision himself, because they disagree about whether they want a boy or a girl. James did not finish the story, but it nevertheless reaches a logical conclusion, ending at the moment when Merrow agrees to paint the portrait. What remains open—in a state of suspense—is the question of the child's gender.

As a story that ends with the creative process about to begin and the artist suspended, as it were, between genders, "Hugh Merrow" offers an appropriate point of entry for a study of James's representation of masculinity and male subjectivity. As Leon Edel notes, James was working on the story, which he called "The Beautiful Child," during the summer of 1902, at virtually the same time that *The Ambassadors* was moving toward publication and he was writing a series of essays on French novelists (Edel, *Master* 128–29). Connections among these various works, especially as they foreground questions about masculinity, can be illuminated in the context of James's concerns at the turn of the century, but they can also highlight the vexed question of masculinity that he pursued from the beginning to the end of his career. In reviewing his responses to French novelists, James was trying not only to create and promote a public authorial self but also to research his private self. Through the intimate process of his reading, he recognized, these writers had inscribed themselves in him. As he writes at the beginning of his 1902 essay on Balzac,

> these particular agents exist for us, with the lapse of time, as the substance itself of knowledge: they have been intellectually so swallowed, digested and assimilated that we take their general use and suggestion for granted, cease to be aware of them because they have passed out of sight. But they have passed out of sight simply by having passed into our lives. They have become a part of our personal history, a part of ourselves, very often, so far as we may have succeeded in best expressing ourselves. (90)

In his essays on the French novelists James repeatedly measured his own "best" writing against the standard offered by such male writers as Flaubert, Zola, and especially Balzac, whom he considered the "father of us all" ("Lesson of Balzac" 120). George Sand, however, forced him to test himself against a much more enigmatic model of gender. Reading and writing about Sand compelled James to reexamine gender questions he had swallowed, digested and assimilated—to bring to the surface of his discourse a complicated gender identity, as well as complex questions about sexual desires, that had passed "out of sight" and *into* his own life.

In James's late work, Leo Bersani argues, there is an insistence that "fictional invention" actually "*constitutes the self.*" Although James's primary subject is freedom, the novels

> dramatize the difficulties of living by improvisation: the incompatibilities among different ways of composing life, the absence of determined values by which to discriminate morally among various compositions, the need to develop persuasive strategies capable of imposing personal ingenuities on the life of a community, and finally, the nostalgia for an enslaving truth which would rescue us from the strenuous responsibilities of inventive freedom. (132)

Coincidentally, the quality that most captivated James in Sand's writing was her power of improvisation—the "force of her ability to act herself out" (Review of *George Sand* 783). She was an "*improvisatrice,* raised to a very high power," he maintained ("Letter from Paris" 705)—indeed, "the great *improvisatrice* of literature" ("George Sand," *Galaxy* 712). What Bersani calls the strenuous responsibilities of inventive freedom has special relevance for James's view of Sand, for the improvisational freedom that James marked in her writing confused him in much the same way that the Archdeans' demands confused Hugh Merrow. As a woman who impersonated a man and was often taken for one, she suggested the possibility that gender and sexuality are fluid—in suspense—subject not only to deconstruction but also to improvisation. She demonstrated the ease of living by improvisation—most compellingly, the ease of reconstructing one's gender. That improvisational ability, however, makes James anxious about "swallowing" her or, having swallowed her, confronting the self that he has improvised and succeeded in best expressing.

In his preface to volume 12 of the New York Edition James explores the attractions and dangers of "improvisation" in one of his notoriously extended metaphors. "Nothing is so easy as improvisation," he remarks, "the running on and on of invention; it is sadly compromised, however, from the moment its stream breaks bounds and gets into flood" (*Art of the Novel* 171–72). The metaphor in this iteration bears no gender inflection, but the passage articulates a double-edged attitude toward improvisation that can help us appreciate those instances when James does experiment with gender and sexual improvisation. "To improvise with extreme freedom and yet at the same time without the possibility of ravage, without the hint of a flood," he cautions himself; "to keep the stream, in a word, on something like ideal terms with itself; that was here my definite business. The thing was to aim at absolute singleness, clearness and roundness, and yet to depend on an imagination working freely, working (call it) with extravagance; by which law it wouldn't be thinkable except as free and wouldn't be amusing except as controlled" (172). The tensions between free play and control, the danger that play will exceed control and "flood" or "ravage" the improviser, register obviously enough. James wants to give his imagination free rein, to let it "work" with "extravagance." Not every reader will construe James's language in gendered or sexual terms—forging connections between his writerly imagination, so intensely placed on display, and his efforts to construct a male identity as a writer. James credited George Sand with extraordinary powers of "improvisation," however, and the issues she raised for him as both a writer and a man provide a touchstone for a gendered interpretation of a passage in which he feels his way toward an improvisational power of his own. Whatever the attractions of improvisation—the freedom and extravagance—James emphasizes the need for control. He worries most about being ravaged and flooded—presumably by his own imagination, which bursts its bounds and subjects him to improvisational freedom that threatens his very sense of identity. That fear of ravage, experienced as a loss of self-control, is precisely what Sand portended for James: a gendered and sexual identity, transgendered and transsexualized, improvised past any point of control.

Although James's fascination with Sand reached a climax during his late period, his interest in her and in questions she raised spanned his career. Those questions appear as early as 1877, with the publication of both his *Galaxy* magazine article "George Sand" and his novel *The American*, in which the hero, Christopher Newman, plays a "new man" who rejects a cutthroat business ethos in favor of self-improvement and feminization in France. In *Notes of a Son and Brother* James fondly recalled that the "sense of the salmon-coloured distinctive of Madame Sand was even to come back to me long years after" (*Autobiography* 404). While James notes something "very masculine" in Sand's "genius," his "final impression of her" is that "she is a woman and a Frenchwoman," and women, he says, "do not value the truth for its own sake, but only for some personal use they make of it" ("George Sand" 712). He not only establishes binary terms (personal-impersonal) for his evolving aesthetic, but also aligns those terms with gender. Yet, despite her personal use of truth (especially the "truth" of her erotic adventures), Sand was "very masculine." James was a man who clearly valued truth for its own sake, but since Sand had already appropriated the very masculine for herself as a woman and as a writer, what of the masculine was left for him? By opening up masculinity to women, Sand obviously complicated it for a man such as James, either by suggesting that femininity was similarly open to men or by simply leaving men suspended, like Hugh Merrow, between genders, neither masculine nor feminine. On the one hand, his later essays make clear, James felt that Sand's example (as the more "masculine" writer) robbed him of his masculinity and even feminized him. On the other hand, Sand forced him to suspend his idea of the masculine: to disassociate "masculine" from "male" and thus from himself—in other words, to interrogate a monolithic masculinity and to accept the possibility of a plurality of masculinities from which he might continually improvise his own. Writing with "all one's manhood" at "one's side" becomes a double-edged sword for James—suggesting a splitting of manhood from James's writing self that enables improvisational freedom from conventional gender constructs but also the possibility of ending up in a no man's land of no manly identity at all.

Feminist criticism of the 1970s and 1980s found James an ambiguous figure, partly because so many of his fictions feature female protagonists whose stories seem rendered from their own points of view. James's attitude toward those characters, of course, could be and was construed negatively, as well as positively. Nan Bauer Maglin scored James for the "disgust and mockery" he felt toward "independent women, the women's movement, and women in general" (219). Sandra Gilbert and Susan Gubar held him up as one of many "embattled" turn-of-the-century males who "struck out against the women whom they saw as both the sources and the witnesses of their emasculation" (36).[1] In contrast, Judith Fetterley praised him for his "ability to place himself on the side of women and in line with their point of view" (116), and John Carlos Rowe cited his "uncanny ability to represent the complex psychologies of women" (*Theo-

retical 90). Joyce W. Warren congratulated him for his "detachment" from American "individualism" and credited him with an ability to create women who are "real persons" (244). Elizabeth Allen added that James's women are not simply "signs for an observant consciousness," but subjects "mystifying and controlling the signifying process" (10). Carren Kaston even wrote to "reclaim James from currently hostile feminist criticism," praising him for his "profound sensitivity to what it was and very often still is like to be a woman" (40).

When biographers and critics turned to questions about James's own gender and sexuality, however, they usually found him lacking. Leon Edel concluded that he suffered from a confused, weak masculinity and "troubled sexuality" (*Henry James* 87). Richard Hall termed him the "golden capon of world literature" and an "old-fashioned masturbating Victorian gentleman who led a narcissistic sexual life" (49, 51). Georges-Michel Sarotte called him "passive and feminine," a "prototypical 'sissy'" (198), while Alfred Habegger considered him a "boy who could not become a man" (*Gender* 256). William Veeder even situated James in an unusual position in a "bizarre version of Freud's family romance" as a feminine orphan ("Feminine Orphan" 20).[2] Perhaps it need no longer be pointed out the implicit biases of these accounts—in favor of a very limited notion of manhood and masculinity that, to be sure, these critics share with many people in the nineteenth century. That limited definition, for example, precludes being both a sissy and a man or, more complexly, experimenting with the many configurations or constructs of manhood that recent men's studies scholars have noted. That is not to say that Henry James found his way easily to nontraditional constructions of gender and sexuality. In fact, James's characterization of himself in gendered terms often warrants such critical disparagement—at least as he constructs, or reconstructs, himself in his autobiographical writings. James plays the weak younger brother, particularly in relation to William, and he emphasizes his failure to measure up to his father's ideals of manhood and achievement. "I never dreamed of competing—a business having in it at the best, for my temper, if not for my total failure of temper, a displeasing ferocity" (*Autobiography* 101). Recalling William's attempts to state the case for an artistic career, James recalls that the "'career of art' has again and again been deprecated and denounced, on the lips of anxiety or authority, as a departure from the career of business, of industry and respectability, the so-called regular life" (268). Even though William seems an early ally, however, James compares himself invidiously to his brother. Had William pursued a "career of art," he implies, he would have done so in a manlier fashion. "'I play with boys who curse and swear!'" he famously recalls his brother as bragging. "I had sadly to recognize that I didn't," James himself confesses, "that I couldn't pretend to have come to that yet" (147). In front of his cousins, he remembers, he couldn't help "feeling that as a boy I showed more poorly than girls" (217).[3]

Taken together, these critical and self-critical assessments paint a portrait of James as an artist whose gender identification is confused and contradictory. Most of these assessments—including James's own—work a variation on the nineteenth-century model of inversion and depend upon some form of binarism (male-female, masculine-feminine, normal-inverted, heterosexual-homosexual) with James either assigned one position (from which to be "embattled" with the other), or considered the battleground between the two. They also depend on some notion of normative male identity from which James, even to his own perception, can only deviate. James, in short, fails to measure up. Kaja Silverman concludes that, despite the "ostensible gender of the biographical Henry James, the author 'inside' his texts is never unequivocally male; situated at a complex intersection of the negative and positive Oedipus complexes, that author is definitively foreclosed from the scene of passion except through identifications which challenge the binarisms of sexual difference" (180). Silverman helps to open up the question of gender identification in James's writing, while separating that question from James's biographical selfhood, but her psychoanalytic approach to the question seems too limiting because it does not account for the playfulness and slipperiness—the verbal performance—of James's language.[4] In fact, the multiple characterizations of James's manliness or lack of manliness suggest that the gender and sexuality to be inferred from his writing are less singular than plural, that his writing is not simply the site of colliding gender monoliths. Indeed, I argue that establishing James's gender and sexual identity is less important than attending to his own interrogation of gender and sexuality.

H. G. Dwight's assertion in 1907 that James was a "woman's writer; no man was able to read him" (438), while intended to signify James's effeminacy, may also suggest the way James unsettled male readers by destabilizing conventional nineteenth-century constructs of male subjectivity. David Halperin notes that the "conceptual isolation of sexuality per se from questions of masculinity and femininity made possible a new taxonomy of sexual behaviors and psychologies based entirely on the anatomical sex of the persons engaged in a sexual act (same sex versus different sex)." The result was that "a number of distinctions that had traditionally operated within earlier discourses pertaining to same-sex sexual contacts and that had radically differentiated active from passive sexual partners, normal from abnormal (or conventional from unconventional) sexual roles, masculine from feminine styles, and pederasty from lesbianism: all such behaviors were now to be classed alike and placed under the same heading" (39). Writing during this period of transition, James illustrates the ambiguities and confusions—the multivalence—of gender and sexuality, and his fiction it seems to me conducts a series of experiments in gender/sexual construction and deconstruction. Repeatedly, James demonstrates the instability of gender identities, largely through what I am tempted to call a game of musical subject positions, in which male characters are redefined—re-identified—in relation to "other," male and female, characters. Triangulating and even quadrangulating male characters such as Rowland Mallet and Prince Amerigo (the bookends, so to speak, in the gallery whose portraits concern me here), James destabilizes male identity by pluralizing male subjectivity.

Within his own person James may have felt insecure in his gender and sexual identification, but as a writer I find him playful and experimental. Recalling the "flowers of perverse appreciation" that he gathered during his brief sojourn as a law student at Harvard, for example, James remembers his preoccupation, as a budding young writer, with the "degree and exact shade to which the blest figures in the School array, each quite for himself, might settle and fix the weight, the interest, the function, as it were, of his Americanism" (*Autobiography* 449). As he tries to settle questions of American male typology—what he campily calls "pearls of differentiation"—he remains coyly unaware, "not dreaming of the stiff law by which, on the whole American ground, division of *type*, in the light of opposition and contrast, was more and more to break down for me and fail" (449–50). This failure of American men to settle themselves neatly into types provides James an opportunity to play with his "pearls" according to the stiff law of his own imagination. The "young appearances" could be "pleasingly, or at least robustly homogeneous," he notes, "and yet, for livelier appeal to fancy, flower here and there into special cases of elegant deviation—'sports,' of exotic complexion, one enjoyed denominating these (or would have enjoyed had the happy figure then flourished) thrown off from the thick stem that was rooted under our feet" (450). This remarkable extended metaphor suggests James's campy playfulness, as well as his awareness of contemporaneous gender and sexual theorizing—and its limitations. He feels some constraints on his imaginative play because some "happy figures" are not yet flourishing, but he seems much more interested than many of his readers in keeping the questions of gender and sexuality open to "elegant deviation"—that is, to improvisation, or performance—especially to deviations that "flower" from the "thick stem" of his own fanciful imagination. He adroitly mixes gendered metaphors in this passage, conflating flower and phallic imagery. The "stiff law" he dimly perceives causes American men to break down—that is, their types to break down, and thus to flower for him. American men, especially those who seem most homogeneously robust, in effect become "pansies."

Masculine homogeneity converts rather easily—almost homophonically—into homosexuality. But the power in this passage is James's own—the phallic power of his imagination to convert robust young men into flowers. "Everything's coming up roses," in the words of the old song. James enjoys the sport of playing with the "sports."

Michel Foucault considers the nineteenth and twentieth centuries "the age of multiplication," featuring a "dispersion of sexualities, a strengthening of their disparate forms, a multiple implantation of 'perversions,'" and he concludes that our "epoch has initiated sexual heterogeneities" (37). Although Judith Butler points out some of the contradictions and unresolved tensions in Foucault's theory of sexuality, her performative theory of gender identity represents the best attempt during the past decade to destabilize gender categories, although applying her theory to men carries certain risks.[5] Calling gender a "kind of persistent impersonation that passes as the real" (vii), Butler's feminist project works to destabilize "woman" and "women" as useful categories. "Rather than a stable signifier that commands the assent of those whom it purports to describe and represent, *women,* even in the plural, has become a troublesome term, a site of contest, a cause for anxiety" (3). Butler destabilizes gender by disassociating it from sexuality, as well as from sexual practice and from desire. "Intelligible genders are those which in some sense institute and maintain relations of coherence and continuity among, sex, gender, sexual practice, and desire" (17). These four quadrants suggest the variables that any identification of sex or gender or sexual practice or desire must take into account. That is, sexual practice is not necessarily a function of sexual or gender identity or even of desire. Gender and sexual identities can be consistent or inconsistent with one another. Gender, Butler asserts, "is always a doing, though not a doing by a subject who might be said to preexist the deed" (25). I want to try to avoid the sort of psychic determinism that even this transgressive paradigm entails and to keep sex, gender, and desire in play as cross-relational categories. Butler's feminist project does not translate seamlessly to a study of masculinity, but her suggestive terms seem appropriate to the queer subject, Henry James. Although he does not refer to Butler or apply the idea comprehensively to questions of gender and sexuality, Ross Posnock advances a useful theory of theatricality to describe James's representation of selfhood. Comparing James to Walt Whitman and Oscar Wilde, Posnock argues that James "converts the bourgeois self of control into a more supple mode that eludes social categories and is open to the play of the fundamental passions" (5). "As James grew into manhood," Posnock concludes, "the gaping and the vagueness of his mimetic behavior found its most 'workable' public mode in theatricality, self-representation that mitigates the reification of identity by letting the contingencies of social interaction continually shape and reshape it"

(185). Posnock's provocative theory of James's theatrical, or mimetic, selfhood resembles Butler's theory of performativity, and the subject positions that James distributes to his male characters certainly represent contested sites at which "sex, gender, sexual practice, and desire," to use Butler's terms, come together in a state of dynamic tension.

I want to be careful here. In her brilliant analysis of the narcissistic foundations of *The Golden Bowl*, Beth Sharon Ash cautions us about accepting a "radically heterogenous" concept of sexuality by reemphasizing the importance of embodiment and an "understanding that the body is not free to change its shape at will. The finitude of gender difference," she goes on,

> does not prevent gender from being constructed in alternative ways in various cultures. And an acceptance of gender difference does not commit one to fictions of unity, stability, and identity, or to a promotion of the hierarchical, oppositional structures of patriarchy. In contrast, the challenge to gender difference posed by the post-modern idea of a "radically heterogenous" sexuality is largely a denial of finitude, embodiment, history—an ideological fantasy based on unlimited autogendering. Such a fiction may be liberating in some ways, but it is also a form of highly aestheticized "play," which tends to avoid responsibility for the socially situated and psychologically invested nature of human interaction. ("Narcissism" 88 n. 4)

My sense of James's representation of gender and sexuality does veer toward the danger zone (in Ash's view) of excessively fictionalizing those characteristics—of creating a form of "aestheticized 'play.'" While I certainly understand that writing is a form of behavior and thereby subject, like other forms of behavior, to certain constraints and determinations, I think that the field of fiction does allow an author like James considerable freedom for writerly play—in this case, experimental play with heterogenous gender and sexual configurations.

This open view of James's relation to masculinity, which I posited in a 1991 *PMLA* article, challenged the assumptions of much James criticism. That essay seems limited now, largely because it pays too little attention to James's engagement with homosexuality. In the past decade critics such as Eve Sedgwick, Kelly Cannon, John Carlos Rowe, Richard Henke, Hugh Stevens, Eric Haralson, Michael Moon, and Wendy Graham have broadened our understanding of James's representations of gender and sexuality—thanks in many cases to the influence of gay, lesbian, and queer studies. Cannon focuses most explicitly on James and masculinity and especially on James's representation of "marginal" male characters, who reflect his interest in unsettling rather than fulfilling the terms of "conventional manhood" (1), but Cannon equates masculinity rather simplistically with aggressiveness and heterosexual passion. Most usefully, however, he argues that these male characters' displacement to the margins signifies both positively and negatively. Marginalization confirms each character's lack of conventional masculine attributes, but it also offers a liberated space where alternative masculinities may be tested. Like James himself, Cannon claims, these marginal males battle society's "conventional image of masculinity (physical aggression, heterosexual activity)" and yearn for "atypicality (androgyny, homosexuality, passivity)" (41). Henke and Rowe come to similar conclusions. Focusing on James's early novels (*Watch and Ward*, *Roderick Hudson*, and *The American*), Henke argues that James "challenges a singular conception of masculine identity" (257), while "exposing the onerous constructedness of the male subject which patriarchy needs to keep hidden in order to preserve the inviolability of masculinity" ("Embarrassment" 271). But Henke also recognizes that James plays with gender constructs and "is capable of seeing gender in more than essentialist terms, as role, performance, the practice of social conventions, or relative constructions" ("Man of Action" 237). In Rowe's analysis of the "other" Henry James he discovers a writer who "achieves a psychic alterity that can take erotic pleasure and intellectual satisfaction from subject positions no longer tied to strict gender and sexual binaries" (*The Other Henry James* 29). All three critics emphasize James's interest in exploring alternatives to conventional gender and sexual paradigms.

Whereas Cannon, Henke, and Rowe touch only lightly on homoeroticism in James's writing, many recent scholars have brought James and James studies out of the closet to the point where we can almost take James's homosexuality for granted. "Something extraordinary began happening to James in the mid-1890s, and more frequently in the next decade," Fred Kaplan asserts in his 1992 biography. "He fell in love a number of times" (401)—each time with a younger man. Kaplan goes on to detail James's relationships with John Addington Symonds, Jonathan Sturges, Morton Fullerton, Hendrik Andersen, Howard Sturgis, and Jocelyn Persse, and these relationships clearly figure behind some of James's fictional works—with Symonds, for example, providing the "germ" for Mark Ambient's character in "The Author of Beltraffio." Although Kaplan argues for the "lack of full sexual self-definition" in these relationships (453), despite the extravagant imagery of James's many love letters, he does emphasize James's longing for emotional companionship and convivial embraces (452). Indeed, like Leon Edel before him, he stresses the literary, or epistolary, essence of these relationships, suggesting James's sublimation of sexual desire in acts of aesthetic appreciation. For her part, in her tour de force analysis of "The Beast in the Jungle," Eve Kosofsky Sedgwick finds James to be a closeted gay male writer who, like his heterosexual counterparts, represents "homosexual panic" and "heterosexual compulsion" (*Epistemology* 196). In later essays, she stresses James's anal eroticism, which she grounds in his notorious problems with constipation, and she considers him "a kind of prototype, not of 'homosexuality' but of *queerness*, or queer performativity" ("Shame and Performativity" 236). Michael Moon, although acknowledging that James has proven "something of a disappointment to some gay readers hoping to find in his work signs of a liberatory sexual program for male-male desire of the kinds available in the writings of some of his contemporaries, such as John Addington Symonds and Oscar Wilde" (*A Small Boy* 31), insists that James's "less readily legible relation to the emergence of homosexual identity in his lifetime" renders his fiction no less encoded with homoerotic significance. Indeed, Moon argues, using James's "determinedly and painstakingly antisensational model of a major queer culture-making career might yield us a considerably different set of templates for delineating both our expectations of queer art and for specifying our terms for its frequently—reliably—expectation-defying surprises" (2). Moon seeks the "'monstrous' and outrageous" qualities in James's writing, and in *A Small Boy and Others* he focuses on the first volume of James's autobiography (from which he takes his own title) and "The Pupil," in which he persuasively decodes "perverse" adult desires for young Morgan Moreen (27).[6]

Hugh Stevens and Wendy Graham also emphasize the homoerotic imaginary in James's novels, and both apply the insights of gay, lesbian, and queer theory in provocative, subtle readings of several Jamesian texts. Stevens, for example, claims that even the early James "was already a *gay novelist*, who created lasting fictions which, ahead of their time, explore the workings of same-sex desire, and the difficulties of admitting such desires, within a cultural formation marked by homosexual prohibition" (115). Graham offers more particularized accounts of James's homosexuality by arguing for his meticulous engagement with contemporaneous events and publications, especially in the emergent field of sexology. Paying careful attention to the sexological discourses of James's era, she considers him a case of gender inversion, with which she thinks he felt "comfortable, up to a point" (9).[7]

These studies of James sexuality and particularly his homosexuality represent the most exciting critical development in James studies over the past decade, and I hope that the present study can add to this understanding. In the process I want to attend carefully to the terms in which James himself understood and represented gender and sexuality and to avoid what Jonathan Ned Katz calls "retrolabeling" (333). In his important recent study of "sex between men before homosexuality" (his subtitle), Katz interests himself in "different historical ways of naming, conceiving, and, ultimately, constructing sexuality, gender, and kinds of persons" (302). Katz, in other words, reads forward from the historical record to the present, resisting the temptation to impose contemporary templates of sexual behavior and identification on the case studies he selects. "We may refer to early-nineteenth-century men's acts or desires as gay or straight, homosexual, heterosexual, or bisexual, but that places their behaviors and lusts within our sexual system, not the system of their time," Katz warns. "Projected on the past, homo, hetero, and bi distort our present understanding" (9). Although he does not mention Henry James, Katz's historical and historicizing project can offer an appropriate theoretical model for examining James's writing as itself an example of gender and sexual theorizing. As Katz explains, the "names people call particular erotic desires and acts play a big role in the shaping of sexuality in an era" (11). In this study I am especially interested in identifying the "names" James employs for "particular erotic desires and acts" and in understanding those names in James's own terms—with connections inevitably to James's own complex sexuality and gender identifications but also with connections to the discursive systems of identification prevalent in British and American culture of the nineteenth and early twentieth centuries.

James's thousands of letters are only now being catalogued, but many of his letters to young men are newly available and form the basis for our new understanding of James's homosexuality.[8] Rosella Mamoli Zorzi has recently published seventy-seven of James's letters to the young sculptor Hendrik Andersen, and Susan Gunter and Steven Jobe have edited a collection of James's letters to Jocelyn Persse, Howard Sturgis, Hugh Walpole, as well as Andersen. That James desired emotional and physical intimacy with men and expressed that in vivid, often achingly sensual terms has become indisputable. His letters to young men from the 1890s and early years of the twentieth century offer poignant, sometimes heart-rending examples of Jamesian desire and his frequent worry that his desire was not reciprocated. What it meant to his self-image or for our reconstitution of his self-image to feel and express himself in these terms is a trickier matter. Consoling Andersen upon the death of his brother Andreas, for example, James famously casts himself in the role of "a brother and a lover" (*Henry James Amato Ragazzo* 88).

> Your news fills me with horror and pity; and how can I express the tenderness with which it makes me think of you and the aching wish to be near you and put my arms round you? My heart fairly bleeds and breaks at the vision of you *alone*, in your wicked and indifferent old far-off Rome, with this haunting, blighting, unbearable sorrow. The sense that I can't *help* you, see you, talk to you, touch you, hold you close and long, or do anything to make you rest on me, and feel my deep participation—this torments me, dearest boy, makes me ache for you, and for myself; makes me gnash my teeth and groan at the bitterness of things. (86)

When James wrote that passage in 1902, he was already feeling anxious about Andersen's feelings for him, and he felt some frustration that Andersen did not write and visit more often. James takes advantage of the occasion, however, to express desire for Andersen in the form of consolation. In offering to take Andreas's place in Hendrik's life, to be "like a brother," James extends an invitation to more than brotherly love—to a relationship in which playing the brother arguably represents the form that playing the lover will take. Conflating two roles and forms of love, James was playing upon one of the most acceptable forms that homoerotic love could take at the turn of the century—a version of "Greek love," which James knew from John Addington Symonds's "A Problem in Modern Ethics."[9] This is not to desexualize James's feelings, for Symonds explicitly celebrates the sexual dimensions of Greek same-sex desire.

Consistently in his letters to young men James expresses his desire for emotional and physical intimacy, but he does so theatrically by dramatizing himself in various ways. Effusive and melodramatic, he wants to hug them, to throw his arms around them and welcome them into his arms, and again and again he signals his readiness to respond to any indication of reciprocated interest. "The least sign or word from you, or intimated wish," he tells Jocelyn Persse, "makes me vibrate with response & readiness—so attached am I to your ineffaceable image" (*Dearly Beloved* 95). As lovers on the make will do, James ups the emotional ante in his letters, representing his own desire as always excessive. "Keep a-wanting of me all you can," he ends a letter to Howard Sturgis, "you won't exceed the responsive desire of yours, dearest Howard, ever so constantly *Henry James*" (149). "I am yours, yours, yours, dearest Hugh, *yours!*" he signs himself to Hugh Walpole (187). Despite the genuine yearning, the heartfelt desperation, in some of these love letters, James also indulges himself in campy metaphorical play that resembles the archness we enjoy in his fiction. "Irresistible to me always any tug on your part at the fine & firm silver cord that stretches between us," he opens a letter to Persse; "at any twitch of it by your hand, the machine, within me, enters into vibration & I respond ever so eagerly and amply! (My image sounds rather like the rattle of the telephone under the effect of a 'call'; but I mean it well, & I mean it, above all, my dear Jocelyn, affectionately!)" (96). The image of James with a cord penetrating his body, attached to a machine that responds to "calls" from Persse almost defies interpretation because the figure is so over the top, but James can top himself, especially when he compares himself to animals.[10] "I have shown you often enough, I think," he writes to Howard Sturgis, "how much more I have in me of the polar bear than of the salamander—& in fine at the time I last heard from you pen, ink & paper had dropped from my perspiring grasp (though while *in* the grasp they had never felt more adhesively sticky,) & I had become a mere prostrate, panting, liquefying mass, waiting to be removed" (158). Playing the literary polar bear with sweaty fingers for Sturgis, James becomes an old elephant for Hugh Walpole. "Beautiful & admirable of you to have threshed through the tropic jungle of your 30 waiting letters to get at *this* elephant," he tells the young man, "who accordingly winds round you, in a stricture of gratitude & affection all *but* fatal, his well-meaning old trunk. I abominably miss you—having so extravagantly enjoyed you; but it's a great enrichment of consciousness, all the while, that we are in such beautiful, such exquisite relation" (193). I am less interested in using these passages from James's letters as evidence for his homosexuality than in pointing out the various poses within a homoerotic discourse that James assumes. This is not quite to say that, where his sexuality was concerned, James was in a state of suspense. He clearly felt desire for other men, although he expressed that desire more openly toward the end of his life. But it would be counterproductive from a literary standpoint to reduce James's sexuality to simple terms when it is the terms themselves that are so provocative. After all, posing himself as a man with a cord penetrating his body for Jocelyn Persse to "twitch" places James in a very different subject-object position than his self-dramatization as an old elephant who will wind his "well-meaning old trunk" so affectionately around Hugh Walpole. James obviously takes pleasure in both poses. Both seem obviously homoerotic, but taken together they reflect a complex, not a simple, eroticized self. And they hardly represent the only poses James enjoyed striking.

James delights in positioning his male characters in such ways that their gender and sexual orientations are reversed, ambiguous, and even multiple. It is important to track both gender and sexuality in James's writing because gender deviance is so often the form that sexual deviance takes during a period in which the theory of inversion offered the dominant paradigm for understanding homosexuality. As Hubert Kennedy has pointed out, the "third sex" theory promoted by Karl Ulrichs in the 1860s and revised by other theorists such as Richard von Krafft-Ebing, Havelock Ellis, and John Addington Symonds did not last long (103), but variations of it have had a significant influence. Although Ellis explicitly rejected Ulrich's female-soul-in-male-body theory as "unintelligible" (183), for example, he retained a more sophisticated version of that theory. Beginning with the observation of a "latent organic bisexuality in each sex" (184), Ellis theorizes that sexual differentiation occurs later—and sometimes imperfectly:

Putting the matter in a purely speculative shape, it may be said that at conception the organism is provided with about 50 per cent. of male germs and about 50 per cent. of female germs, and that, as development proceeds, either the male or the female germs assume the upper hand, killing out those of the other sex, until in the maturely developed individual only a few aborted germs of the opposite sex are left. In the homosexual person, however, and in the psychosexual hermaphrodite, we may imagine that the process has not proceeded normally, on account of some peculiarity in the number or character of either the original male germs or female germs, or both, the result being that we have a person who is organically twisted into a shape that is more fitted for the exercise of the inverted than of the normal sexual impulse, or else equally fitted for both. (184)

Even as they promote a binary theory of inversion, Ulrichs and Ellis find themselves identifying subgroups within their primary groups and thus multiple homosexualities. Interestingly, gender becomes the variable. Deviations within homosexuality are marked with gender characteristics. Even the largely binary taxonomy that Ulrich and Ellis employ, however, has room for multiple homosexualities. In an appendix to *Studies in the Psychology of Sex*, Ellis summarizes Ulrich's subcategories of homosexual men, or "Urnings":

Among urnings, those who prefer effeminate males are christened by the name *Mannling*; those who prefer powerful and masculine adults receive the name of *Weibling*; the urning who cares for adolescents is styled a *Zwischen-urning*. Men who seem to be indifferently attracted by both sexes, he calls *uranodionings*. A genuine Dioning [heterosexual male], who, from lack of women, or under the influence of special circumstances, consorts with persons of his own sex, is denominated *Uraniaster*. A genuine urning, who has put restraint upon his inborn impulse, who has forced himself to cohabit with women, or has perhaps contracted marriage, is said to be *virilisirt*, a virilized urning. (228)

Even this rudimentary proliferation of categories, based largely on the gender differences of the homosexual subjects' object choices, illustrates the difficulty of gender and sexual classification.[11]

John Addington Symonds went further in his "A Problem in Modern Ethics," which James read in 1891, toward liberating gender characteristics from sexual orientation. "It is the common belief that all subjects from inverted instinct carry their lusts written in their faces," Symonds wrote; "that they are pale, languid, scented, effeminate, painted, timid, oblique in expression." This "vulgar error rests upon imperfect observation," he concluded. "The majority differ in no detail of their outward appearance, their physique, or their dress from normal men. They are athletic, masculine in habits, frank in manner, passing through society year after year without arousing a suspicion of their inner temperament" (107). We may cringe today at the distinction Symonds accepts between homosexual males and "normal men," but his celebration of a diverse homosexuality is significant. Furthermore, the implicit idea that masculinity could actually disguise homosexuality, especially in a culture of increasing sexual surveillance, may well have attracted someone like James, fascinated as he was with the problematics of representation and interpretation. Writing homosexually without "arousing suspicion"—James knew how to do that. Even though James inherited a relatively simple model of gender and sexual deviance, his own representations of gender and sexual identity became much more complex.

In this study I would like to keep both gender and sexuality—"sex, gender, sexual practice, and desire," to repeat Butler's terms—in play as variable frames of reference for understanding the ways James explores and constructs male identity in his writing. Ahead of his time, I think James recognized that gender and sexuality existed independent of one another—that desire for variably gendered objects could construct a variably gendered and sexualized subject.[12] No where does such variability bristle so much as in the essays James wrote about George Sand. Sand destabilized masculinity and heterosexuality for James in many different ways. Yet instead of trying to restore conventional gender differences, James attempts to keep masculinity open—multi-directionally, as it were—for both men and women. That is, he does not simply admit Sand under the sign of masculinity but repositions himself in complex and problematical ways within an expanded category of masculinity that must include this transgendered and transsexualized female man.

Before I examine the ways that gender issues are played out in James's Sand essays and in *The Ambassadors*, I want to return to "Hugh Merrow," for James's portrait of the artist as an immaculate father-creator discloses a richly ambiguous connection between art and masculinity. The story seems rooted, as James Gifford suggests, in a male fantasy of parthenogenesis (68). In substituting a single male artist for the couple who have tried unsuccessfully to conceive a child, "Hugh Merrow" works a variation on the primal scenes that Silverman finds in many of James's works. The Archdeans come to Merrow, they tell him, because of the skill he displayed in painting another child: "happy little Reggie Blyth, six years old, erect in a sailor-suit." Granting to Merrow an extraordinary procreative (and phallocentric) power, the Archdeans assure him, "You can have as many [children] as you like—when you can paint them that way!" (*Complete Notebooks* 589, 592).[13] The most intriguing question that "Hugh Merrow" raises, of course, is why James emphasizes the child's undecided gender? The answer, I think, involves the way the child mirrors and even engenders its creators. Because Mrs. Archdean wants a girl, while Mr. Archdean wants a boy, they decide to let Merrow create whichever he thinks he can do best (592). "Which would you rather do?" Mrs. Archdean asks him. "Which would most naturally come to you, for ease, for reality?" (593). Where gender is concerned, the Archdeans will give Merrow, as they say, a "free hand," but this, of course, is precisely the problem. While touting the pleasures of improvisation, James himself had worried about his imaginative "stream" exceeding his control—breaking its bounds and becoming a "flood." Similarly, Hugh Merrow seems to fear the engendering power of his own imagination—that is, the gender determination that his imagination and creative desire, if given a free hand, might "naturally" project onto the painted child. "For little Reggie, you see, I had my model," he tells the Archdeans. "He was exquisite, but he was definite—he lighted my steps. The question is what will light them in such a case as you propose. You know, as you say, what you want, but how exactly am I to know it?" As a male artist, Merrow must worry most, during the creative process, about suspending his masculinity. He must worry that a "naturally" gendered (or perhaps ungendered) self will subvert the socially masculine self that empowers his art. Insofar as an artist's creative products proceed from desire, furthermore, Merrow may worry that, without a model to warrant his production, he may produce something that reveals too much about what comes "naturally" to him. It is no wonder that he tells the Archdeans, "There's such a drawback as having *too* free a hand" (594).[14]

Merrow's anxiety of improvisation, it seems to me, is also James's. Whereas Merrow worries about not having a model to light his steps in the creation of gender, James seems to worry about the effect an ambiguously gendered model (Sand) will have on the "gender" of his own art. As James later points out, George Sand finds that "the free mind and the free hand were ever at her service" (Review of *George Sand* 788). As a woman who improvises a masculine identity, furthermore, Sand raises questions for James about the relation between gender and sexuality. If gender becomes a variable term in Sand's case—subject to performance—does sexuality also become variable? If gender and sexuality both float free of their biological sites, do they also float free of each other? One of the things to which "queer" can refer, according to Eve Sedgwick, is "the open mesh of possibilities, gaps, overlaps, dissonances and resonances, lapses and excesses of meaning when the constituent elements of anyone's gender, of anyone's sexuality aren't made (or *can't* be made) to signify monolithically." Unlike "gay" and "lesbian," she goes on, the very concept of "queer" "seems to hinge much more radically and explicitly on a person's undertaking particular, performative acts of experimental self-perception and filiation" (*Tendencies* 8, 9). Sexual and gender categories began to proliferate at the end of the nineteenth and beginning of the twentieth centuries, as sexology came into its own as a social or behavioral science, and I think James exploited the taxonomic confusion in order to experiment with various sexual and gender identities. Gordene Olga MacKenzie notes that cases that would be defined as "transsexual" today were "originally classified under the categories of homosexuality, sexual perversions, Eonism, androgyny, psychic hermaphroditism and transvestism. Each of these categories contained sub-categories such as cross-dressing, effeminateness, congenital sex inversion, antipathic sexual instinct, uranism, transmutatio sexus, transformation of sex and metamorphosis sexualis" (35).[15] Today, "queer" subsumes these and other categories of gender and sexual difference. Sedgwick hypothesizes that not only masculinity and femininity, but "effeminacy, butchness, femmeness, and probably some other superficially related terms, might equally turn out instead to represent independent variables—or at least, unpredictably dependent ones" ("'Gosh, Boy George'" 16). To consider James a "queer" or any other kind of "deviant" writer does not mean ascribing contemporary terms of gender and sexual identity to him, but using contemporary queer theory to approximate and illuminate qualities in James's writing that, had he translated them into a metadiscourse, would have assumed some other form. Indeed, it means looking closely at James's own richly metaphorical language *as a metadiscourse* on questions of gender and sexuality.

I want to return at this point to James's vexed attempts to come to terms with George Sand, for they illustrate the problems and possibilities of his engagement with questions of masculinity. In the three long essays James wrote about Sand in the last two decades of his life (1897, 1902, 1914), she serves him as an artistic doppelgänger, an idealized, complexly androgynous double. Because as a writer she was "both man and woman," she caused James to falter "again and again" in attempting to describe her (Heilbrun 35, 36). Coming to terms with what he called the riddle or mystery or question of Sand meant researching his own gender identity and the gender of his literary authority. Sand shook James to the very foundation of his gendered and sexual selfhood, prompting him simultaneously to effusive accolades and to a series of discursive gymnastics. She finally induced a bizarre gender reversal in which she became a dubious masculine ideal that placed James in a subject position he experienced simultaneously as male and female, hetero- and homoerotic. Sand compelled James to suspend his conventional male identity and the authorial self he was trying to construct. Insofar as he could not recognize himself and his artistic profile in the masculine Sand, James seemed to feel his identity as a male writer was indeterminate or in suspense.

In the end it is precisely the intersection of Sand's gender and her creative power that poses the greatest problem for James, and the primary way for him to swallow Sand is to transmute her into a man. She was a "woman quite by accident," he maintains in his review of *She and He*; she possessed "the true male inwardness"—indeed, "more of the inward and outward of the other sex than of her own" (748, 750). Her masculinity resided in her "inward impunity," her ability to get "off from paying" for her repeated surrenders to "unconsecrated passion." The history of her "personal passions reads singularly like the chronicle of the ravages of some male celebrity," James claims, because it represents the "same story of free appropriation and consumption" (751, 750). Whereas a "feminine" woman could not have maintained enough presence of mind to have the use of her experience, Sand had, "as liberty, all the adventures of which the dots are so put on the i's by the documents lately published, and then she had, as law, as honour and serenity, all her fine reflections on them and all her splendid literary use of them. Nothing perhaps gives more relief to her masculine stamp," he concludes, than the "rare art and success with which she cultivated an equilibrium." In short, Sand gave off a "peculiar air of having eaten her cake and had it" (752).

The power of Sand's masculinity to disturb James's authorial equilibrium stands even clearer in his 1914 review of Wladamir Karénine's *George Sand*. The main difference between this final essay on Sand and the previous ones is a new cultural perspective in which Sand figures as standard-bearer for the feminist revolution. However, because, for James, feminism seemed to mean both the masculinization of women and women's appropriation of the masculine, it impugned his conception of his own male identity. He claims that the "answer of [Sand's] life to the question of what an effective annexation of the male identity may amount to" leaves "nothing to be desired for completeness" (Review of *George Sand* 781). Transmuting George Sand into a transpersonal masculine ideal was tricky, because Sand's "equilibrium" of masculine and feminine qualities—her female masculinity—threatened to make her more robustly masculine than James himself, who could be left to identify himself with a male femininity. In other words, he would be one of these "who at the present hour 'feel the change,' as the phrase is, in the computation of the feminine range, with the fullest sense of what it may portend" (Review of *George Sand* 779). What Sand's example may portend is a change in men and, more ominously, a change in James's conception of himself as a man.

In admitting that he most recognizes in Sand's "tale," not "the extension she gives to the feminine nature, but the richness that she adds to the masculine," James does not mean that Sand merely affected masculinity or, usurping male prerogatives, acted "like a man" and thus made it possible for a man to act "like a woman." Whereas Sandra Corse says that James "saw in Sand not a person who appropriated men, but who appropriated masculinity itself" (68), I think that James saw Sand's masculinity as going beyond her behavior and thus beyond the "masculine" to the "male." Her performance of masculinity challenged the very idea of gendered identity. "It is not simply that she could don a disguise that gaped at the seams, that she could figure as a man of the mere carnival or pantomime variety," James writes, "but that she made so virile, so efficient and homogeneous a one" (Review of *George Sand* 781). Not only has Sand's gender floated free of her biological nature, but it has also exceeded her performance. She is not in male drag. She is transsexual and transgendered—and "homogeneous" as a man. Her maleness seems to occupy some ontological realm between the essential and the constructed—or is constructed so impeccably (with no "gape" at the "seams") that constructedness and essentialism come to mean the same "real thing." Sand also foreshadowed something more than androgyny, more than a union of opposed gender constructs. She suggested new constructs, new categories—the pluralization of genders. As James observes,

> Nothing could well be more interesting thus than the extraordinary union of the pair of opposites in her philosophy of the relation of the sexes—than the manner in which her immense imagination, the imagination of a man for range and abundance, intervened in the whole matter for the benefit, absolutely, of the so-called stronger party, or to liberate her sisters up to the point at which men may most gain and least lose by the liberation. She read the relation essentially in the plural term. (Review of *George Sand* 781)

Although James begins with the traditional notion that Sand androgynously united masculine and feminine characteristics, he ends more complexly by noting that she read the relation between men and women not as a union of discrete or singular genders but "in the plural term." He emphasizes how, in liberating women from traditional femininity, Sand enables men to "most gain and least lose"—that is, to "pluralize" their manhood. Her "philosophy" thus portends the dissolution not only of gender categories (of behavioral characteristics) but of gender identities. The resulting emergence of a plurality of gender and sexual identities occupying the same subject position would require men to suspend traditional masculinity, as Hugh Merrow is forced to do, in favor of the improvisational freedom to construct a masculine self from a range of possibilities that would include George Sand's female masculinity.[16]

In his 1914 essay James magnifies Sand's personal influence and projects it on the culture at large. The "force of George Sand's exhibition," he says, is

> that effective repudiation of the *distinctive*, as to function and opportunity, as to working and playing activity, for which the definite removal of immemorial disabilities is but another name. We are in presence already of a practical shrinkage of the distinctive, at the rapidest rate, and that it must shrink till nothing of it worth mentioning be left, what is this but a war-cry? . . . Unless the suppression of the distinctive, however, is to work to the prejudice, as we may fairly call it, of men, drawing them over to the feminine type rather than drawing women over to theirs—which is not what seems most probable—the course of the business will be a virtual undertaking on the part of the half of humanity acting ostensibly for the first time in freedom to annex the male identity, that of the other half, so far as may be at all contrivable, to its own cluster of elements. (Review of *George Sand* 780)

James's extravagant imagery in this difficult passage resorts to conventionally masculine language ("war-cry," "business," "annex") to proclaim its lack in the culture at large. Noting that the difference between men and women "must shrink till nothing of it worth mentioning be left,"

James reveals continued anxiety about what "swallowing" the masculine Sand portends for his own masculinity and even suggests a fear of castration. However, by emphasizing what Sand means for men and women in the early twentieth century, rather than simply for himself, James makes the "shrinkage" work to his advantage—bringing cultural masculinity more into line with his own, which has been "drawn over" to the "feminine type."

The change in James's view of Sand between 1897 and 1914 can be located in his 1902 essay, "George Sand: The New Life," as well as in *The Ambassadors*, which was published the same year. Confronting Sand, James resembles Lambert Strether, whose categories are all "taken by surprise" by Marie de Vionnet (NY 21: 271).[17] Because Sand's "annexation of the male identity" could also presage the feminization of James's identity—his "drawing over to the feminine type"—he tries to find a way to accommodate her fulfillment of a masculine ideal without jeopardizing his different masculine authority. It is not surprising, therefore, that he should try to solve Sand's riddle by restoring his own sense of male identity. To do that in his 1902 essay, he invokes a masculine muse, the quintessential male writer, Honoré de Balzac, the "father of us all." James incorporates Balzac's masculine authority—what he later terms the "big Balzac authority" (*Autobiography* 251)—and even interpolates Balzac's words to put Sand in her place and thus reestablish his own gender equilibrium. In effect, James uses one masculine authority (Balzac) to countermand another (Sand) and improvises a position for himself in between—suspended in the masculine.

Balzac's characterization of Sand in an 1838 letter, James maintains, "lets into the whole question of his hostess's character and relations . . . air and light and truth; it fixes points and re-establishes proportions" ("George Sand: The New Life" 772). Self-styled as Balzac's "grateful critic," James says that Balzac "comes nearest straightening the question" of Sand in his observation that she "has in character all the leading marks of the man and as few as possible those of his counterpart." Indeed, she "hangs together perfectly if judged as a man." She *is* a man, Balzac says, because "she wants to be . . . she has sunk the woman . . . she isn't one. Women attract, and she repels; and, as I am much of a man, if this is the effect she produces on me she must produce it on men who are like me—so that she will always be unhappy" ("George Sand: The New Life" 772). Not only does James rely on Balzac's authority, he relies on Balzac's experience and even on Balzac's subjective estimate of Sand's gender identity. Women attract Balzac, Sand repels him (anomalously, given the number of her male lovers). Since Balzac is "much of a man" and repelled by Sand, Sand must also be a man and thus destined to be unhappy because unattractive to Balzac and to men like him. The self-serving "logic" of Balzac's syllogism is obvious enough to require no explanation, but where does this remarkable passage leave James? Is he, like Balzac, "much of a man"? That means being repelled by Sand, since Balzac elides the issue of feeling desire for another man—even a female "man" such as Sand. If he is not repelled by her (his essays, indeed, attest his attraction to her), what does that make James? A woman? A man given to unions "against nature," as he had characterized Sand's union with Alfred de Musset (*"She and He"* 748)? Here, in what James might call the "final nutshell," is the suspense of gender with a bit of a vengeance. In this context—in the context of desire and its distribution across ambiguous gender identities—what kind of man can James be?

With the "distinctive" hanging thus in suspense, James moves quickly in the final pages of the 1902 essay to clarify the question that Sand poses. He admits, in fact, that the "copious" data in Karénine's biography "makes Madame Sand so much of a riddle that we grasp at Balzac's authoritative word as at an approach to a solution." And it is, "strange to say, by reading another complexity into her image that we finally simplify it" (Review of *George Sand* 773). This riddle, he says, "consists in the irreconcilability of her distinction and her vulgarity. Vulgar somehow in spite of everything is the record of so much taking and tasting and leaving, so much publicity and palpability of 'heart,' so much experience reduced only to the terms of so many more or less greasy males" (773). By invoking Balzac's "authoritative word" to solve the "riddle" of what he would later call Sand's "annexation" of male identity, James was invoking a special kind of masculine muse—a phallic, male masculinity to diminish Sand's female masculinity. Whereas James repeatedly praises Sand's writing for its fluidity, looseness, and improvisation, Balzac's is "always extraordinarily firm and hard," possessing a "metallic rigidity" ("Honoré de Balzac" [1875] 38).[18] Balzac has the power of "*penetrating* into a subject"; he is "always astride of his imagination, always charging, with his heavy, his heroic lance in rest" ("Lesson of Balzac" 127, 123). Even more than Sand, Balzac serves James as an omni-masculine figure who also possesses the improvisational power to be a man in the plural term. Balzac has the rare ability to get "into the very skin of his *jeunes mariées.*" Balzac "bears children with Madame de l'Estorade, and knows intimately how she suffers for them, and not less intimately how her correspondent suffers, as well as enjoys, without them." Besides being both mother and father, Balzac also plays the son. Besides "penetrating" subjects and sitting "astride" his imagination, phallocentrically empowered in hyperbolic terms, Balzac can play other male roles. "Big as he is he makes himself small to be handled by her [Madame de l'Estorade] with young maternal passion and positively to handle her in turn with infantile innocence." Such multiple male role-playing comprises "the very flourishes," James concludes, "the little technical amusements of [Balzac's] penetrating power" ("Honoré de Balzac, 1902" 114). Conceiving male authority in obvious phallogocentric terms, James posits a versatile, performative phallus—big or small depending upon the role the writer is called upon to play.

Yet, however deeply Balzac could penetrate the very skin of women, neither he nor his art depended on them. Unlike Sand, who converted transgendered heterosexual experience into art, James's Balzac sounds remarkably like James himself in substituting art for experience. He was "always fencing himself in against the personal adventure, the personal experience," James remarks, "in order to preserve himself for converting it into history" ("Lesson of Balzac" 124). While James regards Balzac as both an omni-masculine ideal who exercised a "lusty energy of fancy" ("Honoré de Balzac" [1875] 53) *and* a man whose art did not require "personal adventures" with women, he attributes Balzac's special authority to a knowledge of women. Writing in 1875, James observes that Balzac "is supposed to have understood the feminine organism as no one had done before him—to have had the feminine heart, the feminine temperament, feminine nerves, at his fingers' ends—to have turned the feminine puppet, as it were, completely inside out" ("Honoré de Balzac" 61). Even though James could admit in 1902 that Sand's great service to women is that her "approximation" of a man was at least to the "extraordinary" ("George Sand: The New Life" 775), Balzac's masculine authority clearly offered James an alternative to Sand and thus a way of killing the suspense into which she had cast his own gender identification. Balzac was able to keep the "feminine organism" at his "fingers' ends"—just across the line that might have portended transgendering—but still understand women from the inside out. Whereas Sand figures as the precursor of the increasingly masculine women James saw around him in the early twentieth century, as early as 1875 he observes that Balzac did "not take that view of the sex that would commend him to the 'female sympathizers' of the day. There is not a line in him that would not be received with hisses at any convention for giving women the suffrage, for introducing them into Harvard College, or for trimming the exuberances of their apparel" ("Honoré de Balzac" 61). Balzac, in other words, provides James with an authorial ideal even more masculine than Sand's.

Much like Basil Ransom in *The Bostonians* or earlier characters such as George Fenton in *Watch and Ward*, Christopher Newman in *The American*, and Caspar Goodwood in *The Portrait of a Lady*, James's Balzac "takes the old-fashioned view" and "recognizes none but the old-fashioned categories. Woman is the female of man and in all respects his subordinate" ("Honoré de Balzac" [1875] 61). Suspended between Balzac and Sand and thus between male and female masculinity, much as Verena Tarrant is suspended between Ransom and Olive Chancellor, James remasculinizes himself by invoking Balzac's authoritative word and transmuting Sand not into a feminine woman but into a repellent female man. Whereas Sand's masculinity originally threatens James's, drawing it toward the feminine type, James finally creates a "new-fashioned" category—a homophobically constructed category of female manhood—to solve the riddle Sand poses for him. That is, James seems finally to project upon Sand the gendered and sexual qualities with which he did not want to identify. Even though Sand's ability to eat her cake and have it at the same time—to exercise her sexuality and "use" it in her writing—align her with the masculine position, she performs the masculine with men who, like Musset, are less than "real" men.[19] Swallowing Sand, then, forces James not only to interrogate his own masculinity but to improvise a new double-gendered masculinity that could accommodate both Sand and himself. Then, by establishing Sand as a female man, James can feel more comfortable with his own identity, confident that masculinity can accommodate both female and male men: Sand and Balzac—and, of course, Henry James, who positively bristles between the two as a man in the plural term.

Laurence B. Holland considers George Sand's affair with Alfred de Musset "the one episode of her career that most fascinated and appalled James" and regards it the source of another Venetian affair—that between Jeffrey Aspern and Juliana Bordereau in "The Aspern Papers" (132). The 1833–34 relationship between the thirty-year-old Sand and a man six years her junior must have had an additional resonance for James between 1897 and 1902, when his first two long essays on Sand appeared, because he was basing a novel, *The Ambassadors*, on an analogous situation. Marie de Vionnet's romance with Chad Newsome forms both the pretext for Lambert Strether's return to France and the context for whatever "treasures of imagination" Strether gleans from his experience (NY 22: 224). Similarly, Sand's romance with Musset provides James with the pretext for confronting issues of sexuality and writing and with the context for his own treasure hunting. Convinced that the Sand-Musset affair is the most "suggestive" in the "annals of 'passion,'" James regards as "treasures of the human imagination" the "poems, the letters, the diaries, the novels, the unextinguished accents and lingering echoes that commemorate" that passion ("George Sand: The New Life" 769).

In turning to *The Ambassadors*, I wish not to argue for Sand's influence on the novel or on the character of Marie de Vionnet but to demonstrate how James's three Sand essays and *The Ambassadors* engage one another in a conversation about the suspense of masculinity suggested in "Hugh Merrow." Both the essays and the novel represent a masculinity that must be reconstructed in the aftermath of a woman's challenge, and when Strether finally realizes that Marie de Vionnet and Chad are lovers, he finds himself—like James in the essays on Sand—facing questions about his own gender and sexuality.[20] James took Strether's first and middle names from Balzac's novel *Lewis Lambert*, and his solution to Strether's suspense resembles Balzac's solution to his own—putting a woman in her place in order to reestablish the masculine identity she has put in jeopardy. As with most of James's ostensible solutions to subjective problems, however, Strether's male identity does not rest easily in any single configuration.

Patricia Thomson has cited several parallels between Sand and *The Ambassadors*, arguing for example that Sand's Stephen Morin in *Mademoiselle Merquem* serves as a model for Strether and as a source of his famous "Live all you can" speech to Little Bilham, and connecting Chad's affair with the older Marie de Vionnet and Sand's affair with Alfred de Musset (235, 242). James's own description of Sand in 1914 as the "supreme case of the successful practice of life itself" (Review of *George Sand* 778) suggests that, like Madame de Vionnet for Chad and potentially for Strether, Sand served a paradigmatic function for James. One early reviewer for the *Literary World* complained that "no business men could find the time" to read *The Ambassadors* (Hayes 406), but the failure of Strether's ambassadorial mission to retrieve Chad for the family manufacturing business and thus for conventional masculinity opens other possibilities for Chad and himself. Those possibilities center upon Marie de Vionnet. Strether's desire to learn the "art of taking things as they came" (21: 83) means learning the very lesson that James had attempted to learn from Sand, for in James's view, "making acquaintance with life at first hand" was the "great thing" that Sand achieved ("George Sand" [*Galaxy*] 716). In both cases, furthermore, the anxiety generated by the lesson is projected upon the woman responsible. James's characterization of Marie de Vionnet as the "party responsible" for the "miracle almost monstrous" of Chad's transformation (21: 167) echoes the "monstrous vitality" that James described in Sand in the same year ("George Sand: The New Life" 774). Both metaphors register the anxiety and the thrill that James felt as he contemplated the metamorphic effect that these women portended for men. As the "fate that waits for one, the dark doom that rides" (21: 167), Madame de Vionnet also suggests James's ominous characterization of Sand as the "rather sorry ghost that beckons [him] on furthest" ("*She and He*" 746). Although Marie de Vionnet, like the earlier Claire de Cintré in *The American*, seems to epitomize French femininity and thus the fulfillment for men of rather conventional masculine ideals (within a heterosexual register), James still confronts Strether with unstable possibilities of gender and sexual identification as he worries over the riddle of what relation Chad enjoys with her.

Eric Haralson notes that Strether's very lack of conventional masculine attributes makes him the "perfect bearer of the novel's argument, its necessarily gentle dissent from uniform masculinity and compulsory sexuality" ("Lambert Strether's" 182). As early as his third night in London, Strether's sense of gender differences faces a significant test that places his ability to fulfill his manly reclamation project in serious jeopardy. To fulfill that mission without being wholly hypocritical or purely mercenary, Strether would have to find Chad himself in need of reclamation—that is, deformed or corrupted. As Strether gives himself over to "uncontrolled perceptions" (21: 50) and lets his "imagination roam" (21: 51) at the theater, however, he recognizes how difficult any such diagnosis will be. He comes face to face with a "world of types" and with a "connexion above all in which the figures and faces in the stalls were interchangeable with those on the stage" (21: 53). In short, he enters a carnivalesque world of performance that "penetrated" him as if with the "naked elbow of his neighbour" (21: 53):

Those before him and around him were not as the types of Woollett, where, for that matter, it had begun to seem to him that there must only have been the male and the female. These made two exactly, even with the individual varieties. Here, on the other hand, apart from the personal and the sexual range—which might be greater or less—a series of strong stamps had been applied, as it were, from without; stamps that his observation played with as, before a glass case on a table, it might have passed from medal to medal and from copper to gold. (21: 53)

Eerily, in view of the blurring between stage and stalls, when Strether turns his attention to the play, he discovers a "bad woman in a yellow frock" making a "pleasant weak good-looking young man in perpetual evening dress do the most dreadful things" (21: 53). Finding himself secretly sympathizing with the victim (whom he identifies with Chad), Strether indicates his own conflicted identification and desire. In analyzing this passage, Hugh Stevens concludes that the "spectacle of the London theatre creates for Strether a breakdown in certainty of sexual meanings, and this instability is experienced by him as not only intimidating, but also creative and exhilarating" (18).[21] Despite its seeming conventionality, the play Strether watches places him in at least two subject positions. In identifying with the "good-looking young man" (Chad) and the position he occupies, Strether seems to acknowledge his own masochistic position in relation to Mrs. Newsome.[22] Insofar as Strether differentiates himself from Chad in this scene, however, he occupies a female subject position as a "bad woman"—indicating, I think, the safest way he can imagine making Chad do "dreadful things" and placing him in a position uncannily similar to the one George Sand occupied for James in her relationship with Alfred de Musset. Marie de Vionnet, of course, plays the role of bad woman in the conventional melodramatic plot that Mrs. Newsome has projected upon her son, while Mrs. Newsome herself, in Strether's imagination, plays that role for him. Strether's imagination proves more subtle, however, as he imagines himself (gender) switching between roles in the play, and risking inversion as even a bad woman seems preferable to jeopardizing the heterosexual terms of subject-object relationship within the male imaginary that he embodies at this early point in the novel.

When he finally sees Chad in Paris, of course, Strether's resolve proves weak indeed. James famously emphasizes Chad's "sharp rupture" (21: 137) of identity and the "emotion of bewilderment" (21: 136) that Strether experiences as a result. "You could deal with a man as himself," Strether thinks; "you couldn't deal with him as somebody else" (21: 136). Paul Armstrong argues that "Chad's difference from himself compels Strether to reconsider the whole issue of the stability and dependability of the world" (67), but the transformation James describes reflects more particular issues, because it pertains explicitly to the question of male identity and the relation between men. If Chad is no longer Chad, is Strether still Strether? Can one truly undergo what James later calls an "alteration of the entire man" (21: 167)? If so, than that potential alteration would include one's gender and sexuality. As several critics have noted, moreover, Strether's response to the first sight of Chad suggests a spontaneous eruption of desire that inverts his ambassadorial relation to the young man and forces him to confront the appropriate gender identity from which that desire can be expressed. Mark Mitchell and David Leavitt, for example, claim that Chad's presence "evokes an intense, if subconscious, desire for the boy" (220). Citing the language through which James represents Strether's response to this encounter and to the excruciating experience of sitting "close to Chad" while the play goes on (21: 136), they conclude that James's prose "chokes an erotic response that the use of words such as 'rush,' 'flush,' 'strained' and 'pressure' only serves to underscore—so much so that the carnal implications of the phrase 'the long tension of the act' ring out loud and clear, despite (or perhaps because of) James's efforts to suppress them" (221). I don't think James tries to suppress anything in this scene, however. Indeed, he goes out of his way to intensify the pressure that Strether experiences by making him sit through the first act of the play after he sees Chad. The proprieties of the theater prevent his reacting except inwardly to the "sharp rupture" his own subjectivity has suffered. James, in other words, keeps Strether, his gender and his sexuality, in suspense.

In one respect, the famous scene in the French countryside, in which Strether learns the sexual truth about Chad's adulterous relationship with Marie de Vionnet, ends some of the suspense that the earlier scene with Chad has created. It constitutes the climactic "rupture" for his ambassadorial mission to France, because it prevents further suppression of the erotic and the destabilizing effect that diversified desire can have on male identity. As "queer as fiction" (22: 257), the scene also transports Strether into the world that the French novel richly evoked for James—that is, the world of Balzac, Flaubert, Zola, and especially George Sand. Marie de Vionnet's switch to French when the question of her true relationship with Chad cannot help invoking Sand's erotized masculine discourse about Musset. Kaja Silverman, furthermore, argues that this scene "encourages identifications which are in excess of sexual difference." As a "primal scene fantasy," it "opens onto both the positive or heterosexual, and the negative or homosexual versions of the Oedipus complex," promoting "desire for the father and identification with the mother, as well as desire for the mother and identification with the father" (165). Strether's gender alignment and sexual identifications, she implies, are paradigmatically dual—female as well as male, homosexual as well as heterosexual.

My concern, however, is less with the gender confusion implicit in this scene than with the possibilities of masculinity the scene opens up (and closes off). Kelly Cannon argues that Chad and Marie de Vionnet "represent the heterosexual union to which the sexually marginalized male comes unprepared physically and emotionally" (19), but he begs the question in that simple, either-or formulation of what responses Strether has available. If Strether identifies with both Chad and Marie, as Silverman points out, he identifies with a feminized masculinity and a masculinized femininity. The scene thus introduces the notion of masculinity "in the plural term." To complicate matters further, Strether himself experiences a gender reversal as he reconstructs the scene. When he finally faces the "deep, deep truth of the intimacy" between Chad and Marie, he sees his former self as female: "he almost blushed, in the dark, for the way he had dressed the possibility in vagueness, as a little girl might have dressed her doll (22: 266)." Strether's figure for himself, which seems (pro)created by the primal scene in which he has participated, raises several issues. Resorting to such infantilizing gender inversion reflects a masochistic self-recognition that he does not measure up to turn-of-the-century ideals of heterosexually empowered manhood. But Strether's figure also has a campy side and enables James to play with his character and his reader across lines of gender and gendered desire. The choice of figures—little girl rather than little boy—prolongs the negative identification of the primal scene, for example. If Strether performs the "little girl," he may attract Chad, as Jeanne de Vionnet ultimately does. Such fantasmatic cross-gendering empowers a heterosexualized play of desire—a classic example of inversion in which desire for a man feminizes the male who desires. The doll-playing fantasy, however, in which Chad and Marie figure as a turn-of-the-century Ken and Barbie, suggests other fantasmatic possibilities. Having "dressed" them, as it were, in the euphemisms of repression, Strether now presumably undresses them as he imagines their sexual intimacy, playing with them separately and together and supposing, as James remarks, "innumerable and wonderful things" (22: 266). Those "things" surely allow Strether to imagine multiple roles and to experiment with a pluralized masculinity and sexual identity. Imagining the "wonderful" things that go on between Chad and Marie de Vionnet certainly involves Strether in the heterosexual imaginary, but in a scene "as queer as fiction" Strether can also occupy Marie's subject and object position—desiring Chad and being desired by him. Perhaps the things that this "bad woman" has done to Chad or made him do to her are not so "dreadful" after all—and truly "innumerable and wonderful" when Strether cross-genders himself to imagine doing them.

In the early scene in which Strether and Waymarsh prepare for bed in a London hotel James stages another campy scene of flirtation or cruising that brings closer to the surface the question of what things—dreadful or wonderful—men might do to other men. Although Strether's mission on Mrs. Newsome's behalf seems designed to enforce a compulsory heterosexuality, Strether flirts with the possibility of homosexual desire and consummation when he puts Waymarsh to bed. "I want to go back," Waymarsh coyly whines, as he keeps his eyes "all attached to Strether's." This direct gaze "enabled his friend to look at him hard and immediately appear to the higher advantage in his eyes by doing so" (21: 30). This direct look between men contrasts with the sort of indirection that cruising relies upon, but it still enables the two men to test their attraction, or "attachment," to each other. "That's a genial thing to say to a fellow who has come out on purpose to meet you!" Strether responds (21: 30). Waymarsh and Strether play with one another across the subject and object of Strether's desire—what he calls "my desire to be with you" (21: 30)—but Strether postpones full disclosure of his desire (whether for Waymarsh or for Mrs. Newsome). "Oh you shall have the whole thing," he teases. "But not tonight" (21: 31). However, when Strether assists Waymarsh to a "consummation" by helping him into bed, pleasuring himself with the "smaller touches of lowering the lamp and seeing to a sufficiency of blanket" (21: 31), he deflects the homoerotic possibilities with which he himself has flirted. Waymarsh appears to him both "unnaturally big and black in bed" and "as much tucked in as a patient in a hospital and, with his covering up to his chin, as much simplified by it" (21: 31).[23] Indeed, despite the gender inversion that seems to accompany this hospital metaphor, Strether enjoys the "feeling" of playing a "nurse who had earned personal rest by having made everything straight" (21: 32). James's metaphors both avow and disavow the homoerotic possibilities with which he and Strether have toyed. As he had at the theater, Strether seems to prefer cross-gendering himself to crossing another boundary, but James surely enjoys playing with possibilities of crossing both gender and sexual lines. From Strether's cross-gendered position as a nurse, he will keep everything "covered up to the chin" and "straight"—causing "straight" to take on meanings that suggest deviations from conventional lines and making Strether seem like a male version of George Sand, inverting himself in reverse.[24]

As we shall see, James frequently opens the possibility of homosocial and homosexual attachment between men but then closes it off in favor of heterocentric plot developments. In this scene James takes pains to keep male-male desire at bay, or to triangulate it through the presence of a woman and Strether's consciousness of his ambassadorial mission. Despite their intimacy and their flirtatious conversation, the two men deflect attention from their situation by discussing Mrs. Newsome—that is, by inserting a woman (albeit a manly one) into what becomes a heterosexually triangulated relationship. "You're a very attractive man, Strether," Waymarsh can observe, but he does so by attributing the observation (and the desire that goes with it) to "that lady downstairs" (Maria Gostrey) and to Mrs. Newsome (21: 32). Waymarsh does push Strether for some kind of commitment, asking why he suggests that his ambassadorial mission is also for him. Strether tries to have the dilemma both ways, but Waymarsh's question obviously causes him some anxiety. James describes him as impatient and "violently" playing "with his latch" before he replies, "It's for both of you." Waymarsh turns over "with a groan" at this point and exclaims, "Well, *I* won't marry you!" (21: 34). Strether escapes from the room in which he might have been closeted for the night with Waymarsh before he can complete his reply, leaving the matter in a state of some suspense. By the end of the first four chapters, in fact, James has opened Strether's sense of gender and sexuality in several ways—placing him in this suggestively intimate relation with Waymarsh and, through Maria Gostrey, causing him to notice the relative asexuality of his relationship with Mrs. Newsome.[25]

Eve Kosofsky Sedgwick's account of James's representation of compulsory heterosexuality in "The Beast in the Jungle," furthermore, bears on Strether's predicament in the last part of *The Ambassadors*. In writing his essays on Sand, James wrestles with his own sexuality and returns again and again—compulsively, as it were—to the most striking example of compulsive heterosexuality he has encountered. At the same time, as a woman who was also a man, George Sand could project a special type of both heterosexuality and homosexuality—a woman who transgenders herself not to be with other women, but to be with men. As James writes in his 1897 essay, "to feel as George Sand felt . . . one had to be, like George Sand, of the true male inwardness; which poor Musset was far from being. This, we surmise, was the case with most of her lovers, and the truth that makes the idea of her *liaison* with Mérimée, who *was* of a consistent virility, sound almost like a union against nature" ("*She and He*" 748). For James the Sand-Musset affair represented gender reversal, with Musset playing a feminine, or at least a less than masculine role. Musset is "unmanly," in James's view, because he "cries out when he is hurt; he resorts frequently to tears, and he talks much about his tears" (Review of *Biographie* 610). James surmises that Sand appropriates the male role and male identity by being more masculine than her male lovers, who, like "poor Musset," are thereby cast in the female role. But the issue for James is more complicated, for when he does imagine a male with a "consistent virility," he must also imagine an "unnatural," or homosexual, union with the masculine Sand. In this respect, then, the Sand-Musset affair does not sound "like a union against nature," since both lovers are transgendered. Whereas the Sand-Musset relationship suggests an inverted heterosexuality, the Sand-Mérimée affair represents a homoerotic heterosexual union between a masculine woman and a masculine man. Gender and sexual constructs have become fluid indeed, as James's transgendered George Sand experiences both homosexual and heterosexual desire for men.

James's dilemma about being feminized or homosexual resembles Strether's quandary as he confronts the Chad Newsome-Marie de Vionnet relationship, which he, like James, although for different reasons, views as unnatural. It would be a stretch of logic to argue that the fictional lovers' differences in age and nationality stand in for the reversed gender positions in Sand's love affairs, but the point is not that Strether must identify himself as one or the other, masculine or feminine. The novel, like James's essays on Sand, represents more complicated possibilities, suspending male identity between masculine and feminine poles and "cutting," or intersecting, it with a spectrum of desire. The male body in both cases becomes the site of gender and sexual indeterminacy. Male subjectivity, predicated upon a range of gendered object choices, comes to occupy a "no man's land" of suspense. Maleness becomes a construct while writing about it presages gender improvisation. In his remarkable characterization of Strether's state of mind (in his preface to the New York Edition of the novel), James figures his hero's subjectivity as a "clear green liquid" in a "neat glass phial," but he goes on to stress the liquid's changeability and so to establish a protean subjectivity. The liquid, "once poured into the open cup of *application*, once exposed to the action of another air, had begun to turn from green to red, or whatever, and might, for all he knew, be on its way to purple, to black, to yellow. At the still wilder extremes represented perhaps, for all he could say to the contrary, by a variability so violent, he would at first, naturally, but have gazed in surprise and alarm; whereby the *situation* clearly would spring from the play of wildness and the development of extremes" (*Art of the Novel* 314). Strether may seem like an unlikely candidate for such internal violence at the "still wilder extremes," but many readers would say the same about Henry James and his representation of gender and sexuality.

Although James observes that it would have "sickened" Strether to "feel vindictive" toward Chad (22: 295)—that is, like an angry and punishing father—the scene in the country, which "disagreed" with Strether's "spiritual stomach" (22: 265), does enable him to restore some gender equilibrium. But an equally important scene, especially in light of James's essays on Sand, occurs when Strether visits Madame de Vionnet for the final time, because in her presence Strether feels "freshly and consentingly passive" (22: 278)—much like James in Sand's "presence" before Balzac intervened. While Strether's reconstruction of the scene in the country has made him feel girlish and demoralized, the scene in Madame de Vionnet's apartment, like James's invocation of Balzac in the 1902 essay, restores him to a manly place. There he assuages his need for punishment by imaginatively projecting Madame de Vionnet's demoralization. His picture of her as "exploited" and "afraid" for her life, as a "maidservant crying for her young man" (22: 284–85), differs radically from James's depiction of Sand. Marie's tears and sobs, which remind Strether of sounds that "come from a child," contrast sharply with Sand's "inward impunity" even as they recall his own girlish infantilization. "Nothing perhaps gives more relief to [Sand's] masculine stamp than the rare art and success with which she cultivated an equilibrium," James observed. "She made from beginning to end a masterly study of composure, absolutely refusing to be upset, closing her door at last against the very approach of irritation and surprise" ("*She and He*" 752). In his 1914 review James conscripts Sand into the ranks of feminist activists as a woman who dealt with life "exactly as if she had been a man" (Review of *George Sand* 779–80). In contrast, Madame de Vionnet, Strether thinks repeatedly, is a woman. Indeed, she is a representative of women, and thus, in his view, "to deal with [her] requires the ability to walk on water" and demands that he act the part of a man (22: 285). In constructing himself as Marie's savior, of course, Strether also switches the object of his ambassadorial desire. His original mission was designed as an intervention in a "monstrous" heterosexual union, the prerequisite for Chad's deprogramming and installation as head of the family business. Saving Marie from Chad rather than Chad from Marie frees Strether from his obligation to Mrs. Newsome and from the arguably masochistic relationship he enjoys with her, and it reverses his relation to Chad and Marie. Switching sides, however, does not eliminate the double identification or double desire that Strether has experienced. This transposition, Strether's movement to Marie's side, simultaneously fulfills and disavows the desire he feels in Chad's presence. Reversal enables and prevents inversion. That is, Strether identifies with

Marie at the very moment when doing so makes him safe from acting upon any desire for Chad. As transposable objects of desire, then, Marie and Chad are really objects of foreclosed desire. Strether's reversal of loyalty forecloses upon the possibility of any affair of his own—with either of them.

James's arguably successful effort to solve the riddle that George Sand posed for his masculinity can illuminate the end of *The Ambassadors*, because the suspense that Strether's "sharp fantastic crisis" creates for his gender identity ends in much the same way as James's over the course of the three Sand essays. When Strether turns down Maria Gostrey's veiled proposal by explaining that he is following a logic of getting nothing for himself out of the "whole affair," his response is as untrustworthy as Maria's claim that he returns to America with only his "wonderful impressions" (22: 326). James Gifford considers Strether's refusal a "renunciation of heterosexuality," but he also points out that such a renunciation "only makes his self-imposed (homo)sexual exile all the more pitiable" (84). In other respects as well, Strether chooses a modest life as a man, like John Marcher, to whom little is likely to happen. He will return from Paris with "treasures of imagination" (22: 224) and with his masculinity at least tentatively and imaginatively in place—but unchanged. In fact, when he fills the interval between his final meetings with Marie and Chad by escorting Maria Gostrey about Paris, he enjoys this "happy interlude" the more for his being able to play the "kindly uncle" to Maria's "intelligent niece from the country" (22: 291). He gets for himself, then, what James got from Balzac: an independent, unaffiliated, uncompromised manhood. In contrast to Sand, who follows a policy of "free appropriation and consumption," of having her cake and eating it too, Strether embraces this logic of renunciation. As James says of Balzac, Strether is "always fencing himself in against the personal adventure, the personal experience, in order to preserve himself for converting it into history" ("Lesson of Balzac" 124). For, in rejecting Maria's proposal, Strether rejects one masculine role (lover or husband) in order to play another (bachelor uncle)—thus aligning himself, in James's view, with Balzac rather than with Sand. With the "breach" between himself and Mrs. Newsome apparently "past mending" (22: 324), Strether seems likely to play the bachelor for the rest of his life.

When Hugh Merrow asks what will "light" his steps in choosing the gender of his subject, Mrs. Archdean suggests that his interest in the "artistic question itself" will determine his decision (*Complete Notebooks* 595). Although we cannot know how James might have resolved Merrow's dilemma, *The Ambassadors* and his essays on Sand all show him allowing his imagination to be "lighted"—bifocally at least—in the masculine. Not that Merrow would simply have painted a boy, for the essays and the novel make clear that being masculine and being male are not always easily compatible. When Merrow tells Captain Archdean that Mrs. Archdean "dreams of a little girl in your likeness, while you dream of a little boy in hers," the Captain advises him to paint a figure resembling them both (*Complete Notebooks* 595–96). But Merrow is skeptical about this possibility. Feminizing the male or masculinizing the female in an androgynous union—all three options seem dubious solutions to James's problems with Sand.

Even more than "Hugh Merrow" and *The Ambassadors*, James's essays on Sand not only open but hold open questions about gender and sexuality. Most important, they show James interrogating the notion that a male artist's gender simply engenders his writing. They suggest, rather, that the artist constructs a gendered and sexual identity in the act of engendering the work of art—indeed, that he knows his own gendered and sexual self only in retrospect, by reading or viewing what he has created. But if gender, and particularly masculinity, is that fluid—something to be read, or "swallowed"—then the artist will always be in a state of suspense about himself. Merrow's anxiety about "having too free a hand" thus mirrors James's anxiety about what it means to "swallow" a writer like Sand and thereby have her "pass into" his life. Swallowing Sand, a masculine female writer, suggests a complex—inverted—homoerotic identification. That is, the inverted gender identity that Sand seems to embody for James forces a vexed desire and sexual identification upon the desiring subject and writer—James himself—who would have to swallow a writerly power he identified simultaneously as masculine and female, heterosexual and homosexual.

The Ambassadors and the essays on Sand show James reconstructing a masculine identity by putting women in their places within a newly expanded masculinity. As he reads and writes about Sand, James offers himself up as a blank space on which Sand inscribes herself, but in the process of inscription Sand also subjects herself to revision. In a similar fashion, the self that his encounter with Sand constitutes for James also becomes subject to revision, most significantly through the incorporation—a transcription—of a superior male authority. In this complex rhetorical staging of gender complications, Sand and the Jamesian self she recreates are written over like a palimpsest by Balzac, a bachelor type complete in himself and able to play male and female roles. James does not simply identify with Balzac, however, and thereby disinvest himself in Sand; rather, he finds himself suspended between the possibilities represented by these two precursors—in the masculine, to be sure, but masculine in the plural term.

James's explorations of what it means to be masculine "in the plural term" and to write with all one's manhood at one's side result, I think, in a state of suspense in which male identity, configured in terms of gender and sexuality, remains fluid. "Really, universally, relations stop nowhere," James wrote in the preface to *Roderick Hudson*, "and the exquisite problem of the artist is eternally but to draw, by a geometry of his own, the circle within which they shall happily appear to do so" (*Art of the Novel* 5). This book examines James's effort to keep male gender and sexuality in such a state of suspense, even as he experiments with various "geometries" of relationship that "appear" to stabilize them. Chapter 1 examines *Roderick Hudson* as an early experiment in exploring multiple male identities in a context of relations that "stop nowhere"—or at least offer sufficient variety to compel various male identifications. Setting up a rectangle of character relations (Rowland Mallet, Roderick Hudson, Christina Light, Mary Garland), James distributes desire along each axis, reflexively constructing multiple male identities. Brook Thomas argues that for James "no essential self exists outside of exchanges, and yet precisely for that reason all exchanges are interpersonal and thus affect the very nature of the self. This is because . . . a self cannot achieve definition without a 'space *between*' that only interpersonal relations can provide, while, at the same time, interpersonal relations are impossible without an emptiness *within* the self, an emptiness making one vulnerable to penetrations—and dominations—by another" (736). In the Mallet-Hudson relationship James employs his protégé theme to test the power of homoerotic desire to reconstruct a male self. That man-making process is complicated by the presence of female characters, especially Christina Light, who engender other, heterosexual, male selves.

Chapter 2 examines *The American* as an experiment in constructing a new manhood by reconstructing a particular male character type, the self-made businessman Christopher Newman. Newman might seem one of the least likely candidates in James's fiction for such a reconstruction project, but I think James is bent on both satirizing such a self-made man and genuinely exploring the possibilities for alternative manhood that such a character affords. Turning to Gilbert Osmond (*The Portrait of a Lady*) in Chapter 3, I examine one of James's subtlest portraits of a gentleman—the flip side, so to speak, of Christopher Newman. In fact, James pointedly characterizes Osmond by virtue of what he is *not*, and on the face of it Osmond seems most *not* like Newman—a kind of anti-Newman, or "newer new man." Chapter 4 focuses on *The Bostonians* and James's unreconstructed southerner, Basil Ransom. With glances at cross-dressing in *Adventures of Huckleberry Finn* and Thomas Dixon's *The Leopard's Spots*, as well as in northern caricatures of the captured Jefferson Davis in drag, this chapter argues that James repeatedly subverts Ransom's masculinist reconstruction project by blurring the boundaries between racial and gender identities and between heterosexual and homosexual desires.

Each power position that Ransom imagines reverses upon itself, implicating him in heterosexual and homosexual economies of exchange and subjecting him to socially constructed feminine as well as masculine identifications that often carry racial implications.

In *Dandies and Desert Saints* James Eli Adams characterizes masculinity as a "rhetorical transaction" (11) and speaks of male "rhetorical self-fashioning" (15). By positing a transactional model of masculine construction, Adams adds an important dimension to any discussion of literary representations of gender issues. James, too, recognizes the importance of rhetorical situations—the way that subject-object relations configure and reconfigure male subjectivity, which subjects itself as it were to interpretation, to being read through the desire of another subject. In chapter 5 I discuss four of James's stories about writers and artists ("The Author of Beltraffio," "The Lesson of the Master," "The Middle Years," and "The Death of the Lion") and his deployment of what I call "homo-aesthetic" desire in acts of writing and reading between men. Homoerotic desire emerges in these stories as the product of intersubjective transactions—as a function of a male reader response. In Eric Savoy's terms, male writing "cruises" its male readers, whose erotic responses to these "homotexts" establish temporary, homo-aesthetic relationships to the writers themselves ("Hypocrite Lecteur" 20). Through the medium of writing, in other words, James ascribes a homoerotically charged male subjectivity to the writer-reader transaction. As he does in the novels, James mediates these male-male relationships by dispersing male desire among several gendered objects and thereby diversifies the male subjectivity that different object choices reflect.

Scholars such as David McWhirter and Hugh Stevens have discovered an underlying masochism in James's writing, and in the final chapter I examine Prince Amerigo in *The Golden Bowl* and the sadomasochistic economy of relations in which he finds himself ensnared. Paradoxically, James deploys a masculinity of mastery from the site of an abject manhood. Amerigo performs the sadistic male—masochistically, on demand.

Insofar as James's autobiographical writings have a plot, the climax of James's self-representation as a male subject occurs at the beginning of chapter 11 in *Notes of a Son and Brother*. Although James had written disparagingly of himself, particularly in contrast to his father and brother William, suddenly he writes with some confidence as he rediscovers the governing principle of this "personal history, as it were, of an imagination" (*Autobiography* 454). He is the "man of imagination, and of an 'awfully good' one," even as he worries that he will not quite be able to "catch" that figure for his use. "He had been with me all the while," he seems to realize, "and only too obscurely and intimately—I had not found him in the market as an exhibited or *offered* value." Although he worried about money throughout his career and certainly recognized the "value"—often a small one—of his writing, he persistently resisted identifying with prevailing models of business manhood. The "man of imagination" James can imagine being, therefore, must find his value and his values elsewhere than in the market, and insofar as business markets comprise the world outside the creative self, the obvious alternative site at which to locate the man of imagination is inside the self. "I had in a word to draw him forth from within rather than meet him in the world before me," James writes, and "to make him objective, in short, had to turn nothing less than myself inside out" (*Autobiography* 455). In the context of this study, of course, the image of James turning himself "inside out" resonates in several registers, suggesting romantic inspiration, the contortions involved in identifying against the norm, but also gender and sexual inversion. "What was *I* thus, within and essentially, what had I ever been and could I ever be," James concludes, "but a man of imagination at the active pitch?" (*Autobiography* 455).

In his preface to volume 15 of the New York Edition, a volume containing "The Figure in the Carpet," James poses a challenge to critics. "I had long found the charming idea of some artist whose characteristic intention, or cluster of intentions, should have taken all vainly for granted the public, or at the worst the not unthinkable private, exercise of penetration" (*Art of the Novel* 228). "I came to Hugh Vereker," he says, by way of a "generalisation"—namely, that criticism is "apt to stand off from the intended sense of things," so he posited a critic, an "intent worker," "who should find himself to the very end in presence but of the limp curiosity." The "drama" that Hugh Vereker's story describes—a drama of criticism, of the "aspiring young analyst whose report we read"—is that "at a given moment the limpness begins vaguely to throb and heave, to become conscious of a comparative tension." As an "effect" of this "mild convulsion," James concludes, "acuteness, at several points, struggles to enter the field, and the question that accordingly comes up, the issue of the affair, can be but whether the very secret of perception hasn't been lost" (*Art of the Novel* 229). James had fun writing the long passage from which I have quoted these excerpts. Can there be any doubt that he relished the wordplay, that he experienced what Sedgwick calls "exhibitionistic enjoyment" ("Shame and Performativity" 229), in the idea of "embodied" intentions vainly seeking a public readership able to "penetrate" them, the image of the critic's "limp curiosity" that begins to "throb and heave" and whose "convulsion" imperils the "very secret of perception"? In his brilliant analysis of this passage and James's tale as a whole, Eric Savoy archly refers to James's lesson for readers as a "sort of critical Viagra" and an object lesson in camp, the "ludic self-parody that James increasingly turned to in his prefaces to the New York Edition" ("Embarrassments" 231, 230). As much as anything else Savoy honors the writerly pleasures of James's text—the laughter that must have bubbled inside him in the act of composition. James poses a serious challenge for his readers, especially his male readers, as he indulges in parody and self-parody and the fun and games of unsettling relationships between words and meanings. Reading James for fun demands no "limp curiosity." Venturing into the funhouse of James's fiction we run the risk of getting "lost among the genders and the pronouns" ("The Death of the Lion" 296). We shall need all our manhood at our sides, where of course we face the danger and the opportunity of losing it altogether. I hope I am man of imagination enough for the job—especially in the plural terms that James's suspense of masculinity requires.

Chapter 1
Configuring Male Desire and Identity in *Roderick Hudson*

Before launching into a largely favorable review of *Roderick Hudson* (1875) for the *New York Times*, the anonymous critic summarized James's career—citing first the "Jr." that connected him to his better-known father and then his esoteric appeal to the "more cultivated and thoughtful part of the reading public." "He has shown no indications," the reviewer complained, "of qualities of a robust natural growth" (Hayes 3). James's lack of writerly virility hampers his ability to distinguish male and female characters from one another, and the critic cites his stylistic inability to differentiate between genders. Complaining that the characters in *Roderick Hudson* all talk "pretty much in the same way, the way of Mr. Henry James, Jr.," the reviewer archly observed that Rowland Mallet "might be a male Mary Garland, and Mary Garland a female Rowland Mallet, Esquire" (Hayes 7). In effect, the *Times* reviewer places James in a position that anticipates Hugh Merrow's in his later, unfinished story—in the position of having his own gendered identity inferred from the objects, or characters, he creates. Failing to find the right gendered voices for his male and female characters undermines his claim to a "robust" gender identity of his own. Although the reviewer hoped that James would develop more masculine features—that is, more "original traits," as he "attains conscious strength and wins confidence in his powers by their exercise" (Hayes 3)—the jury, so to speak, seems to remain out. He finally praises *Roderick Hudson* as "one of the best novels produced in America," but he also notes the "conscious primness" of James's style, which he finds "too often apparent" (Hayes 7). James himself, of course, recognized that *Roderick Hudson* tested his writerly and manly power. Suppressing acknowledgement of *Watch and Ward*, he considered *Roderick Hudson* his "first attempt" at a "long fiction with a 'complicated' subject" (NY 1: vi), and certainly his representation of gender and sexuality, distributed provocatively among male and female characters, figures prominently among those complications. "Really, universally, relations stop nowhere," he would write in the New York Edition preface to *Roderick Hudson*, "and the exquisite problem of the artist is eternally but to draw, by a geometry of his own, the circle within which they shall happily appear to do so" (1: vii). If in fact relations "stop nowhere," the individuals involved in those relations find themselves continually challenged to redefine or re-identify themselves "in relation."

Roderick Hudson offers the best early example of James's "protégé theme" (Martin, "'High Felicity'" 101) and his earliest extended effort to plot the narrative trajectory of male homoerotic desire—how men identify themselves in relation to each other. Rowland Mallet recognizes that his "genius is altogether imitative," even though he has not yet "encountered any very striking models of grandeur" (1: 4), but in Roderick Hudson he obviously finds a "model of grandeur" in whom he can invest considerable energy—playing patron, living vicariously through the other man's achievement, and testing his own attraction to his protégé.[1] In addition to experimenting with paths of desire and identification, the narrative also illustrates James's early effort to explore a range of masculine behavior and masculine roles, because the male-to-male relationship is doubly complicated by the presence of two women: Christina Light and Mary Garland. In an excellent recent essay on homosocial bonds in the novel, Nomi Sofer argues that James was "acutely aware" that the "homosocial cannot exist outside of the compulsory heterosexuality of patriarchal society and realistic fiction" (192), but I think the relational and identificatory possibilities he explores in *Roderick Hudson* are more supple and versatile. They certainly include the homoerotic, not just the homosocial, but in exploring the potential of mutually fulfilling homoerotic relationships, James does explore their many complications. Rowland Mallet, for example, finds the male object of his desire—his "model of grandeur"—entangled in a romantic and sexual relationship with a woman (Christina Light), while he himself at least considers the "possibility of a throb" with another woman (Mary Garland) to whom his protégé is formally engaged. Relations in *Roderick Hudson*, as well as the identifications they engender, may not stop "nowhere," but their various configurations do enable James to experiment with multiple gender and sexual performances.

The double-stranded love plot, or hetero-text, that James creates necessarily complicates the more important male-to-male relationship—in effect, covering or repressing the homosocial and homoerotic subtext of the novel. Mallet's desire for and efforts to identify with another male are blocked by Roderick's relationship with two women, both of whom Rowland himself at least in some sense desires. Put another way, Mallet faces the challenge of reconciling his idealized image of the artist with the distressing image of the artist-with-a-woman, while his own relationship to the male artist figure is doubly mediated. Although Sofer argues that *Roderick Hudson* displays "profound pessimism about heterosexuality"—indeed, that "heterosexual obsession" in the novel "has the power to destroy men's lives" (186)—I think the four-sided configuration of characters enables James to experiment with several alternative relationships and their implications for male identity, even as the relationship between a male center of consciousness and a "doubled" love object comprised of male artist and female subject remains at the center of his attention. My goal, therefore, is to examine James's two male characters and the interplay and negotiation between homosocial and homosexual, heterosocial and heterosexual discourses, out of which their male identities are constructed.

In moving his two male characters from Northampton to Rome—from the "centre of Christendom" to the "mere margin," as Mrs. Hudson suggestively puts it—James paradoxically can center his attention more intensively on alternative relationships between and among his major characters. I "approve of a certain tension of one's being," Rowland tells his cousin Cecilia. "It's what a man is meant for" (1: 50). And that tension inheres for Rowland, it seems to me, in the dispersion of desire along various lines of gender and sexuality. By situating his male center of consciousness within a complex configuration of relationships, furthermore, James explores several potential male identities and roles. With Mary Garland, for example, Rowland feels encouraged to be the sort of "soft," genteel male—an "athlete of continence" (Rosenberg 139)—stereotyped by social historians as the Christian Gentleman. Christina Light in contrast demands a more aggressive male type—a "big" man of the sort James would create in Christopher Newman, Caspar Goodwood, and Basil Ransom. None of those characters is simply reducible to type, but each of them does outwardly conform in many ways to the instrumental Masculine Achiever. Rowland's relationship with Roderick, on the other hand, promises a more comprehensive type of masculinity—the sort of intimate brotherhood, or comradeship, that Melville illustrated in the Ishmael-Queequeg marriage and Whitman described in *Leaves of Grass*. Liberated from a competitive, dominant-submissive posture, such relationships can be founded on principles of mutual benevolence and the breakdown of hard ego boundaries.

Early reviewers of *Roderick Hudson* found neither Rowland Mallet nor Roderick Hudson particularly good examples of manhood. Roderick lacks "true manliness," one reviewer complained (Hayes 5), while Rowland "fails to produce an impression of vital individuality." He remains "almost a lay figure, a stiff model of oppressive excellence and wisdom, always saying and doing exactly the right thing at the right time," and, as noted above, might even be regarded as a "male Mary Garland" (Hayes 6, 7). Another reviewer, terming Rowland a "fairy godmother" to Roderick (Hayes 9), considers Roderick himself a "weakling" and labels his conduct "unmanly and unbearable." "He was not meant for a finished product," that reviewer concludes. "Only a butterfly existence could suit such a character" (Hayes 10). Such snide remarks derive, I think, from the reviewers' unease with the relationship between Rowland and Roderick—their intuition that gender and sexuality are linked for men. Gender identity—manliness or virility—depends upon heterocentric identification. What we would now call homosexual identification portends gender inversion. Thus, another reviewer, noting the "anomalous relation of these two young men," recognized somewhat euphemistically that they were "sometimes comrades on the footing of good fellowship" and, with considerable relief, "sometimes separated into a modest and most conscientious and responsible patron, and a ward now wholly self-surrendering and endearing" (Hayes 14)—in other words purified of any whiff of "good fellowship." The reviewer who complained that Roderick lacked "true manliness" also noted the "perplexing little triangular arrangement of personages" in the novel (Hayes 4) and explained Roderick's lack by his inability to inspire sufficient desire in Christina Light. "The virile force to which her feminine nature longs to render due submission," this reviewer reasoned, "she does not find in his brilliant but unstable, untrustworthy nature" (Hayes 5). From our perspective, of course, the idea of an "unstable, untrustworthy nature" registers more positively than negatively—suggesting the liberation of individual identity from prescribed gender and sexual roles and opening up the possibility of "brilliant" alternative performances. I would not argue that James and his readers easily found their way to such a reading, but I do think James was working toward alternative configurations of male gender and sexual identity—that he deliberately and experimentally wanted to create "unstable" male characters that destabilized conventional male roles and identities.

Twentieth-century critics have tended to discuss the male characters in *Roderick Hudson* by opposing Roderick and Rowland in order to identify unresolved conflicts either in James's own male identity or in his conception of male character. Leon Edel suggested, for example, that James had "abstracted the incandescence of his genius and placed beside it his decorous, cautious, restrained self, or his mother's warnings beside his own desires" (170).[2] More usefully for my purposes, several critics break free of such binary approaches and seem to recognize the inherent instability in the complex relationships James configured. As Oscar Cargill puts it, relationships in *Roderick Hudson* result in "Christina's vague yearning for Rowland, who yearns for Mary, who will not have him but is passionately devoted to Roderick, who, ultimately bored by her, burns for a casually responsive Christina" (26). Ronald Emerick expands the range further by analyzing Christina's love for Rowland: "To 'Rowland loves Mary Garland loves Roderick loves Christina' must be added 'loves Rowland' to complete the rectangle of romantic relationships" (353). And Robert K. Martin has added "Rowland loves Roderick" and read the novel as "the story of a man who fell in love with a handsome young artist, adopted him as his protégé and took him to Italy" ("'High Felicity'"101).³

Martin makes what now seems an obvious case for the homoerotic dimension of Rowland's attraction to Roderick, for there is little question that Roderick and Rowland excite one another. Roderick's "face flushed," and he "stammered," "panted," and got "greatly excited" when Rowland offers to take him to Rome. His arm trembles in his benefactor's (1: 34, 35). When Rowland admires Roderick's work in his studio, the "light of admiration was in Rowland's eyes, and it caused the young man's handsome watching face to shine out in response" (1: 37). Hugh Stevens also argues that the novel "makes homoerotic affection more than a casual aspect of Rowland Mallet's character. In its foregrounding of questions of legal status, and its exploration of Rowland's melancholic resignation, the novel specifically explores the cost of relinquishing same-sex attraction" (67). Indeed, Stevens sees *Roderick Hudson* as inaugurating the tragic homosexual paradigm in James's fiction, arguing that the novel portrays a "'masochistic economy,' an economy in which desire is never gratified and always punished, but in which a certain pleasure derives from that very punishment" (83).

"Outing" Rowland Mallet, however, represents only a necessary first step in exploring James's construction of male identities in the novel. *Roderick Hudson* does not simply reflect the closeting or frustration of male desire but the distribution of desire within a vexing economy of male-male and male-female relationships. The mutually creative, as well as conflicted, nature of the male-to-male bond becomes complexly entangled with male-female relationships. As Stevens puts it, the "radical masochistic economy of *Roderick Hudson* derives from complex and multiple movements of ungratified desire and unstable identifications. For Rowland's desire for Roderick, and Roderick's desire for Christina, comes full circle (or full triangle) in Christina's desire for Rowland" (80). Before sexology and legal definitions of sexual identity exerted their coercive force, James experiments in *Roderick Hudson* with the identificatory, or reflexive, power of male desire—the power of object choice to engender a male self. Moving his characters to the liberatory climate of Italy, James enables himself to play with various possibilities for gender and sexual identification.

Rowland Mallet serves James not only as a center of consciousness, but also as a "center of manliness"—a subject position, if you will, through which various constructs of manhood can circulate. Although Kelly Cannon rightly claims that Rowland "fails to meet the masculine norm because he cannot muster sufficient heterosexual passion for Mary Garland" (9), such a view of Rowland's limitations and of the norms and alternatives with which James works is itself much too limited. Not content to represent Rowland's masculine sensibility within any simple binary, James attempts to educate it, first through relationship with Roderick, and then through the challenges posed by Christina and Mary. Roderick in effect mediates Rowland's relationship with each of the women, placing himself "between women," while the women mediate Rowland's relationship with Roderick, placing themselves "between men."

As James initially characterizes him, Mallet appears waiting for some outside force to change his life. Identified as he is with his money and with conventionally masculine systems of business exchange, he feels ready to invest self and money in some alternative speculation. He is "waiting till something takes [his] fancy irresistibly." "I'm holding myself ready for inspiration," he tells his cousin Cecilia in reporting his intention to visit Europe, but he worries that if "inspiration comes at forty it will be a hundred pities to have tied up my money-bag at thirty" (1: 4). Claims such as Poirier's that Rowland is simply an "observer who, like Ralph Touchett, must subsidize the kind of life he cannot lead" seem short-sighted, given the open field for investment that James initially posits for his central character (20). For in Mallet (and in the "drama" of his consciousness) James depicts a male character whose intellectual and emotional energy, while narcissistically invested in an enclosed self, nonetheless awaits something to stimulate an opening and presumably an outpouring of the "money-bag" of hoarded emotion. Jonathan Freedman considers the "neurasthenic" Mallet to represent the "conflict between a Calvinist insistence on a life of vigorous activity and the aestheticist privileging of a life of pure contemplation" (138). Mallet himself seems to recognize that conflict and to seek a means of reconciling those two impulses.[4] He certainly recognizes the vacuity of his present life and feels the need to channel suppressed energy into self-expression. He pointedly tells Cecilia that he is tired of narcissistic self-enclosure: "tired of myself, my own thoughts, my own affairs, my own eternal company." "True happiness," he recognizes, "consists in getting out of one's self" and, moreover, being able to "stay out" (1: 7). Although he could simply be rationalizing his inactivity and covertly expressing a desire to uncloset himself (anticipating a character such as John Marcher in "The Beast in the Jungle"), he explains that his problem has simply been the lack of an "absorbing errand": "I want to care for something or for somebody. And I want to care, don't you see? with a certain intensity; even, if you can believe it, with a certain passion." Although Cecilia interprets this to mean that he simply wants to "fall in love" (1: 7), the issue is more complicated, because love is only one of several bases for relationship in *Roderick Hudson*. The terms of desire that Mallet uses, furthermore, clearly suggest an alternative to a strict "money-bag" economy of investment and profit at the expense of others. Whether oriented heterosocially or homosocially, caring for something or somebody suggests selflessness more than selfishness and a basis for human relationship that James pointedly distinguishes from the economic basis of American business society.

As he looks in the mirror, Mallet characterizes himself half-facetiously as a "man of genius half-finished. The genius has been left out, the faculty of expression is wanting; but the need for expression remains, and I spend my days groping for the latch of a closed door" (1: 8). He does in fact spend the rest of the novel seeking ways to invest and to "open" himself to experience by getting and staying outside the closed door, or closet, behind which he has secreted himself. In this regard, he registers a typical male scenario in post-Civil War America. Feeling cultural pressure to achieve business success and to fall in love and marry, he wants some other definition of maleness, some other male self that can serve as a "model of grandeur." He accepts the idea that "true happiness" requires investment of energy in "something or someone," but he seeks an alternative to the two choices most readily available and encouraged by his culture: a woman or a business career. "Roderick will repay me," he tells Mary. "It's a speculation" (1: 77). Indeed, Rowland is in some sense as much a sculptor as Roderick—a "fairy godmother," in one reviewer's arch terms (Hayes 9), with the power to transform Roderick's Cinderella into a princely sculptor. Mallet feels bored to have his "hands always so empty," so he "embraced the idea that something considerable might be made of Roderick" (1: 48), even though his cousin Cecilia warns him that he will have his "hands rather full" with the younger man. The challenge for Mallet inheres in the terms—the discourse of aesthetic capitalism—he uses to express his desire. Can he keep his "speculation" in Roderick as free as possible from the dominant-subordinate, potentially exploitative temptations of profiteering capitalism? To speculate in another man is risky in all sorts of ways—even before the criminalization of homosexuality—and James seems specially interested in the ethical and psychological challenge of such male-male investment.[5] What effects can such male-to-male desire have on both relationships and individual identities? Can male desire be compatible with self-achievement? In effect, can Rowland care enough about Roderick to keep his hands off and allow his protégé to develop freely—to own his own labor? Roderick will later declaim to the Italian sculptor Gloriani that he wants to "produce the sacred terror; a Hera that will make you turn blue, an Aphrodite that will make you turn—well, faint" (1: 117), so freeing him from patronizing control could quickly turn the tables on Rowland's project—placing him in a masochistic position, as Wendy Graham notes, in relation to a sculptural male sadist. In her view Roderick "intends for his 'divine forms' to replicate the experience of being shattered into sexuality; his bravura manner belies a hidden identification with the viewer's frisson, the sublime thrill of aesthetically induced pain and fright" (129–30).

Although Mallet and Hudson are very different from one another, each represents an alternative to conventional masculinity. Having never been "accused of anything more material than a manly stoutness" and with hair the "fairest shade of yellow" and a "complexion absurdly rosy" (1: 13), Mallet is a kind of Fair Gentleman. Although he served, like the later Christopher Newman and Basil Ransom, as an officer during the Civil War, "if not with glory, at least with a noted propriety," he feels none of those later characters' hunger for "driving a lucrative trade" (1: 15). In fact, he considered his post-college stint in his father's counting-house to be "small drudgery" (1: 14). Hudson, of course, seems very different. Active and energetic, he does "everything too fast," according to Cecilia, and he himself feels "something inside" that "drives" him—some "demon of unrest!" (1: 20). Neil Schmitz considers Roderick a typical Jacksonian male; his "aesthetic tall talk" is the "dangerous hyperbole of the male hysteric" (155).[6] At the same time, Hudson is no conventional Masculine Achiever in the manner of Newman or Goodwood. Indeed, this "remarkably pretty boy" (1: 17), with his "soft and not altogether masculine" voice (1: 21) and "extraordinary beauty" (1: 23), reminds Rowland of "some beautiful, supple, restless, bright-eyed animal, whose motions should have no deeper warrant than the tremulous delicacy of its structure" (1: 31). In these physical terms, he is as much an alternative to conventional masculinity as Mallet, and like his patron he rejects the "repulsive routine" of the business world (1: 24). He experiences exasperation at having to fill a "double place" for his mother ever since his brother Stephen, a model of the "useful man," was killed in the war. "It's a good deal to ask of a man," he complains, "especially when he has so little talent as I for being what he's not." From his mother's point of view and from his culture's, he recognizes, his brother was "much more the right thing" (1: 41). His mother demands that he "must be to her everything that [his brother] would have been"—in short, someone who "would have made fifty thousand dollars and had the parlour done up" (1: 42). In putting the matter so bluntly, James obviously represents the conflict he himself felt between business and an artistic career, but he has also diagnosed in remarkably stark terms the tensions experienced by many late-nineteenth-century American men.

James does more, however, than simply represent a simple choice between business and art for his two unconventional male characters, because in putting them together in a homosocial and erotically charged relationship, he explores the possibility of dynamic male identities that develop through the vehicle of male-male relationship. In this complementary relationship between men, Rowland provides the "voice of taste and authority," while Roderick offers an "indefinable attraction—the something tender and divine of unspotted, exuberant, confident youth" (1: 30). In fact, Hudson seems to require of Mallet what Mallet requires of "something or someone"—a goad to self-expression, a form for self-expression and self-expenditure to take. Whereas Mallet hoards his energy, however, Hudson expends energy like Walt Whitman in bursts of exaggerated utterance, as when he announces his intention to become "the typical, original, aboriginal American artist" (1: 33). Furthermore, while Mary Garland confidently announces that sculpture is "work for men" (1: 346), given the "row" with his mother that follows Roderick's decision to accompany Rowland to Rome, James appears to be signaling the emergence of a male figure at odds with women—an artist empowered homoerotically and phallocentrically in the masculine by another male. Roderick wants to "strike out hard" and "do something violent and indecent and impossible—to let off steam" (1: 71)—but he rejects conventional masculinity and conventional masculine models.[7] He commits himself to high art, becoming an "aesthete *gloriosus*" in Richard Ellman's felicitous term (214). Roderick is an artist to "his fingers' ends," James observes (1: 29), and during his apprenticeship he has used his sculptural "fingertips" to form male rather than female figures. Disengaging Roderick from women (despite his engagement to Mary), James explores the possibility of a homo-aesthetic creativity—empowered by the investment of male subjectivity (and Rowland's speculative desire) and focused on male subjects. In volunteering himself to be Roderick's patron, Rowland ensures that he will possess and become the privileged viewer of Roderick's productions. Investing his own desires in Roderick's art, he enables male desire to circulate through sculpted objects to the male subjects triangulated with them—a "speculation" indeed—and thus to configure homoerotic desire reflexively.

Roderick's first sculpture, a bronze statuette called *Thirst*, represents a "youth of ancient fable—Hylas or Narcissus, Paris or Endymion"—whose beauty is the "beauty of natural movement" (1: 17). Robert Martin, noting the mention of Hylas (beloved of Hercules), argues that the sculpture's function is to "make the reader aware of a homosexual (or homoerotic) relationship between the two men" ("'High Felicity'" 103).[8] Mallet immediately takes *Thirst* into his possession—as if simultaneously introjecting homo-aesthetic desire and slaking his own "thirst" for Roderick by incorporating, or swallowing, an object Roderick has created. The four mythological figures to which James compares the statue, moreover, all represent an ephebic ideal that he would have known both from experience and from his reading.[9] James knew that body type, and his use of it early in the novel emphasizes Roderick's position as both a male subject and object: creator of desirable male bodies through his sculpture, object in his own right of Rowland Mallet's attention and desire.

James would have found in Walter Pater's account of German art historian Johann Winckelmann's interest in Greek sculpture authorization for admiring beautiful male bodies and seeking intimate male friendships—a model for the homo-aesthetic friendship of critic and sculptor he represented in *Roderick Hudson* and belatedly discovered when he met Hendrik Andersen. That Winckelmann's "affinity with Hellenism was not merely intellectual, that the subtler threads of temperament were inwoven in it," Pater avows, "is proved by his romantic, fervent friendships with young men. He has known, he says, many young men more beautiful than Guido's archangel. These friendships, bringing him into contact with the pride of the human form, perfected his reconciliation to the spirit of Greek sculpture" (191).[10] Roderick's sculptural relationship with Rowland uncannily anticipates James's relationship with Andersen, the American-born sculptor he met in Rome in May 1899. "The moment James climbed the stairs into Andersen's sun-filled Roman studio," observes Fred Kaplan, "he began a memorable relationship that was to clutch at his heart for the next five years" (447). As if replicating the behavior of his own protagonist, James immediately became Andersen's patron; he insisted upon purchasing Andersen's portrait bust of a young boy, Count Alberto Bevilacqua, which looked much like Andersen himself (Kaplan 447).[11] In his letters James pointedly used Andersen's sculptures to mediate his own desire for the sculptor himself. Before closing his 9 May 1906 letter with the tender "goodnight, dearest Hendrik. I draw you close and hold you long and am ever tenderly yours" (*Henry James Amato Ragazzo* 160), James offers Andersen extended advice about sculpting nudity:

I should go down on my knees to you, for instance, to individualize and detail the *faces*, the types ever so much more—to study, ardently, the question of doing that—the whole face-question. I should cheekily warn you against a tendency to neglect *elegance*—to emphasize too much the thickness and stoutness of limb, at the risk of making certain legs, especially from the knee down, seem too short etc.—and arms also too "stocky" and stony. The faces too blank and stony—the hair, for me, always too merely *symbolic*—and not living and *felt*. These offensive things I should say to you—in such a fashion that you would but love me better and our friendship would be but the tenderer and closer. (158–60)

In this remarkable passage James overtly negotiates an ardent verbal relationship with Andersen through his sculptural criticism. Down on his knees before the sculptor, James examines the sculpted bodies and encourages Andersen to forego the symbolic register for the fully and individually embodied. James designs this "offensive" advice, moreover, to have a similar—more "living and *felt*"—effect on his own relationship with Andersen.

In his ability to sculpt an ideal male nude Roderick proves more successful than Hendrik Andersen, whom James would criticize for his inability to differentiate his nude figures by gender in terms uncannily similar to those used by one critic of *Roderick Hudson*. "I sometimes find your sexes (putting *the* indispensable sign apart!) not quite intensely enough differentiated—I mean through the ladies resembling a shade too much the gentlemen." Divesting the penis of its phallocentric signifying power, James expands the coverage of his critical gaze to encompass other body parts. Citing the figure of a ballerina, James criticizes Andersen's failure to allow her "sufficient luxury" of hip, "or, to speak plainly, Bottom." "She hasn't *much* more of that than her husband, and I should like her to have a good deal more" (162). Focusing though he does on a female figure and her "Bottom," James closes his letter by expressing his desire to "take" Andersen to his "heart" and to "feel" his arms around him—making it clear that here too he uses sculptural criticism to express his desire for Andersen himself. James had established a similarly mediated relationship between Roderick Hudson and Rowland Mallet, but that relationship founders when Roderick turns from sculpting male to sculpting female figures.

Roderick's ability to "differentiate" between genders reflects itself in his early sculptures, which reveal an interesting range of male figures with obvious roots in the crises of post-Civil War American culture: a "colossal head of a negro tossed back, defiant, with distended nostrils," a bust of his dead brother (killed in the Civil War), and of course the bust of his boss at the bank, Barnaby Striker, which Roderick climactically smashes with a hammer in order to signal his break with American commercialism and his passionate commitment to his European excursion with Rowland (1: 38). That gesture, and especially James's observation that the bust "cracked into a dozen pieces," which "topple" upon the floor, foreshadows the violence latent in the homosocial relationships on which James centers so much of his attention. Striker is by his own account "every inch" a "self-made man" (1: 62), so in busting his bust—with a mallet, no less—James signals his own effort to redefine the terms of artistic achievement and male identity, liberating both from conventional models of masculine achievement.[12] Given his initiatory relationship with Rowland, Roderick promises to be more an artistically "man-made man" than a self-made man after the business model.

Ironically, at the moment they decide to leave for Italy together, Mallet and Hudson interest themselves in Mary Garland, creating what an early reviewer termed a "perplexing little triangular arrangement" (Hayes 4). Mutual attraction to Mary offers heterosexual cover, of course, even as it positions her between them and thus enables them to relate to each other in romantic terms. As Wendy Graham puts it, "the excitement produced by homosocial intimacy gets vented through heterosocial channels" (104). Rowland's attraction to Mary compensates for his "odd feeling of annoyance with Roderick for having peremptorily taken possession of his nature" and also derives from her embodiment of the "comfort" and "safety," the "perfect absence of temptation" in Northampton (1: 67). Although the *New York Times* reviewer complained that James rendered Rowland a "male Mary Garland," Mary actually offers Rowland a more complex male role. She speaks for work and for doing—for having a profession and being a "producer" rather than "observer" (1: 74–75)—while simultaneously discouraging the character excesses of marketplace achievement. Indeed, she offers Rowland the possibility of combining feminine and masculine traits—of becoming a male version of herself—and thereby reconciling what Rosenberg terms the "irreconcilable conflict between the imperatives of the Masculine Achiever and the Christian Gentleman" (150).

Roderick's engagement to Mary derives more from excess energy than from love, but it also springs from the deflection of desire from investment along conventional gender lines. You "came and put me into such ridiculous good-humour," he tells Rowland, "that I felt an extraordinary desire to spill over to some woman, and I suppose I took the nearest" (1: 82). Suggesting the compulsive and compulsory heterosexuality that Eve Sedgwick describes in *Epistemology of the Closet*, Roderick credits Rowland with evoking his "extraordinary desire to spill over" in his art and in his relationships, but he looks to "some woman" in whom to invest his "extraordinary desire." Given the exaggerated male self Roderick becomes in the process of leaving a business career in America for an artistic career in Europe, however, his engagement to Mary seems capricious. James recognized the anomaly. "It is not really *worked-in* that Roderick himself could have pledged his faith in such a quarter, much more at such a crisis, before leaving America," he commented two decades later in the Preface to the New York Edition, "and that weakness, clearly, produces a limp in the whole march of the fable" (*Art of the Novel* 17).

This "obscure hurt," so to speak, to Roderick's fable and male self cannot be healed simply by his finding a more desirable love object. The double engagement to Mary Garland (if Rowland can be considered engaged to her in imagination) serves several purposes: providing American ballast for the European quest of these male characters, but also "normalizing" and covering their masculinity and heterosexuality at the very moment they embark upon a relationship in the "margin." Most importantly, however, the double engagement shows how complexly James was trying to imagine possible relationships and possible male roles. In retrospect, in the New York Edition preface, he suggested those intentions in the process of regretting Mary's comparatively unconvincing appeal to Rowland. The novel does not truly convince us, James remarks, that "Rowland's destiny, or say his nature, would have made him accessible at the same hour to two quite distinct commotions, each a very deep one, of his whole personal economy" (*Art of the Novel* 17). Torn between Roderick and Mary—between investing his economic, intellectual, and emotional "money-bag" in a relationship with a man or with a woman—Rowland's character is such that, as James puts it, "each of these upheavals of his sensibility must have been exclusive of other upheavals, yet the reader is asked to accept them as working together" (*Art of the Novel* 17–18). Most striking in this statement is the tension between James's first and final intentions. Whereas he acknowledged creating a male figure (Rowland) who invested himself in two relationships—a unique kind of androgynous or bi-directional ideal in which desired male and female objects work together—in retrospect he regretted making that possibility available and wished instead to make Rowland choose between Roderick and Mary. The "whole sense of the situation depicted," he now believed, "is that they should each have been of the strongest, too strong to walk hand in hand" (*Art of the Novel* 18).[13]

For all practical purposes, of course, Rowland does seem to choose. Resigning himself to "three interminable years of disinterestedness" in Mary (1: 80), he directs his attention and his money to Roderick's education and career, speculating in Hudson and investing himself in a symbiotic, homosocial relationship in which male "youth and genius hand in hand" (rather than a man and a woman) produce the "most beautiful sight in the world" (1: 90). Roderick's "unfailing impulse to share with his friend every emotion and impression" makes their "comradeship a high, rare communion" (1: 90–91). For much of the novel, on the other hand, James seems to have made a choice of his own, as if resisting the full implications of such emotional intimacy between men—as if Roderick and Rowland were "too strong" (too obvious) to "walk" homotextually, so to speak, "hand in hand." He seems more interested in Roderick's separate artistic development than in Rowland's experience, as if determined to define his own male aesthetic more narcissistically than relationally and to embed it within a traditional, instrumental male economy—as if trying to compensate aesthetically for the business model of male achievement with which Roderick had broken when he smashed the bust of Barnaby Striker. Roderick transmutes everything he experiences into art with the "instinct of investing every gain of sense or soul in the enterprise of planned production" (1: 93). Even Roderick, however, feels some inner conflict about what happens to him in Europe, as if unable to maintain an entrepreneurial model of art outside of America.

Roderick evolves as both subject and object, sculptor and sculpted object, and the personal changes he experiences in Italy register on his body, as if it were still in the clay. Shortly after his arrival in Rome, for example, he becomes convinced that he has a new body: "Surely I haven't the same face. Haven't I different eyes, a different skin, different arms and legs?" (1: 86). He projects this self-sculptured sense of protean possibility—the "grand genius of me!" (1: 88)—into his early sculptures. He thinks of sculpture Whitmanically—the way Whitman thought of poetry—in terms of embodiment and size. "We stand like a race with shrunken muscles," Roderick claims, "staring helplessly at the weights our forefathers easily lifted." "I mean to go in for big things; that's my notion of art" (1: 116). Indeed, Roderick's first stage of artistic development represents a homo-aesthetic phase of sculpting male bodies. A logical extension of his thirsty male figure, his first Roman sculpture is an Adam inspired by his watching, ensconced in a gondola with Rowland, a "brown-breasted gondolier make, in high relief against the sky of the Adriatic, muscular movements of a breadth and grace that he had never seen equalled" (1: 91). This triangulated scene in which two men gaze at another man's semi-naked body serves James as a means of mediating a relationship he would find it difficult to name, and it recalls a passage in an 1869 letter that James wrote his brother William from Venice. The Venetian population, "on the water, is immensely picturesque," he had written, and he singles out the "bare-chested, bare-legged, magnificently tanned and muscular" men (*Letters* 1: 142). Roderick, too, feels mesmerized. Jumping up after two hours of observation, in a kind of epiphany of phallogocentric inspiration, he declares that the "only thing worth living for was to build a colossal bronze and set it aloft in the light of a public square" (1: 92). Determined to "hand over his passions to his genius to be dealt with" (1: 93), he "wrestled all day with a mountain of clay in his studio." He was "passionately interested, he was feeling his powers," and he believes that his powers, "thoroughly kindled in the glowing aesthetic atmosphere of Rome," will never dissipate. He keeps models in his studio "till they dropped with fatigue" (1: 102) and finally shapes the "miraculous," life-sized Adam, a sculpture he was "never afterwards to surpass" (1:103). When put into the Carrara marble that Rowland has chosen, this product of Roderick's powerful passions passes "formally into Rowland's possession" (1: 104)—Rowland's first tangible return on the "speculation" he is making in Roderick's career. An example of intersubjective male triangulation, this scene of creativity reflects uncanny cooperation between male desires. Mutual male gazing at another man engenders Roderick's creativity, which is doubly sponsored by Rowland's money and desire, and the result is a colossal male sculpture that circulates between patron and protégé. The sculpture functions as both object of a homoerotic and homo-aesthetic coupling—a surrogate child after the fashion of the Archdeans' design in the later "Hugh Merrow"—and an idealized male subject, a phallocentric ideal of masculine embodiment.[14]

Robert Martin's provocative notion that Christina Light will "ensnare" Roderick and "take him away from his older lover" ("'High Felicity'" 104), like other characterizations of her as a "femme fatale," downplays the important challenges Christina poses for Roderick's art and the range of options James explores for his male character.[15] The ambiguous agent of both finishing and corruption (like Marie de Vionnet in *The Ambassadors*), Christina frustrates Roderick's phallocentric aesthetic, his desire to objectify and idealize her. Determined to "care only for the beauty of Type" and to create only "divine forms" (1: 116, 118), Roderick cannot accommodate Christina's complexity. Her volatile subjectivity simply resists easy abstraction. Even as a model, Christina resists efforts to make her other than she is. She is "fatal to the pictures" of her (1: 155) because her appearance simply cannot be reduced to any "divine form." The Italian sculptor Gloriani compares her to Salome (1: 190). The American painter Augusta Blanchard says she "looks half like a Madonna and half like a ballerina" (1: 195), while Madame Grandoni considers her an actress who "believes in her part while she's playing it" (1: 196). Even as an object for others, in short, Christina transcends rather than conforms to any "Type." Her performance of her self, especially her gendered self, exceeds common categories. She is "never the same, and you never know how she'll be," in Roderick's words—"because there are fifty of her" (1: 187). A variation on the improvisational George Sand, Christina Light suggests multiple possibilities for manhood in relation. The man able to respond to each of the "fifty" Christinas would have to improvise multiple male selves.

Ironically, Roderick's artistic powers flag when he turns to sculpting female figures and when he tries to metamorphose into the kind of man Christina demands. After he meets her in Baden-Baden, he confesses that his nature and will—and his sexual orientation—have been shaped for good. Although he acknowledges that there are "all kinds of uncanny underhand currents moving to and fro between one's will and the rest of one—one's imagination in particular"—he has concluded that a "certain group of circumstances" have conspired to "snap" his "power to choose" like a "dry twig" (1: 141). Roderick's logic is a little difficult to follow, but the transformation he describes might fairly be termed a "fall" into heterosexuality. His earlier exuberance, sponsored by "underhand currents" that liberate his powers of object choice, has given way to a circumstantially constructed imaginary that naturalizes desire by heterosexualizing object choice. As Roderick announces resignedly to Rowland, "One conviction I've gathered from my summer's experience . . . is that I'm damnably susceptible, by nature, to the grace and the beauty and the mystery of women, to their power to turn themselves 'on' as creatures of subtlety and perversity. So there you have me" (1: 141–42).

James uses Christina Light, in other words, to naturalize and normalize Roderick's desire and male identity, but also to signal the decline of his evolving male (arguably homoerotic) aesthetic. Her beauty is so extraordinary, James observes, it is as if "nature had produced it for man's delight and meant that it should surrender itself freely and coldly to admiration" (1: 151). Inspired by his vision, Roderick begins to model a new, female figure, a "woman leaning lazily back in her chair" whose image effectively triangulates and thereby forecloses upon the expression of male-to-male desire that James had earlier represented. Although Rowland gladly took possession of Roderick's "Adam," he does not like this replica of the Capitoline Aggrippina because it "differed singularly from anything his friend had yet done" (1: 143). Roderick, James implies, can't do women, and as he falters in his studio, he puts his new manhood at risk. "Be a man," Rowland tells him, with some annoyance at his whining, "and don't, for heaven's sake, talk in that confoundedly querulous voice" (1: 149). Roderick himself recognizes that, six months before, he could stand up to his work "like a man" (1: 147). In the famous scene in the Coliseum in chapter 13, Christina cries out for a man "cast in a bigger mould than most of the vulgar human breed," but this demand that Roderick reincarnate himself as one of his own "big things" comes with a catch. She only wants a man who can give her a "feeling" that will cause her to "send Prince Casamassima and his millions to perdition" (1: 261). Heterosexual and market-driven, Christina's voice effectively constructs Roderick's desire and the male subjectivity behind it. This rather trite example of a *belle dame sans merci*, sapping male strength and creativity, contrasts with the power of Roderick's relatively undifferentiated desire during the early part of the novel. Even though Christina later complains that the "world's idea of possible relations, either for man or woman, is so poor—there would be so many nice free ones" (1: 409)—James uses her agency and the influence of Roderick's conscience to reconstruct his imagination along conventionally heterosexual and hetero-aesthetic lines. Roderick may be observed "ardently shaping a formless mass of clay" into a replica of Christina (1: 170), but Christina also shapes Roderick into a particular kind of man, enforcing the prescriptive authority of compulsory heterosexuality. Rising to the challenge Christina offers, Roderick asserts his manhood in just the terms Christina has outlined. She had demanded a man with the "voice of a conqueror" (1: 261). Attempting to achieve such a voice, Roderick thunders, "Sit down!" when she tries to prevent his "gallant" gesture of plucking a flower from the wall some twenty feet above them (1: 265).

Although James focuses primarily in *Roderick Hudson* on his two male characters, he uses Christina Light to explore a heterosexual model of manhood by which both Roderick and Rowland can be judged. In fact, in the lengthy conversation with Roderick at the Coliseum (with Rowland eavesdropping), Christina attempts to define such a masculine ideal. James often uses female characters as magic mirrors for men, reflecting men as they might want to view themselves, and Christina's portrait of a gentleman sounds terribly conventional. She describes and, for Roderick, would seemingly inscribe the portrait of a male rescuer who can sweep her away to safety and offer a pointed alternative to Prince Casamassima, who, she later tells Rowland, "never walks" and must be carried up the Faulhorn in a palanquin—"like a woman" (1: 489, 490). Portraying herself as a "poor weak woman," she wants a "man who's strong" and will "neither rise nor fall" by anything she says, a "great character" with the "voice of a conqueror" (1: 260–61). Anticipating Maggie Verver in *The Golden Bowl* in her desire for a man at least on the edge of sadism, she admits that she could desire a "man of extraordinary power who should wish to turn all his passions to account" (1: 262), and she claims that the language she would like to hear from a "person offering [her] his career" would express a "confidence that would knock [her] down" (1: 263). The masculinity that Christina's subjectivity inscribes seems too clearly erected on the prostrate form of "other" manhood—designed to cover and compensate for the "weak" terms that her "strong" character eclipses. The reviewer for the *New York Times*, for example, responded in precisely these conventional terms to Christina's eventual decision not to marry Roderick. "With all her admiration of his genius and of himself," this reviewer concluded, "she feels that he is not quite manly. The virile force to which her feminine nature longs to render due submission, she does not find in his brilliant but unstable, untrustworthy nature" (Hayes 5). However limited the *Times* reviewer's notion of "true manliness" (Hayes 5), it gibes with the notion James attributes to Christina. In contrast to the potentially selfless investment that Rowland seemed eager to make in Roderick's artistic power, Christina's desire to see Roderick's passions turned "to account" encourages male competition and a battle (over her) to the death. It also inscribes a compulsive, even compulsory heterosexual ideal—a portrait of a conventional American Adam who would knock her down rather than eat the apple she offered him.

Although James uses Christina Light to educate both male characters in appreciating women in other than aesthetic or economic terms, he objectifies an archaic masculine ideal through her reflective subject position that neither man can fulfill. Roderick's response to Christina's sketch, for example, is an "incoherent wail" (1: 263), followed by the foolhardy gesture of trying to scale the high wall of the Coliseum to pick a rare blue flower for her—an attempt that the vigilant Rowland prevents (1: 266). Even though Rowland admires the "ardent authority" of Roderick's gesture, his action also prevents Roderick's becoming the kind of man Christina apparently wants. At the same time, James surely means Roderick's new swagger to be viewed ironically as a misunderstanding of Christina's wish.[16] "Roderick was far from hanging his head as might become a man who had been caught in the perpetration of an extravagant folly," he observes from Rowland's point of view; "but if he held it more erect than usual our friend believed that this was much less because he had made a show of personal daring than because he had triumphantly proved to Christina that, like a certain person she had dreamed of, he too could speak the language of decision" (1: 266–67). Acting out of an archaic masculine ethos rather than out of the sort of strength of character that would be above such impetuous displays, Roderick mistakes bravado for self-confidence and ironically reveals himself to be as "scant" as Christina has suspected (1: 263).

James replicates this scene of at least a potential "fall" in Rowland's later vision of Roderick plunging to his death into a gulf of annihilation (1: 314). As it evolves, Rowland's fantasy triangulates desire, as he imagines Mary Garland "standing there with eyes in which the horror seemed slowly, slowly to expire" and being left by default to him (1: 315). James explores the complexities of this triangulated or quadrangulated relationship for much of the rest of the novel. As he imagines Mary's subjectivity and desire for Roderick, he considers her "abject for some last scrap" of the "feast" of her dream of marriage. He resists this vision, however, because it causes a gender inversion—rendering Mary a "mere male in petticoats" (1: 449)—but that female-to-male inversion obviously masks the male-to-female inversion that Rowland can imagine for himself. Either way, James associates abjectness with maleness, and in fact Rowland later feels "abject" before Mary, as he imagines her "throwing herself back into Roderick's arms at his slightest overture" (1: 474). In view of his earlier fantasy and especially his very similar readiness to jump at Roderick's beck and call, Rowland appears doubly abject before Roderick. He occupies a "girl's" position—Mary's—particularly when he broaches the subject of his intentions to Roderick. He feels "inconsistent and faint-hearted"—like a rejected suitor. "Roderick had made him promises," James notes, "and it was to be expected that he should wish to ascertain how the promises had been kept" (1: 475).

Although Roderick characterizes his relationship with Christina as a "blest idea shaping itself in the block," but now "suddenly split and turned rotten" (1: 481), Roderick himself furnishes the best example of rot and waste. When he dies at the end of the novel, he resembles a ruined sculpture, a "vague white mass" that "lay tumbled upon the stones," while Rowland occupies the sculptor's position. Although James quickly notes that Roderick is "singularly little disfigured" (1: 523), Rowland initially resists this example of abject male embodiment. He cannot bring himself to touch Roderick's body. "An attempt to move him would attest some fatal fracture, some horrible physical dishonour," so Rowland's one gesture is to close Roderick's eyes.[17] The result is a modest, Galatea-like animation, at least in Rowland's imagination: "The eyes were the eyes of death, but in a short time, when he had closed them, the whole face seemed to revive. The rain had washed away all blood; it was as if violence, having wrought her ravage, had stolen away in shame. Roderick's face might have shamed her; it was indescribably, and all so innocently fair" (1: 524).

Robert Martin considers Rowland responsible for Roderick's death insofar as he fails to love Roderick by accepting the "full human implications, including the sexual, of the master-protege relationship" ("'High Felicity'" 102)—fails, in other words, to offer Roderick the sort of healing touch that James later imagines giving and receiving from Hendrik Andersen. In shutting Roderick's eyes, Rowland symbolically breaks the circuit of male gazing. He transforms himself in this gesture into a voyeur, something like Whitman's twenty-ninth bather in being invisible to the other man whose body is fully displayed to his eyes and hands. The sort of tentative looks between men, in which desire is read and erotic subjectivity inferred, is not possible in this scene. Roderick may be exposed, but he remains unconscious of his exposure.[18] Fully displayed on his back to Rowland's male gaze, Roderick's death renders him statue-like, and Rowland's gaze and any desire it may express remain narcissistically contained. Left alone with Roderick, however, Rowland feels guilty for the way he has treated his friend but also, it is certainly possible, for the feelings he experiences at the site of his abject body. He loses himself in "dark places of passion" within himself, and he "lashes" himself for his conduct toward Roderick with a "scourge of steel" (1: 525). "If overt homosexuality is not generally narratable as itself in the nineteenth century, in what forms might such desires be narrated?" asks Scott Derrick. One such form, he suggests, is the "plot of disaster and death, which authorizes a violent and genocidal penetration of the male body, and which also produces emergencies that authorize the expression of tenderness and the giving of care" (90).[19]

The trace of blood, the one sign of the "internal economy" that James would later admonish Hendrik Andersen to emphasize in his art, must be removed before Roderick can in a sense come back to life.[20] In this undertaking the body must be purified—the eyes closed, traces of the insides removed. James was a long way from the passionate outburst of his letter to Andersen in representing the "blood-flow *under* the surface" of his characters, even though Mallet spends seven long hours with the body, a gap in the narrative that James refuses to fill even as he calls attention to this extended moment between men: "The most rational of men was for an hour the most passionate. He reviled himself with transcendent bitterness, he accused himself of cruelty and injustice, he would have lain down there in Roderick's place to unsay the words that had yesterday driven him forth on his lonely ramble" (1: 387). Only indirectly, through a fantasy of substitution and guilty self-abuse does James express the erotic charge that this moment carries—a dream come true as nightmare in which male desire has free rein to play with the abject, dead body of another man.

Christina's marriage to Prince Casamassima, of course, brings both Roderick's and Rowland's European experience to a climax. With Christina lost to him, Roderick feels divided within himself and alienated from the world around him. Sensing a "perfect vacuum" in his mind (1: 432) and a "crack in his brain" (1: 459), he projects the split in himself on Christina, mistakenly blaming her because she "didn't come up to [his] original idea of her" (1: 480). On the one hand, he celebrates her inspirational effect. She "makes my heart beat, makes me see visions" (1: 501), he tells Mallet. On the other hand, because he depends for inspiration on Christina, after her marriage he feels as if an "essential spring had dried up within him" (1: 445), and he regresses as both an artist and a man. At Rowland's urging he calls for his mother and for Mary and he begins to like, "almost as he had liked it as a boy, in convalescence from measles, to lounge away the hours in an air so charged with feminine service" (1: 353). He even sculpts a bust of his mother—the last sculpture of his career—signaling, it seems to me, how thoroughly he has shifted his creative energy away from the possibility of a mature artistic, as well as passionate, relationship (whether to Rowland, Christina, or Mary Garland).

Rowland Mallet has a relationship to Christina Light, not simply as Roderick's guardian, but in his own right, and while Roderick's suggestion that Christina may have had some romantic interest in Rowland (1: 505) seems farfetched, James uses Rowland to explore another potential male-female relation and, thereby, another construct of masculinity. From the first Rowland disapproves of Christina, and his moral compunction consistently interferes with his ability to understand her character. Whereas for Roderick she represents a potential lover and model for his art, for Rowland she remains essentially a text that he tries to read and interpret—like Daisy Miller for Frederick Winterbourne—and at first he is prone to conforming her to the terms of texts previously read. While he does give her some credit for being the "author" of her self and of her roles, he can credit her sincerity only by believing her the victim of her own fantasies. When she tries to explain her religious upbringing, for example, Rowland finds her inauthentic. He

> had already been sensible of something in this young lady's tone which he would have described as an easy use of her imagination, and this epitome of her religious experience failed to strike him as an authentic text. But it was no disfiguring mask, since she herself was evidently the foremost dupe of her inventions. She had a fictitious history in which she believed much more fondly than in her real one, and an infinite capacity for extemporised reminiscence adapted to the mood of the hour. She liked to carry herself further and further, to see herself in situation and action; and the vivacity and spontaneity of her character gave her really a starting-

point in experience, so that the many-coloured flowers of fiction that blossomed in her talk were perversions of fact only if one couldn't take them for sincerities of spirit. (1: 278)

In Rowland's extended metaphor Christina sounds much like George Sand, "the great *improvisatrice* of literature" ("George Sand" [*Galaxy*] 712), both in her resistance to easy classification and in her power of "extemporizing" a "fictitious history"—that is, writing her own story and, presumably, her own role in it. Rowland's cynical attitude toward Christina's story parallels Roderick's lack of emotional engagement, and the critical distance he maintains from her prevents him from appreciating her desire to escape the "text" in which she is bound. In effect, he himself creates a "fictitious history" of Christina that he prefers to any she might "invent" for herself. But in a novel that uses women (as in Christina's Coliseum speech) to mirror and even construct male subject positions, it is tempting to see in Rowland's resistance to Christina's fictitious history a resistance to possibilities for his own. In other words, his grudging appreciation for Christina's performance of herself suggests his own tentative performativity—the performance of a gendered selfhood that would be open to multiple enactments. Christina can imagine alternative roles for men, as well as for women, but she complains that the "world's idea of possible relations, either for man or woman, is so poor—there would be so many nice free ones." She tells Rowland that she "should like" Roderick as "something else" besides a lover and wishes that he would play the role of her brother and never again talk to her of marriage (1: 409). Here, too, James explores the possibility of alternative male roles, as if posing the challenge to his male characters through Christina to discover alternatives to male roles predicated on views of women as either aesthetic or economic objects.

Rowland's reaction to Christina's marriage, therefore, is worth noting because of its difference from Roderick's. Unlike Roderick, who only seems able to cry out in pain, Rowland seems to appreciate Christina's plight and, while admitting a tendency to "see things melodramatically" (1: 417), he sees her, at least partly, from her point of view. He objects to Roderick's accusations about her "infernal coquetry and falsity" (1: 429), becoming her champion much as he had earlier been Roderick's. Whereas Roderick simply judges her a "ferocious flirt" who has cynically led him on (1: 430), Rowland believes that she has acted desperately to make the best of her limited options. The change that occurs in his relationship with Christina signals a developing capacity for appreciation and an "intimate" relation—not in a romantic or sexual sense, but in an ability to understand a woman's behavior from her own point of view. Rowland's new "vision" of Christina, furthermore, does not occur capriciously within his own imagination. It derives from a conversation with her—in other words, from his willingness to let her define herself. As James puts it, "that last interview had sown the seeds of a new appreciation" (1: 488). Appreciating Christina herself rather than some "idea" of her, Rowland reveals himself, in Oscar Cargill's words, "the more mature and more masculine of the two men" (30). By the end of the novel, in fact, Rowland has fulfilled the masculine role that Christina defined for him earlier. He has become a "faithful friend," an "intimate friend—a friend to whom one could tell everything" (1: 209). This particular brand of masculinity, of course, deviates from the norm in some of its qualities—appearing much closer to the ideal of Christian gentility, for example, than to a model of masculine achievement. Being faithful means being a man in a very limited sense.

Rowland appears much more successful, of course, as a sympathetic "reader" of women than he does as a lover of either women or men. His astute judgment about Mary Garland, as he compares her favorably but not unfairly with Christina, represents one of the finest discriminations in James's early fiction despite its traditional masculine self-interest:

> There are women whose love is care-taking and patronising and who attach themselves to those persons of the other sex in whom the manly grain is soft and submissive. It did not in the least please him to hold her one of these, for he regarded such women as mere males in petticoats, and he was convinced that this young lady was intensely of her sex. That she was a very different person from Christina Light didn't at all prove that she was a less considerable one, and if the Princess Casamassima had gone up into a high place to publish her dismissal of a man who couldn't strike out like a man, it had been hitherto presumable that she was not of a complexion to put up at any point with what might be called the Princess's leavings. It was Christina's constant practice to remind you of the complexity of her character, of the subtlety of her mind, of her troublous faculty of seeing everything in a dozen different lights. Mary had never pretended not to be simple; but Rowland had a theory that she had really a finer sense of human things and had made more, for observation and for temper, of her scant material of experience, than Christina had ever made of the stuff of her wild weaving. She did you the honours of her intelligence with a less accomplished grace, but was not that retreat as fragrant a maiden's bower? (1: 449–50)

Rowland appreciates Mary partly, of course, because she resembles him; she is more an observer than a "wild" actor. In resisting the idea that Mary is "care-taking and patronising," however, Rowland indirectly refuses to define himself as a man who needs such a maternal woman—that is, as someone in whom the "manly grain is soft and submissive," a "male in petticoats." Contrasting Mary with Christina Light, Rowland also refuses to define himself as a "wild" man—an archaic, phallic male who could "strike out like man." At the same time, this passage suggests that he possesses remarkable openness about gender and an appreciation of varieties of masculinity and femininity. Even though Rowland does prefer those subtle qualities of mind that he and Mary possess, in the process of coming to terms with Mary's womanhood—and thereby with his own manhood—he neither denigrates Christina nor idealizes Mary. As Philip Sicker astutely observes, he is "the first of James' heroes to perceive his beloved as something other than a timeless icon" (46). Whereas Roderick's idealizing founders on his recognition that Christina is never the same because there are "fifty" of her, Rowland seems to appreciate his first impression that in Mary's face "there were many possible ones" (1: 53). Whereas Roderick boasts of being impervious to Mary's influence (1: 424), thus revealing himself as a feckless romantic whose infatuation with the beautiful and with a great beauty prevents other relationships, Rowland holds both Mary and Christina in a kind of dynamic tension with one another. And maintaining a "certain tension in one's being," we should recall, is "what a man is meant for."

In the last extended conversation between Roderick and Rowland, James contrasts his two male characters to the latter's advantage. While Roderick accuses him of being wholly ignorant of "nerves and needs and desires and a restless demon within," Rowland rightly judges these accusations to be the "high insolence of egotism" (1: 506). "I've loved quite as well as you," he maintains; "indeed I think I may say rather better, since I've been constant. I've been willing to give more than I received. I've not forsaken one mistress because I thought another more beautiful, nor given up the other and believed all manner of evil about her because I hadn't my way with her. I've been a good friend to Christina Light, and it seems to me my friendship does her quite as much honour as your love!" (1: 506–7). James does not necessarily rationalize a preference for friendship instead of love for women. Although clearly Rowland's "friendship" for Christina Light is superior to Roderick's "love" for her, James leaves open the question of Rowland's capacity for romantic love—the question of his "love" for Roderick and for Mary Garland. And in that regard, Roderick's observation that Rowland's silence about his feelings for Mary because of her engagement is "like something in a bad novel" certainly hits home (1: 511). Indeed, although Roderick's earlier accusation that women "scarce have an existence" for Rowland because he has "no imagination of them, no sense of them, nothing in [him] to be touched by them" is surely an exaggeration (1: 504), Rowland's feelings for Mary remain as mysterious as his behavior.

On one hand, Rowland certainly calculates his chances with Mary, anticipating that she will grow "weary of waiting for Roderick to come to his senses" (1: 460–61), and he is willing to go "half-way to meet her" if she suddenly declares her disillusionment with her fiancé (1: 474). He is also capable of tricking Roderick into declaring his feelings for Mary (1: 477), and, convinced that "Roderick had shattered the last link in the chain that bound Mary to him" when he asks her for money to visit Christina in Interlaken, he experiences the "movement of irrepressible elation" and "barely" stifles a "cry of joy" (1: 503). He has accumulated enough repressed passion for Mary that he can imagine Roderick plunging to a violent death and Mary "standing there with eyes in which the horror seemed slowly, slowly to expire, and hanging motionless hands which at last made no resistance when his own offered to take them" (1: 315). Rowland's appreciation of Mary, in fact, does not develop as much as his appreciation for Christina Light. To be sure, while he seemed initially attracted to Mary because of her association with the "tranquil spot" of Northampton and its "perfect absence of temptation" (1: 67), he recognizes her capacity for change when he sees her in Rome. "She was older, easier, lighter; she had, as would have been said in Rome, more form. She had thus, he made out, more expression, facial and other, and it was beautifully as if this expression had been accumulating all the while, lacking on the scene of her life any channel to waste itself. It was like something she had been working at in the long days of home, an exquisite embroidery or a careful compilation, and she now presented the whole wealth of it as a kind of pious offering" (1: 324). The domestic imagery of his appreciation, however, suggests preference for a cloistered life much nearer the "centre of Christendom" than the "mere margin," and a life in which even the opportunities for observation are restricted. Furthermore, the patience with which he waits for some sign that his suit might be successful suggests more than anything else a man who cannot speak the "language of decision." Indeed, at times he appears in pathetic contrast to the brash Roderick, as when, "in his high modesty," he dares not risk the "supposition that Mary could contrast him with Roderick to the advantage of his personal charm" and thinks that "his consciousness of duty done had a hand to hold out for any such stray grain of enthusiasm as might have crumbled away from her estimate of his companion" (1: 473).

Thus, while Rowland does seem to develop an appreciation for Mary's subtle virtues—fulfilling the terms of what Roderick called a "completely plastic vision" of her as a subject—it is hard to imagine what expectations or hopes he can have that justify his being the "most patient" of men (1: 527). When Mary implored him to search for Roderick during the violent storm in which he was killed—thus manifesting, to Rowland's mind, her readiness to "sacrifice" him—he felt the "comfort of certainty" that she no longer cared for him at all (1: 517). And later he obviously smarted under the recognition that, "during the awful journey back to America," she had "used him, with the last rigour of consistency, as a character definitely appointed to her use" (1: 526, 527). James had noted after Rowland's last conversation with Roderick that his "extraordinary acute sense of his rights had been replaced by the familiar chronic sense of his duties" (1: 515), but a sense of duty will not account for Rowland's behavior in later years.

Consistently the observer, he appears at the end of the novel without the possibility of any "intimate relation" of his own. The alternative Mallet faces and embraces anticipates the endings that many of James's characters make—renunciation of passionate experience. Renunciation, or reconciliation to a life without a viable love object, occurs with a twist in *Roderick Hudson*, however. In arguing that "Rowland's heterosexual love interest is merely a 'compensation' for the failure of the homosocial ideal" (197), Nomi Sofer undervalues Rowland's homoerotic investment in Roderick, although she does suggest provocatively that Roderick's "mistake is succumbing to the kind of 'unsafe' heterosexual passion that is incompatible with homosocial relationships instead of choosing the 'safe' female object of desire who would enable, rather than disrupt, the primary bond between men" (200). The tacit advice, that Rowland and Roderick remain in the closet and cover their relationship by heterosexual marriage, certainly has historical precedents. And the configuration for which Rowland finally settles does involve triangulation. Boasting of his "patience," Rowland spends much of his time in repeated, yet unproductive, rounds of visits to Northampton to see Mary. With Roderick's death he has lost the pleasure of vicarious experience, and he recognizes that his "personal world" is now "as void and blank and sinister as a theatre bankrupt and closed" (1: 526). His visits to Northampton confirm him in the role of a bachelor whose sexuality remains in a state of suspense because he has no apparent love interest. Like the narrator of "The Aspern Papers" in his visit to Juliana Bordereau, Rowland may visit Mary because she offers indirect emotional intimacy with Roderick—the power that James later attributed to the "publishing scoundrel" to "look into a single pair of eyes into which his [Aspern's] had looked or to feel a transmitted contact in any aged hand that his had touched" (8).

Critics who long for a neater ending to *Roderick Hudson* or play "matchmaker" for the four major characters fail to appreciate the complexity of James's conception of both gender and relationships. Romantically considered, for example, the "open" ending of the novel recognizes that individual character cannot be easily completed relationally. Similarly, while James sketches both Roderick and Rowland as alternatives to prevalent masculine types, especially to the Masculine Achiever, he clearly finds no easy way to reconcile or synthesize the differences between them. As an experiment in masculinities, *Roderick Hudson* contains no viable "model of grandeur." Manhood that might be negotiated homosocially or homosexually in transactions between men gives way before heterosexual inscriptions of masculinity that prove self-destructive (in Roderick's case) and self-abnegating (in Rowland's). Nevertheless, James goes a long way in the novel toward educating his two male characters about relations with women, even if their relation with each other seems to receive progressively less attention. More importantly, in deliberately blurring the lines of conventional relationships in the novel—each of the four major characters is "intimately" related to each other—James explores the potential of many different character pairings, even as he leaves many of them in a state of suspense.[21] The absence of "transactions" between extremes in *Roderick Hudson*, then, can be viewed as a strength rather than a weakness. It suggests James's continuing openness to possibilities of masculinity and relationship, his unwillingness to stabilize the meaning of manhood. What he remembered as he composed the Preface to the New York Edition of the novel was "the questions begotten within the very covers of the book, those that wander and idle there as in some sweet old overtangled walled garden, a safe paradise of self-criticism" (*Art of the Novel* 10). In raising more questions than he answers about the meaning of masculinity in *Roderick Hudson*, James creates suspense that he would spend the rest of his writing career trying not to resolve.

Chapter 2
Nursing the Thunderbolt of Manhood in *The American*

Looking back to the "Europe" he knew thirty or forty years ago in his New York Edition preface to *The Reverberator, Madame de Mauves, A Passionate Pilgrim, and Other Tales,* James recalls an imaginative field dominated by American girls like his own Daisy Miller (NY 13: xvi). When he turns his attention to the men, "the non-European, in these queer clusters, the fathers, brothers, playmates, male appendages of whatever presumption," such male figures resolve themselves—are "visible and thinkable"—into a single type: "the American 'business-man'" (13: xvii). Even from the distance of thirty or forty years, a successful writing career behind him, James feels a sense of inadequacy. Before the "American business-man," he declares, "I was absolutely and irredeemably helpless, with no fibre of my intelligence responding to his mystery. No approach I could make to him on his 'business side' really got near it. That is where I was fatally incompetent, and this in turn—the case goes into a nutshell—is so obviously why, for any decent documentation, I was simply shut up to what was left me" (13: xvii).[1]

James means to explain why he focused early works such as "A Passionate Pilgrim" and *Madame de Mauves* on American girls. He ignores his literary efforts, especially in *The American* (1877), to get "near" the American business man in the person of Christopher Newman, a character whose name alone suggests interesting possibilities for invention, literary play, and gendered novelty, even as the character in the flesh seems initially an unlikely candidate for masculine reinvention. Although James creates Newman in obvious contrast to Roger Lawrence (in *Watch and Ward*), Rowland Mallet, and Roderick Hudson (although as a westerner he does resemble Roger Fenton in *Watch and Ward*), I do not agree with Richard Henke's assertion that Newman is the "embodiment of masculine perfection" and a "remarkably well-adjusted male figure" ("Embarrassment" 275). Newman is certainly different, but even *The American* shows James experimenting with nontraditional, particularly "non-phallic" masculinities, as Kaja Silverman uses the term (3). In the reeducation project he undertakes with Newman, James seems bent on decentering the phallus as the privileged signifier of masculinity and opening male identity and male subjectivity to alternative performances of manhood. He does so, moreover, within the discursive context of nineteenth-century male typology, interrogating and attempting to reconstruct two of the prominent male character types that I discussed in the Introduction—what social historians have called the Masculine Achiever and the Christian Gentleman. As I noted, Charles Rosenberg maintains that Victorian sexuality can be characterized not so much by its repressiveness as by "a peculiar and in some ways irreconcilable conflict between the imperatives of the Masculine Achiever and the Christian Gentleman" (150), and it is tempting to see that conflict represented in the contrast James draws between such characters as Christopher Newman and Urbain or Valentin de Bellegarde in *The American*. Newman, like Caspar Goodwood in *The Portrait of a Lady* (1881) and, to a lesser extent, George Flack in *The Reverberator* (1888), certainly appears to be a classic, even exaggerated, portrait of a Masculine Achiever, while the Bellegarde brothers give the Christian Gentleman ideal a French twist.[2] The point in adducing these models, however, is not to "trace" such character types in the novel, but simply to provide a frame of reference within which different male characters can be understood. At least intuitively aware of these cultural ideals, James worked a series of variations on them, experimenting with masculine identity and behavior and attempting their reconstruction. In *Notes of a Son and Brother* James repeatedly recalls his failure to measure up to a "business" model of manhood. "To attend strictly to business," he observes, "was to be invariably *there*, on a certain spot in a certain place; just to be nowhere in particular, to *have* to be nowhere, told the queer tale of a lack or of a forfeiture, or possibly even of a state of intrinsic unworthiness" (*Autobiography* 305). In *The American*, however, James attempts to forge terms for a "new" manhood by educating an American "business" man without making him vulnerable to accusations of "queerness" or "lack" or "intrinsic unworthiness." He tries to liberate Christopher Newman from triangulated relationships that contaminate his masculine performances. In that respect, *The American* might be considered a search for a male utopia in which the exchanges that constitute male identity have been disinfected, so to speak, of complicating others. That search is alternately androcentric and gynocentric, rather than heterophobic or homophobic. In Newman's relationships with Benjamin Babcock and Valentin de Bellegarde, for example, James explores what might be called the power of homosocial man-ufacture—the possibility of constructing a man in cooperative rather than competitive relation with other men. In Newman's relationship with Claire de Cintré, on the other hand, James attempts (less successfully we shall see) to disengage romantic transactions between men and women from the homosocial market economy in which they are embedded and to explore the terms of what might be called a "pure" heterosexual masculinity.

Most early reviewers accepted Christopher Newman as an archetypal American, a Christopher Columbus rediscovering the Old World, and they usually noted his manliness. The *Atlantic Monthly* reviewer, for example, called Newman a "keen, hardy, broad-hearted but intensely commercial American" (Hayes 31). The *Appleton's Journal* reviewer termed him a "fine, manly fellow, physically and mentally, with unimpaired sensibilities and plenty of aspiration of a practical and democratic kind" (Hayes 43). And the reviewer for the *Eclectic Magazine*, faintly echoing Walt Whitman's famous self-portrait in the 1855 version of "Song of Myself," complimented James on the "situation" he had created—"that of an American, a self-made man, fresh from the crudities of his wild Western home, confronted with the aristocratic prejudices and the inflexible social standards of the most exclusive society of the Old World" (Hayes 44). The reviewer for *Scribner's Monthly* could hardly contain his praise for Newman as an ideal American male. "Big, rich, frank, simple-hearted, straightforward, and triumphantly successful," this reviewer gushed, "he satisfied us entirely by his genuine and hearty manliness, and he seemed to carry in his very blood a genius for success in any direction toward which his modest strength might be turned" (Hayes 39). So pure an exemplar of the American race (carrying his "genius" in his "very blood"), this reviewer's Newman also carries an imperialistic power, for "it would have seemed the most natural thing in the world for him not only to marry Madame de Cintré, but to become the guiding head of the whole house of Bellegarde" (Hayes 39). Given the power of conquest they recognize in Newman, reviewers felt disappointed at the ending James wrote because it undercut their sense of Newman's manliness. Newman "was emphatically a man of action," Thomas Sargeant Perry wrote in the *Nation*, "who felt that he wanted something and at once put out his hand for it." Given Newman's instrumental confidence, Perry reasoned, a "man of his sort cannot sacrifice his life's happiness, and, what is more, that of the woman he loves, for a mere whim." Indeed, Perry felt especially chagrined that James seemed to validate the Bellegardes' confidence that Newman would prove a "week-kneed adversary" (Hayes 30)—as if James had sold out his manly character to the French. The *Scribner's Monthly* reviewer, in fact, acknowledged the anger he felt at James's "failure to comprehend the character he had created." "Any man with the force of character needed to make the manufacture of washtubs a stepping stone to a great fortune, whether he were an American or not," this reviewer argued, "would have had that in him which would have driven him even to a desperate effort to reclaim a promised wife" (Hayes 40). The *New York Times* reviewer went even further, but his complaints about the ending capture the backwoods spirit of

James's characterization—the melodramatic inflationary rhetoric of Southwestern humor. "It would have been better for Mr. James' literary fame," this reviewer cautioned, "to have blown the convent up with nitroglycerine, and had Newman carry off Mme. de Cintré on an engine captured and managed for that purpose by the hero himself, than to have allowed him to end his love affair in what is vulgarly termed a fizzle" (Hayes 28). These extravagant responses to Newman's character and especially the keen, all-American disappointment that James fails to realize Newman's manly potential suggest how strongly some readers identified themselves with this portrait of "The American." James would come close to fulfilling this reviewer's fond fancy some nine years later when he ended *The Bostonians* in such a melodramatic manner. In this case, however, he obviously had other ideas about the plot his American New Man would inscribe. The reviewers' complaints, it seems to me, reflect a failure of understanding that has its roots, I would argue, in a narrow conception of American manhood. James does create an archetypally manly American, but he has more interest in unsettling that new man's manly character than in simply letting it drive the "engine" of his plot.

Invested as he is with such cultural import, in fact, Newman has garnered relatively little attention as a man—that is, as a potentially "new" man, James's revision of American manhood. The most significant exceptions are Carolyn Porter and Eric Haralson. Although she notes the "virtually innate masculinity with which James tries to invest him" (119), Porter emphasizes Newman's feminization, particularly at the end of the novel, when the Bellegardes insult and humiliate him and, in contrast to Valentin de Bellegarde, he accepts his loss. In his brilliant assessment of Newman's complex manhood, Haralson too emphasizes what Silverman would call "male masochism"—the beating fantasy (from Freud) that James effectively imposes on him. James "was subliminally leagued with Newman's punishers," Haralson argues ("James's *The American*" 483), because he resented the "rugged maleness" with which Newman would "reclaim the purloined mantle of patriarchy" (488) and feared the incest taboo Newman threatened to violate in his proposed marriage to Claire de Cintré. In *The American*, Haralson concludes, "a child—a new man—is being beaten in due proportion to his desire and seeming capability to seize the power of the father" (489). In effect, the very qualities that the *Scribner's* reviewer extolled make Newman a target for the jealous James. In contrast to Porter and Haralson, who emphasize Newman's performance of conventional masculinity—as well as its punishment, and even castration—I see James's portrait of this New Man as more experimental. Newman becomes the site, if you will, of a kind of open-market free-for-all among competing male subjectivities, and, as I did in the previous chapter, I want to focus on Newman's manhood-in-relation. Unlikely though it is as anything other than a source of low comedy (an updated version of Royall Tyler's *The Contrast* or James Kirke Paulding's *The Lion of the West*), James's implication of Newman in a romantic-gothic love story offers a rigorous test of manly possibilities. Can a primitive man like Newman really reform himself sufficiently to qualify as Claire de Cintré's husband? Can American masculinity really be made that flexible? Central though it is, Newman's relationship with Claire is not the only significant relationship in *The American*, and it will prove valuable to examine Newman in relation to other men, especially Benjamin Babcock and Valentin de Bellegarde. James seems to be trying to liberate manhood from the sort of triangulation, or quadrangulation, that complicated *Roderick Hudson*—as if seeking a "pure" heterosexuality (an unmediated male-female relationship) and "pure" homosociality (a utopic male bond).

In experimenting with Newman, of course, James poses himself a remarkable challenge because, as Haralson puts it, Newman "marks the limit of 'true' manliness among James's men" (475), reflecting James's variation on the "muscular" Christian manhood expounded by Charles Kingsley ("James's *The American*," 476–77). In *The American Scene* (1907), James remarked that "No impression so promptly assaults the arriving visitor of the United States as that of the overwhelming preponderance, wherever he turns and twists, of the unmitigated 'business man' face, ranging through its various possibilities, its extraordinary actualities, of intensity" (409). In his initial conception and description of Christopher Newman, James seems to be transcribing rather than revising the "business man" or Masculine Achiever stereotype. An "evangelist of the American doctrine of success," in James D. Wilson's terms (84), Newman also has his roots, like William Dean Howells's Silas Lapham, in the Civil War and the Union victory. His business success derives directly from battlefield leadership and the survival ethos he has learned to take for granted.[3] A brigadier general in the Union army, this "powerful specimen of an American" was "in the first place, physically, a fine man." "Long, lean, and muscular, he suggested the sort of vigour that is commonly known as 'toughness'" (*The American* [1879] 33), and this physical portrait seems to confirm Anthony Rotundo's conclusion that a "bodily ideal of manhood" became the "dominant ideal" in the second half of the nineteenth century ("Body and Soul" 26).[4] Newman is also a westerner, at least by his recent experience, and it is worth remembering that the American West of the period was a legendary site of violence and danger.[5] The year before James published *The American*, after all, Sioux warriors killed General George Armstrong Custer and his cavalry at the Battle of The Little Bighorn and Wild Bill Hickok was killed playing poker in a Deadwood saloon in the Dakota Territory. Newman appears in the novel out of this violent western background, even as he efficiently represents the coincidence of masculinity and business success. In effect, he has capitalized and capitalized *on* his manhood, investing his energy not only in business but also in his own physical self.[6] "He appeared to possess that kind of health and strength," James notes, "which, when found in perfection, are the most impressive—the physical capital which the owner does nothing to 'keep up'" (34). Hyperbolically phallocentric, Newman's spermatic economy—his fund of bodily "capital"—seems more precisely a spermatic alchemy, providing an endless supply of energy for life's business. Indeed, Newman ironically reverses the qualms of nineteenth-century masturbation warnings by finding it difficult to relax.

Despite his hero's maintenance-free manhood, James clearly means to do something new with Newman, if not exactly to feminize or invert him, at least to open his character and his masculinity to new experiences and new configurations—that is, to a post-Civil War reconstruction.[7] In some respects Newman's story resembles the one James had told in *Roderick Hudson*—the story of a relatively formless, energetic American abroad who becomes embroiled in a gothic-romantic love plot. If *The American* lacks an equivalent to Rowland Mallet, a patron and central consciousness, that is because Newman himself represents a cross of sorts between Masculine Achiever and Christian Gentleman—a business-oriented Roderick Hudson struggling to become a Rowland Mallet. As noted above, James suppresses the homosocial male bond he had centralized in *Roderick Hudson,* moving it to the margins (in Newman's relationships with Babcock and Valentin) and focuses instead, as he would do in *The Bostonians,* on his hero's relationship to women. The result is not simply Newman's feminization, as Porter claims, but the possibility—no mean feat in view of his excessive manhood—of his becoming a "ladies' man."[8] What kind of "new" man would an "old" man like Newman have to become, James seems to ask, in order to qualify himself as Clair de Cintré's husband? What kind of man can the female gaze create if a male subject becomes its object? Claire's brother Valentin advises Newman that his "best chance for success will be precisely in being, to her mind, unusual, unexpected, original. Don't try to be any one else; be simply yourself, out and out" (161). Under Newman's special circumstances, of course, *being* himself is not something he can "simply" be, but Valentin's advice does provide an important parameter for gauging Newman's protean pretensions as he tries to come "out" and "be" a successful suitor. For more often than not Newman puts pressure on himself to be "other" than he is.

In recalling his "first glimpse" of his subject in his New York Edition preface (*Art of the Novel* 21), James conflates two key scenes from the novel: the events that would send Newman to Europe and those that would send him home, both involving opportunities for revenge not finally taken and thus instances of Newman's acting against his own "original" instincts. In other words, the scenes that, for James, empowered and impelled his narrative recalled the sites of Christopher Newman's greatest power—greatest precisely because not used or expended. James's logic of vengeful economy recalls by analogy the spermatic economy of nineteenth-century sexual discourse, in which men were advised to conserve their limited supply of sperm in order to ensure an ample supply for procreation. As James suggestively explains his recollected vision of Newman, "He would hold his revenge and cherish it and feel its sweetness, and then in the very act of forcing it home would sacrifice it in disgust" (*Art of the Novel* 22). Phallically configured as it is, Newman's revenge becomes an autoeroticized object of desire, a thing in which a tactile pleasure can be taken, but its "sweetness" can only be enjoyed insofar as it is not used. Indeed, using that sweetness, "forcing it home," is not simply to risk using it up but to render it an object of "disgust." That is the point James himself wishes to "force home," because he mentions it several times. One's "last view" of Newman, he says, "would be that of a strong man indifferent to his strength and too wrapped in fine, too wrapped above all in other and intenser, reflexions for the assertion of his 'rights'" (*Art of the Novel* 22).

The economy of energy that James propounds in the Preface, as well as his investment in Christopher Newman, is more complicated than this simple spermatic economy suggests, however. James's act of recollection enables him to repossess a youthful version of himself, and that act of imaginative repossession depends for its appeal on an intimate and complex identification with his hero. Whereas Newman's power can be enjoyed only as it is not spent, James's remembered impression of authorial power depends on its almost orgasmic spending within a homo-aesthetic economy. "It was all charmingly simple, this conception," he remembers, "and the current must have gushed, full and clear, to my imagination, from the moment Christopher Newman rose before me" (*Art of the Novel* 23). Reiterating his emphasis that "the essence of the matter would be that he [Newman] should at the right moment find them [the Bellegardes] in his power," James pointedly makes his own power identical with Newman's. He "would come out strong and would so deeply appeal to our sympathy. Here above all it really was, however, that my conception unfurled, with the best conscience in the world, the emblazoned flag of romance" (*Art of the Novel* 25). James enjoys this recollection in a bittersweet mood, however, as if recollection itself depleted the strength of his conception. "I lose myself at this hour," he added,

in a certain sad envy of the free play of so much unchallenged instinct. One would like to woo back such hours of fine precipitation. They represent to the critical sense which the exercise of one's whole faculty has, with time, so inevitably and so thoroughly waked up, the happiest season of surrender to the invoked muse and the projected fable: the season of images so free and confident and ready that they brush questions aside and disport themselves, like the artless schoolboys of Gray's beautiful Ode, in all the ecstasy of the ignorance attending them. (*Art of the Novel* 25)

Here, as he had earlier, James reverts to an innocent, artless state—a carnivalesque state of homosocial freedom and play. He can unfurl his romance with the "best conscience in the world," largely by desexualizing the process of writing, and so save himself from the "disgust" that accompanies forcing his idea home upon the reader.

When Newman recounts the conversion experience that brought him to Europe, he describes his recoil from a similar "disgust," a recoil as much as anything else from an aggressive masculinity that would force itself home—upon another man. Smarting from a "very mean trick" played upon him by a business rival, Newman finds himself on Wall Street with the chance to put the other fellow's "nose out of joint"—to the tune of sixty thousand dollars. "I owed him a grudge, I felt awfully savage at the time," Newman says. "If I put it [the money] out of his way, it was a blow the fellow would feel, and he really deserved no quarter" (56). Newman, of course, resists this vengeful impulse. He experiences a "mortal disgust" for the whole business and wants to "wash" his hands of it. The idea of losing the sixty thousand dollars seems "the sweetest thing in the world" (57). Newman experiences this spontaneous revulsion as a personal rebirth—a dissociated state in which he feels himself divide in two. "I seemed to feel a new man inside my old skin," he concludes, "and I longed for a new world" (57). So radical a violation of standard male business and behavioral practices is this experience that Newman suspects himself of being insane. "Perhaps I was [insane]," he tells his friend Tom Tristram, "but in that case I am insane still" (57). In diagnosing a potentially pathological manhood—pathological not in its original manifestation but in its arguably feminized reincarnation—Newman earmarks the challenge James has posed himself in his character: finding some state of equilibrium that will "normalize" his new manhood.

The new world for which this New Man longs, of course, is the Old World, and the novel opens, as it were, on Newman's first day of school. Despite the "aesthetic headache" he experiences from straining his attention and dazzling his eyes in the Louvre in the novel's opening scene (33), Newman seems determined to rehabilitate and re-educate himself in European terms. James goes to great lengths to emphasize his elasticity, his desire to "expand," as he puts it, to "the full compass of what he would have called a 'pleasant' experience" (103). He conceives his project, especially his plan to acquire a wife, in conventionally masculine terms, but James seems determined to keep his archetypal hero off-balance, to unsettle any male role he performs. Even though Newman retains the active power of purchase conferred by his "long purse" (104), he feels himself in a largely passive position—as a kind of empty vessel that will be filled and formed by his experience. In fact, in considering this program of cultural self-improvement a "proceeding properly confined to women, foreigners, and other unpractical persons" (103), Newman self-consciously assumes a female subject position.[9]

Instead of simply inverting his hero within a conventionally male-female binary, James attempts to alter the terms of gendered valuation, to blur the boundaries between genders and to open new possibilities for manhood. In not being conventionally masculine, in other words, Newman does not by default become feminine, even though he "poses" in a female position.[10] Newman's education in alternative masculinities requires female instruction—by Mrs. Tristram and of course Claire de Cintré, a woman as archetypally European as Newman is American. Variously described as a "princess in a fairy tale," a "great white doll of a woman," and, like Galatea, a "statue which had failed as stone, resigned itself to its grave defects, and come to life as flesh and blood," Claire challenges Newman to sublimate his masculine energy in acts of aesthetic appreciation—in short, to "pose" in the feminine. Objectify her though he will, however, Newman also looks to Claire as an artist, a female Pygmalion who will recreate him as a gentler man. He can imagine himself an object that her female gaze renders transparent, and he "had a feeling that if she could only read the bottom of his heart, and measure the extent of his good will toward her, she would be entirely kind" (164). It is "Madame de Cintré's 'authority,'" James notes, "that especially impressed and fascinated Newman; he always came back to the feeling that when he should complete himself by taking a wife, that was the way he should like his wife to interpret him to the world" (165). More appropriative than androgynous, Newman would surrender his power of self-expression—becoming an object of female desire—but he retains his confidence that Claire will express or "interpret" him in a readerly fashion, the way he himself would want to be read.

In fact, Newman vacillates in his conception and response to Claire. An ideology of masculine achievement often eclipses any impulse of open appreciation, and the fear of victimization that James exemplifies in Tom Tristram and in Valentin de Bellegarde inhibits subjection to female authority. Newman may be "ready to accept the admired object in all its complexity" (165), but when he outlines his prescription for a wife to Mrs. Tristram, he only too pointedly betrays his Wall Street materialism. "I want a great woman," he admits. "I stick to that. That's one thing I can treat myself to, and if it is to be had I mean to have it. What else have I toiled and struggled for all these years? I have succeeded, and now what am I to do with my success? To make it perfect, as I see it, there must be a beautiful woman perched on the pile, like a statue on a monument." "I want to possess," he concludes, "the best article in the market" (71). A woman as investment in a bull market of male self-improvement—Newman would inflate himself by a process of accumulation, pumping up his male ego through the conspicuous consumption of a beautiful woman he earns through competition with other men. "I made up my mind tolerably early in life that a beautiful wife was the thing best worth having, here below," he confesses. "It is the greatest victory over circumstances. . . . It is a thing every man has an equal right to; he may get it if he can. He doesn't have to be born with certain faculties on purpose; he needs only to be a man. Then he needs only to use his will, and such wits as he has, and to try" (72). James's transcription of free market rhetoric into the European marriage market obviously complicates his efforts to reconstruct Newman's male identity and create a "new man." Rather than decentering the phallus as the primary signifier of Newman's manhood, James seems to recenter it—shifting the terms of masculine self-aggrandizement but not the form. To be a man, even a new man, still means erecting a monumental male self—feeling the "old skin," to invert Newman's earlier statement, around a "new man."

Put another way, Newman's original conception of his marital mission seems embedded within a competitive homosocial economy that positions him, as it were, between men and women. I want to return to Newman's evolving relationship with Claire de Cintré, but first I want to examine Newman's relationship with other men. Perhaps Newman's tendency to settle into traditional *masculine* "poses" might be unsettled, James seems to hypothesize, by breaking him away from the homosocial and *heterosexual* relationships that inscribe such postures and initiating him directly into unmediated homosocial and potentially *homosexual* relationships. Perhaps, in other words, homosocial market-place competition for women might be converted into homosocial comradeship in which men and masculinity, as in Ishmael's squeezable tub of spermaceti, blur and melt together.[11] Through the dynamic of male mirroring, especially by Benjamin Babcock and Valentin de Bellegarde, James explores what it means for Newman to be a man's man, as well as a "ladies' man." In transpositioning or double-positioning Newman, James thereby explores the proposition, in Eve Sedgwick's terms, that for a "man to be a man's man is separated only by an invisible, carefully blurred, always-already-crossed line from being 'interested in men'" (*Between Men* 89).

Writing to Mrs. Tristram during the guide-book tour he takes shortly after seeing Claire for the first time, Newman recounts his companionship with Babcock, the Boston minister who finds him as unworthy a model as he himself has found Tristram. As "different as possible" from Newman, with his "exquisite sense of beauty" and delight in "aesthetic analysis" (106), Babcock plays Christian Gentleman to Newman's Masculine Achiever and seems to mirror him back to himself in a negative light. Cheryl Torsney provocatively reads the Babcock-Newman interlude as James's disguised account of his own homosocial and homoerotic relationship with Charles Sanders Peirce in 1875–76 ("Henry James" 166). As an episode in Newman's manly evolution, however, this brief male friendship seems designed to destabilize Newman's heterosexual project by positioning him between heterosexual and homosexual identifications. For imaginative counterweight, Newman carries Claire's image with him during this whirlwind tour, and he refers Babcock to Claire. He had looked into a "great many other eyes" in the four-month interval since he met Claire, James notes, "but the only ones he thought of now were Madame de Cintré's" (113). Indeed, as he sees himself in Claire's eyes, Newman obviously sees the possibility of a new female-identified male self. He reminisces about his "past life" during which he "had nothing in his head but 'enterprise,'" and he experiences his "present attitude," he tells Tom Tristram, as a "rupture" from that past self. Estranged from Claire, he feels the "pendulum swinging back," even as he has mixed feelings over the prospect (113). He feels "decidedly proud" of some of his achievements, but he "admired himself as if he had been looking at another man"; the "business of money-getting appeared extremely dry and sterile" (114). Divided from his past self through Claire's fantasmatic agency, Newman also feels divided in the present, thanks mainly to Babcock's criticism. "He told me I was low-minded, immoral, a devotee of 'art for art'—whatever that is," Newman reports (116). That astonishing characterization—the hypermasculine Newman, of all people, reincarnated as an aesthete—caricatures the American's projected self-portrait. But if Newman plays flexible "femme" to Babcock, he gets to play "butch-femme" with an Englishman he meets shortly after this break up with Babcock. The Englishman, however, also gives him up "in disgust," Newman reports. "I was too virtuous by half; I was too stern a moralist," he informs Mrs. Tristram. "He told me, in a friendly way, that I was cursed with a conscience; that I judged things like a Methodist and talked about them like an old lady. This was rather bewildering. Which of my two critics was I to believe? I didn't worry about it, and very soon made up my mind they were both idiots" (116). Newman's confusion and suspension between two such different male interpretations of his character and his suspension simultaneously between those two male critics and an internalized image of Claire exemplify James's desire to keep Newman's male character open to fresh possibilities and new constructions, even as Newman's confidence that neither of his male critics understands him suggests determination to remain free of homoerotic inscription and thus open to heterosexual compulsion.

Even though he characterizes Babcock to Mrs. Tristram as a "sweet little fellow" and "the nearest approach" to Claire he has encountered on his tour (116), Newman seems unwilling to become the man that Babcock would make him. For whatever reason, James suppresses the homoerotic potential of this relationship in favor of a multivalence that so diversifies Newman's subjectivity that it ceases to assume any form at all. Babcock objects particularly to Newman's openness, or un-constructedness, his willingness to live in a state of suspense. "He liked everything," Babcock complains, "he accepted everything, he found amusement in everything; he was not discriminating, he had not a high tone" (106). Where Babcock tries, in his own words, "to arrive at the truth about everything" (109), Newman possesses a "gross intellectual hospitality" (106) and will "agree to anything" (109). As he tells Babcock in response to the latter's question about his choice of words to characterize a young woman who had an affair with one of his college classmates, "There are a great many words to express that idea; you can take your choice!" (107). Newman's almost post-structuralist openness to multiple meanings, a multiplicity of choices for characterizing a woman, applies as well to his own sense of maleness. His "personal texture" is "too loose to admit of stiffening" (108). He refuses at this point in the novel to settle into any single male character, to let Babcock "infuse" him with a "little of his own spiritual starch" (108). That is, he refuses to "stiffen" into a traditional masculine posture. The last straw for Babcock appropriately involves another example of Newman's confusing gender distinctions. Announcing that he wants to return to Milan because he didn't "do justice to Luini," Babcock suspects that the painter is not of the "first rank." Newman, however, thinks differently. Luini, he exclaims, is "enchanting" and "magnificent." "There is something in his genius that is like a beautiful woman. It gives one the same feeling" (110).

It is tempting to see homophobic repression in this episode—"homosexual panic," in the term Torsney takes from Eve Sedgwick ("Henry James" 171)—and to see openness as rationalizing homophobia, but Newman himself seems more confused than panic-stricken.[12] Desire and the object choices it entails compose a blurred male self that can experience the "same feeling" by contemplating a beautiful woman as by examining Luini's paintings. And if Babcock can "approach" Claire for sweetness and desirability, then Newman's perch on male subjectivity seems unstable indeed, at least insofar as the object choices available to him can reconstitute that subjectivity. Newman's romantic interlude with Babcock opens several questions, therefore, about his male identity and his masculinity. The point, it seems to me, is not simply to open the question of Newman's homosexuality, which James quickly closes off through his almost compulsive investment in a heterosexual relationship with Claire, but to note his resistance to any definite self-representation in the masculine, including any version of the homosexual. The Babcock episode leaves Newman suspended—between Babcock and Claire, homosexual and heterosexual desires, male-male and male-female economies.

Newman suspends his aesthetic judgment, much to Babcock's chagrin, but he also seems intent upon confusing and destabilizing the terms of his gender identification—specifically, decentering the phallus as the primary signifier of his maleness. That purpose is highlighted in the figure of the "grotesque little statuette" that he sends Babcock to commemorate their brief friendship—a representation of a "gaunt, ascetic-looking monk" with a "fat capon" hung around his waist, visible through "one of the rents of his gown." Although the narrator seems reluctant to suppose that Newman "intended a satire upon Babcock's own asceticism" (112), James's point is clear. Babcock, whose name suggests "bob/bobbed cock" or "baby cock," represents a very limited masculinity, an impotent maleness with a limited capacity to spend itself. Citing the statuette's delicacy, Torsney speculates that the monk may even be "gendered female," thus "previewing the fair-complected Claire" ("Henry James" 173). Although she argues that the statuette therefore embodies castration anxiety and "represents the loss of the sort of manhood and virility for which Newman stands, foreshadowing his own metaphoric castration by the Bellegardes, and also, potentially, with Babcock" ("Henry James" 174), I think that in refusing to accept a dose of Babcock's moral "starch" and to stiffen into a fixed male self, Newman tries to keep his investment options open. The result, as he himself characterizes it in his letter to Mrs. Tristram, is a state of suspense—a male selfhood positioned somewhere between "an old lady" and a "low-minded, immoral" art-for-art's-sake devotée: both "new men," to be sure, but neither likely to marry Claire de Cintré.

Whereas Newman resists Babcock's man-making efforts, he finds himself reversing roles in his relationship with Claire's brother Valentin. On his face, Valentin plays the "ideal Frenchman" of "tradition and romance" (143), a "*gentilhomme*" and thus a model of the man Newman aspires to become. Whereas Newman seems ready, at least initially, to play a male Galatea to Claire's female Pygmalion and to become an American gentleman, in his relationship with her brother he has the chance to play manmaker by refashioning Valentin in his own image—in effect, to make a self-made man. In this respect I disagree with Richard Henke, who argues that Newman "proves to be a particularly lethal role model for Valentine [sic]" ("Embarrassment" 277), because I see Valentin himself as a model for Newman. To be sure, Valentin flirts with the attraction of playing Galatea to Newman's Pygmalion and subjecting himself to Newman's man-making power, but instead he turns the tables on his potential patron and re-embeds him in the gothic-romantic subplot that prescribes rigid, polarized male postures.[13] Valentin feels genuinely attracted to Newman and to the brand of manhood Newman represents, admitting that Newman is the only man he has ever "envied" (141), and his willingness to accept Newman's suit signals his own desire, screened through his sister, for the man he so admires. You "have used your will and you have made your fortune," he marvels. "Happy man, you are strong and you are free" (146). Using Valentin in much the same way he had used Rowland Mallet—to valorize an instrumental manhood by making it an object of male desire—James also provides Newman, as he had Mallet, with the chance to patronize a younger male protégé. Although Newman's invitation to "come over to America" so that he can get Valentin a "place in a bank" sounds ludicrous (268), Valentin (and presumably James himself) feels the attraction even as he feels sheepish about accepting the offer. "It appears to me really a very bright idea," he admits with obvious qualification. "It would look as if I were a strong man, a first-rate man, a man who dominated circumstances" (298). Of course Valentin's enthusiasm is nothing compared to Newman's, and James remains more interested in the reflexive effects of this idea on Newman than on its influence on Valentin. "Newman's imagination began to glow with the idea of converting his bright, impracticable friend into a first-class man of business," James notes. "He felt for the moment a sort of spiritual zeal, the zeal of the propagandist. Its ardour was in part the result of that general discomfort which the sight of all uninvested capital produced in him; so fine an intelligence as Bellegarde's ought to be dedicated to high uses. The highest uses known to Newman's experience were certain transcendent sagacities in the handling of railway stock" (299). Recalling Walt Whitman's boast to "blow grit" within his "impotent" readers (70), Newman's boosterism makes him a man-making Midas, and his extravagance, like Whitman's, saves him from absurdity, linking him with a western humor tradition of brag. The inflated rhetoric of manly achievement proves contagious. "Dip me into the pot and turn me into gold," Valentin commands (300). Newman's desire to remake Valentin offers a creative, homosocial alternative to a procreative, heterosexual relationship and also suggests a reaction (formation) to the danger of his own remaking. Replicating himself by making another man in his own image validates his entrepreneurial manhood (his "original" self) even as it thwarts his reformation as a feminized man, while homosocializing capitalist rhetoric enables Newman to repeat himself narcissistically within a monological masculine discourse.

Although Virginia Fowler claims that Newman's "aggressive and wholly materialistic masculinity" (53) has equally "destructive effects" on both Claire and Valentin (54), because his arrogant desire to "Americanize and masculinize" the European and feminine Valentin "triggers" his despair and leads directly to his fatal duel with M. Kapp (56), I think James's satire cuts both ways. Fowler, like Henke, ignores Newman's efforts to dissuade

Valentin from participating in the duel, for example, and also the way James uses him to measure the stupidity of such archaic masculine rituals. Being a gentleman in *The American*—at least a "*gentilhomme*"—proves fatal for Valentin largely because he identifies his manhood homosocially and heterosexually. Like Tom Tristram, Valentin represents a cautionary manhood, another example of subjection to female authority. "Oh, the women, the women," he complains, "and the things they have made me do!" (144). In that complaint Valentin obscures the homosocial sources of his behavior. He feels genuine relief, it appears, when Stanislas Kapp triangulates his relationship with Noémie Nioche. "The matter now," he tells Newman, "is that I am a man again, and more a fool than usual. But I came within an inch of taking that girl *au sérieux*" (291). Feeling himself a man, or male subject, only within this homosocial matrix—only insofar as he defines himself in relation to M. Kapp, who was "very stiff" and "evidently meant to force his offence home" (301)—he explains his decision to duel axiomatically: "Why, a man can't back down before a woman" (306). In drawing an invidious contrast between Valentin and Newman, arguing that the former "at least avenges his honor as a man," while the latter allows himself to be feminized and rendered impotent, particularly by Madame de Bellegarde (118, 119), Carolyn Porter assumes James's affiliation with a monolithic masculinity. Thus, when Newman fails to press home an advantage, when he accepts his loss rather than avenges his insult at the end of the novel, he imperils his masculinity. In my view, however, James imperils the "masculine" values that Porter accepts without question. He satirizes Valentin's archaic sense of honor—his readiness, in Newman's terms, to be an "ass" because his great-grandfather was (309)—and undermines Newman's similar masculinity in the process in order to explore the tension between female-authored manhood and manly manmaking. Of course, Newman's metaphor also suggests, paradoxically, the connection between that archaic economy of male honor and a homosocial, even homosexual, economy of conquest. Making himself an "ass" for Stanislas Kapp makes Valentin complicit in his own homosexual rape—to having his own abjectness "forced home" upon him. Despite his continued desire to keep his options for education open, Newman resists the idea of making himself that vulnerable.

Even as he seems open to female "authority," therefore, Newman's wholesale investment in the prospect of marriage to Claire de Cintré and in the male self such a marriage entails suggests a clear-cut choice of manly roles—provisional resolution of the suspense into which the Babcock and Valentin episodes cast his manhood. James is walking a tightrope between the sort of emasculation he represents in Tom Tristram, or Valentin's fatal inversion, and the hyperbolic phallicism that characterizes Newman's most confident moments. And Newman's marriage proposal to

Claire assumes a very traditional structure: the active male, gathering himself to a point; the passive woman, listening patiently. Newman utters his words "with great directness and fullness, and without any sense of confusion. He was full of his idea, he had completely mastered it, and he seemed to look down on Madame de Cintré, with all her gathered elegance, from the height of his bracing good conscience" (167). Christina Light might have jumped at this chance to be "knocked down" by such manly words, but Claire is more reserved. Moreover, in an image he will use again when Caspar Goodwood proposes to Isabel Archer in *The Portrait of a Lady*, James emphasizes the latent aggression in such male behavior and registers male potency on the body of a woman. The effect on Claire is "very painful," he notes, and she sits looking at Newman "with her lips parted and her face as solemn as a tragic mask" (167). Newman's long prosecution of his case suggests how completely he wishes to perform a traditional masculinity. Full of himself, he subjects Claire to a monologue, the "longest" speech that he had "ever made," that almost completely eclipses her subjectivity. Rather than enter into a dialogue, Newman speaks for her. He answers objections he attributes to her, for example, when he asserts that *she* cares nothing for the differences between them that so upset her family. He cannot "imagine why the liberal devotion he meant to express should be disagreeable" (168), largely because Claire has ceased to be an individual with a mind of her own and has become an ideal that precedes and now supersedes her. Finally, Newman emphasizes his power to provide things for her—a power derived, of course, from the masculine achievements for which he felt "mortal disgust" earlier in the novel.

As he explores the type of man Newman can be in relation to Claire, James seems to settle for traditional masculine poses. He does not synthesize multiple masculinities so much as he features their polarization. Haralson notes that Newman "oscillates between manly defiance and childlike compliance from beginning to end" ("James's *The American*" 483), and Newman does swing wildly between extremes, either empowering himself phallocentrically in hyperbolic terms or prostrating himself to women. When Claire accepts his proposal, for example, and then struggles to explain her decision, Newman cuts her off and speaks for her. "Your only reason is that you love me!" he murmurs (244). When he revised the scene for the New York Edition, James went out of his way to stress Newman's phallic instrumentality. Instead of murmuring, Newman "almost groaned for deep insistence; and he laid his two hands on her with a persuasion that she rose to meet. He let her feel as he drew her close, bending his face to her, the fullest force of his imposition; and she took it from him with a silent, fragrant, flexible surrender which—since she seemed to keep back nothing—affected him as sufficiently prolonged to pledge her to everything" (NY 2: 272). Newman repeats his performance later in the novel. When he visits Claire at Fleurieres and she remains firm in her resolve not to marry him, he reverts to masculine type. In a scene that James will exaggerate at the end of *The Portrait of a Lady* in the "white lightning" kiss that Caspar Goodwood gives Isabel Archer, Newman becomes predatory and violent, forcing himself upon a resistant woman: "he drew her towards him and clasped her to his breast. He kissed her white face; for an instant she resisted and for a moment she submitted; then, with force, she disengaged herself and hurried away over the long shining floor. The next moment the door closed behind her" (*The American* [1879] 356).

Newman's reaction to Claire's acceptance of his second proposal, furthermore, only confirms his traditional, proprietary notions of marriage. Although his crowing about having telegraphed the news of his engagement to friends in America and about wanting to cry the news "on the housetops" (249) might be attributed to a kind of "Whitmania," it clearly makes the event a public one—entering it into the market, as it were. That is, Newman's behavior confirms his determination to crown his own achievements—what James calls his "somewhat aggressive impulse to promulgate his felicity." Feeling as if he could "break all the windows," he wants to "make the heads of the house of Bellegarde feel him" (251). Newman, in other words, continues to see things as a conflict or competition, the goal being to make the best deal and thus enjoy consequent appreciation in the value of his male self. That self, or subjectivity, moreover, is fully embodied. Feeling himself felt by others, Newman validates his own manhood. In the process he positions himself in the sort of homosocial and heterosexual economy that Eve Sedgwick describes in *Between Men*, commodifying Claire as a trophy for which he must compete with other men. When he meets Urbain de Bellegarde, he "felt himself suddenly in personal contact with the forces with which his friend Valentin had told him that he would have to contend, and he became sensible of their intensity."[14] Newman hardly shrinks from the challenge. In his role as suitor he takes an aggressive tack and in this scene appears eager to cross swords, as it were, with Urbain—eager to "stretch himself out at his own length, to sound a note at the uttermost end of *his* scale" (186).

James makes some effort to liberate Newman's love-making from the homosocial economy in which Urbain de Bellegarde's authority implicates him. "The idea of having this gentleman mixed up with his wooing and wedding," James observes, "was more and more disagreeable to him" (210–11), and he finally informs the man, "I am not marrying you, you know" (213). The goal of achieving a "pure" heterosexuality—a heterosexual manhood not triangulated by an "other" male presence—proves elusive, however, because Newman has conceived his marital campaign in classically homosocial terms. His pursuit of Claire fails as much as anything else because he never forges a relationship with the woman herself—subject-to-subject. Put another way, James does not find a way to construct a new manhood within a male-female economy. When he experiments with a pure, heterosexually-defined masculinity, he imperils not only Newman's manhood but his selfhood, finally calling into question his power to construct a stable self at all.[15]

Shortly before he proposes to Claire for the second time, Newman responds to her observation that he would not like to resemble her brother Valentin by asserting, "I shouldn't like to resemble anyone. It is hard enough work resembling oneself"—by which he means, as he explains, "doing what is expected of one. Doing one's duty" (234). This admission suggests the extent to which James envisions male selfhood as a construct that can be inscribed by others (in the form of "duty"), but it also suggests the potentially catastrophic consequences that a radical reconstruction might entail upon this male self. Valentin had advised Newman that his best chance for success was to "be simply yourself" (161), but this, of course, is precisely the problem Newman faces throughout *The American*—the paradox of performing himself, as it were, to gain the power to be "other" than he is, a "new" man. As he prosecutes his suit, in fact, he feels less and less authentic. When he visits the Bellegardes' for dinner, James notes, "for the first time in his life" he was "not himself." He "measured his movements, and counted his words, and resolved that if the occasion demanded that he should appear to have swallowed a ramrod, he would meet the emergency" (208). In that extravagant image, which conflates materialistic rhetoric with a spermatic economy, James underlines the change in Newman as he determines to be a ladies' man. Unwilling to "stiffen" for Benjamin Babcock into any single masculine construct, he is now, metaphorically at least, willing to suffer bodily violation, to be stiffened or even raped—indeed, to stiffen himself. Whereas James's comparison of Newman's feelings toward Claire to a "young mother's eagerness to protect the sleep of her first-born child" (223) suggests a positive feminization of his character, even as it positions him in a parental role, Newman's willingness to play the chameleon evidences the absence of selfhood more than the presence of protean power. As he tries to talk Claire's mother out of her objections to his suit, for example, Newman seems ready to twist himself into unnatural shapes. "What if I am a commercial person?" he asks. "I will be any sort of person you want" (321). And later, as he tries to talk Claire herself out of entering the Carmelite nunnery, he vows, "I must change—if I break in two in the effort!" (354). Newman's refusal to "stiffen" in any single masculine self here suggests indeterminacy more than flexibility, a state of perpetual suspense or dissociation that prevents rather than enables self-construction.

For the rest of the novel James emphasizes Newman's inability to penetrate the doors and walls that separate him from Claire. In Haralson's Freudian terms, James conspires with the Bellegardes to punish Newman for coveting the "power of the father" ("James's *The American*" 489), reducing him in the process to the level of a beaten, wailing child (481). Viewed another way, James seems to have written himself into a corner—to have emplotted an inflexible manhood that can only swing between phallically empowered or impotent extremes because, with Valentin's death and Claire's incarceration, the possibility of a new manhood-in-relation has been foreclosed. In writing the stage version of *The American*, James determined to save Newman's marriage to Claire, but in the novel he policed the boundaries of Newman's manhood, protecting the borders of his self-enclosed male identity from any intrusions that might reconstruct him in relation to others.[16] Whereas Newman had hoped to find "more of the world"—whether "this world or the next"—in Claire's eyes, her self-imprisonment means that he will find no "I," as it were, in her mirroring gaze. "It was as if [Newman] had his hand on a door-knob and were closing his clenched fist upon it," James writes; "he had thumped, he had called, he had pressed the door with his powerful knee, and shaken it with all his strength, and dead damning silence had answered him" (357). The result toward the end of the novel is Newman's increasing isolation. Although most critics emphasize the moral dilemma he faces in deciding whether to publicize the Bellegardes' alleged crime, Newman's contemplation of vengeance, when psychologically considered, locks him more and more within himself and repossesses a primitive, self-authorizing form of power he had foresworn.[17] He "seemed to himself to be riding his vengeance along the Milky Way," James observes (390), and he characterizes him repeatedly in phallic-aggressive terms—stiffened so to speak into a single, archaic masculine "pose." To compensate for his weakness, he re-empowers himself through a process of simple inversion—beating those who have beaten him and thus committing himself to an adversarial relational economy. "I want to bring them down—down, down, down!" he cries to Mrs. Bread. "I want to turn the tables upon them—I want to mortify them as they mortified me. They took me up into a high place and made me stand there for all the world to see me, and then they stole behind me and pushed me into this bottomless pit, where I lie howling and gnashing my teeth! I made a fool of myself before all their friends; but I shall make something worse of them" (375). In fact, much of the language James uses to describe the embattled Newman makes him a caricature of aggressive masculinity—stressed as a masturbatory phallicism, a saber-rattling in which Newman plays nursemaid to his own phallic power. He was "nursing his thunderbolt," James says;

> he loved it; he was unwilling to part with it. He seemed to be holding it aloft in the rumbling, vaguely-flashing air, directly over the heads of his victims, and he fancied he could see their pale upturned faces. Few specimens of the human countenance had ever given him such pleasure as these, lighted in the lurid fashion I have hinted at, and he was disposed to sip the cup of contemplative revenge in a leisurely fashion. (393)

Contemplating vengeance offers autoerotic pleasure, leaving Newman to define and pleasure himself narcissistically in a fantasy world of his own making, even as it positions him ironically where he has attempted to place himself—as a gentlemanly man of "leisure."

Newman does not finally unleash his thunderbolt upon the Bellegardes. His spermatic economy—even in its vengeful form—requires saving rather than expending energy. As Banta says, he resists revenge "not because of a compassionate wish to forego hurting others, but rather to savor the power and pleasure of his own beleaguered decency" (365). But in forswearing revenge at the end of the novel, much as he had at the beginning, he reopens the question of his male identity and suspends himself all over again, it seems to me, between male roles. To press his advantage over the Bellegardes, as he had recognized upon the earlier occasion in America, would be to foreground a male self that he has wished to temper, if not repudiate. Although he is "tingling with a passion" just before his final meeting with the Bellegardes, James observes that "it was extremely characteristic of him that he was able to moderate his expression of it, as he would have turned down a flaring gas-burner" (409). Similarly, when he visits Madame d'Outreville, ostensibly to reveal the Bellegardes' crime, he resists the temptation because he recognizes the "folly" of doing so (424) and doesn't "want to say anything unpleasant" (425). His adaptation to a mannered manhood in this drawing-room scene subverts as it threatens to invert the manly posture he had earlier assumed. Although Newman feels a "sudden stiffening of his will and quickening of his reserve" as he leaves the Duchess's (424), he worries that his reluctance to "spend" his energy on revenge may have inverted and exposed him, and he wonders if "he was not an ass not to have discharged his pistol" (425).

Although Porter sees Newman's reconciliation to his loss of Claire as a surrender of masculinity, James shows him struggling not be unmanned and searching for new terms with which to define himself. He feels tempted to continue as a "ladies' man," mirrored to himself through Claire's feminizing gaze and committed to "making it a religion to do nothing that she would have disliked" (439), but he seems to recognize the futility and self-denial that such behavior would entail. "It would be lonely entertainment," James observes, "a good deal like a man talking to himself in the mirror for want of better company" (439). Internalizing Claire's image as a substitute for some other object of desire would lock Newman into an unproductive, narcissistic fantasy world. Recognizing as he sits in Notre Dame cathedral that "now he must take care of himself" because Claire is forever "out of the world," he leans his head on the chair in front of him for a long time. When he "took it up again," James notes, "he was himself again" (446).[18] Feeling guilty for wanting to hurt the Bellegardes, he leaves the darkening church "not with the elastic step of a man who has won a victory or taken a resolve, but strolling soberly, like a good-natured man who is still a little ashamed" (446). Although James suggests in pointing out Newman's good-nature that he has changed—becoming a Good Man if not a New Man—his situation at the end of the novel differs little from his situation at the beginning. His story circles back upon itself as, once again, he feels repelled by or ashamed of the vengeful self that has surfaced. What does it mean, after all, for Newman to become "himself again," given how much work it is for him even to "resemble" himself? At the very least, Newman has a lot more work to do before he can achieve a truly new manhood. Being "himself again" raises all over again the questions and opportunities James had set up at the beginning of the novel. Newman ends the novel with his manhood, as it were, still in a state of suspense that James refuses or finds himself unable to end. Whereas the homosocial subplots with Babcock and Valentin seemed to promise greater openness and flexibility—the possibility of remaking manhood—the heterotextual plot closes off such possibilities, leaving Newman caught between limiting extremes. Although James had explored the possibility of a "pure" homosociality and a "pure" heterosexuality, Newman's solitude at the end of the novel suggests his failure to realize either possibility.

Chapter 3
Sheathing the Sword of Gentle Manhood in *The Portrait of a Lady*

From the opening paragraph of *The Portrait of a Lady*, in which he notes that the persons concerned with making tea time "an eternity of pleasure" were "not of the sex which is supposed to furnish the regular votaries of the ceremony" (3), James opens up the question of male identity and performance. William Veeder uses this passage to claim that "no one in James is in fact 'masculine,'" because "everyone is effeminated by culture and mortality" ("Feminine Orphan" 51), but I think James's representation of manhood in *The Portrait of a Lady* is more complicated than such a masculine-effeminate contrast allows.¹ While James does identify expansiveness and an adventurous, freedom-loving spirit with Isabel Archer and make Gilbert Osmond the votary of restriction, domestic duty, and social form—thus inverting the nature vs. culture, male vs. female conflict of many nineteenth-century American novels—not even the arguably "effeminated" Osmond rests easily in a single gendered position.² Indeed, the pattern that gender dynamics trace in *The Portrait of a Lady* bears an unexpected resemblance to the pattern we observed in *The American*. James seems determined to pluralize male identity and subjectivity by transpositioning his male protagonist, but the attempt seems to founder by the end of the novel. Despite obvious differences, Christopher Newman and Gilbert Osmond both suffer relapses, so to speak, and reconstruct themselves largely in phallocentric terms. This is not to say that such reconstructive efforts are wholly successful. As we have see in *The American*, Newman's manhood rests uneasily in a state of suspense at the end of the novel. A new man of a different sort, Osmond's old manhood also tests James's ability to prevent masculine representations from hardening into a single form. Priscilla Walton has deftly recovered Christina Light's story from the dominant male narrative in *Roderick Hudson*, and I think a similar archaeological project is warranted for the men's stories represented in *The Portrait of a Lady*. James would claim in his preface to the New York Edition of the novel that his "germ" was the "sense of a single character, the character and aspect of a particular engaging young woman" (*Art of the Novel* 42), and he devotes no attention at all in that preface to the male characters who, along with Madame Merle, Pansy, Henrietta Stackpole, and others, provide the "right complications" for Isabel's situation (*Art of the Novel* 53). Central though Isabel Archer's story certainly is, James tells a second story in the novel, filling a veritable gallery with "portraits of gentlemen": Caspar Goodwood, Lord Warburton, Ralph Touchett, Ned Rosier, and Gilbert Osmond. One reviewer, in fact, almost wished that James had entitled the novel "The Portrait of Two Gentlemen," because he considered the pictures of Ralph Touchett and Gilbert Osmond rarely equaled in fiction (Gard 93). If James fails to resolve the contradictions in Christopher Newman's masculine performance as a "terribly positive gentleman" or to reconstruct the archaic masculine ethos that Newman embodies, he does not abandon his experiment in reforming manhood. He changes his tack in *The Portrait of a Lady*, marginalizing the instrumental, conventionally masculine achiever in the characters of Goodwood and Warburton and centering his attention on the gentlemen of leisure—Ralph Touchett and Ned Rosier, and most prominently Gilbert Osmond. James would claim that the "high price of the novel as a literary form" resides in its power to

range through all the differences of the individual relation to its general subject-matter, all the varieties of outlook on life, of disposition to reflect and project, created by conditions that are never the same from man to man (or, so far as that goes, from man to woman), but positively to appear more true to its character in proportion as it strains, or tends to burst, with a latent extravagance, its mould. (*Art of the Novel* 46)

Understanding masculinity and male subjectivity in *The Portrait of a Lady*, especially in their more "extravagant" performances, requires close attention to subject-object relations—man to man, as well as man to woman.

William Veeder claims that, through Osmond, James "takes part in an examination of values which continues throughout the nineteenth century and can be summed up in the question 'What is a gentleman?'" (*Henry James* 145). And portraits of gentlemen abound in *The Portrait of a Lady*, linking James to other Victorian efforts to define "the gentleman."[3] Daniel Touchett is an "old gentleman" (5). Lord Warburton offers a "specimen of an English gentleman" (66); he is also a "noble gentleman" (164) with the "general air of being a gentleman and an explorer" (298). Ralph Touchett, on the other hand, is a "gentleman of leisure" (90), while the aggressive Caspar Goodwood, a "gentleman who had accumulated a considerable fortune in the exercise of [the cotton] industry" (119), is a "perfect gentleman"—not to mention a "splendid man" (126). As "pretty as an angel" (198), Ned Rosier hardly seems like Goodwood's younger double, but James describes him as a "perfect little gentleman" (371), even if he is "much more of the type of the useless fine gentleman than the English nobleman," Warburton (429). None of these male characters, however, so persistently performs the "gentleman" as Gilbert Osmond. A "gentleman who studied effect" (235), Osmond is a "quiet gentleman" (255), as well as a "poor gentleman" (257), who characterizes himself hyperbolically as "the most fastidious young gentleman living" (273). Mrs. Touchett always "thought him so much of a gentleman" (282), and during her fireside vigil even Isabel seems prepared to consider him "the first gentleman in Europe" (444). With every male playing the gentleman, the term effectively deconstructs—opening gentle manhood to plural performances. The question of being a gentleman seems necessarily in suspense.

Caspar Goodwood plays an important role in *The Portrait of a Lady*, but his portrait as a Christopher Newman reincarnation betrays the anxiety of that influence—a character who seems to have "stiffened" into a single, inflexible pose. "Straight, strong, and fresh" (337) in the first edition of the novel, but "straight, strong, and hard" in the New York Edition (4: 43), Goodwood feels somewhat insecure in his manhood because he has not had the chance to prove himself as a soldier. He "keenly regretted that the Civil War should have terminated just as he was grown old enough to wear shoulder-straps, and was sure that if something of the same kind would only occur again, he would make a display of striking military talent" (120). Goodwood epitomizes energetic manly striving even if he was too late to prove himself a man in battle. Owner of several cotton mills in Massachusetts, with a "great talent for business," for "managing men," and for "making people execute his purpose and carry out his views" (120), Goodwood seems an unreconstructed, and unreconstructable, Newman—an old, even archaic, masculine type whose personal energy seems centered solely in the phallic order. Leon Edel calls him "monotonously masculine" and recognizes why Isabel feels terrified by his "sheer sexual force" (*Henry James* 259). Even though Isabel "wished him not an inch less a man than he was" (121), she obviously recognizes that Goodwood is no "athlete of continence," in Charles Rosenberg's term (139). She understands the threat he poses to her integrity, as he defines himself oppositionally against women—a "ladies' man" with little respect for women, who would rather see Isabel dead than married to another man (338). He "seemed to take from her the sense of freedom," James writes. "There was something too forcible, something oppressive and restrictive, in the manner in which he presented himself" (118–19).

Carren Kaston calls Goodwood a "rapist lover" whose behavior "justifies Isabel's fearful associations of eroticism with violence" (54), and as Anthony Mazzella has noted, James made him even more insistently phallic when he revised his portrait for the New York Edition (609–11). In that later version Goodwood has a "kind of hardness of presence, in his way of rising" before Isabel, and he "expressed for her an energy—and she had already felt it as a power—that was of his very nature" (NY 3: 162). As "firm as a rock," according to his own characterization, his love-making possesses the power to lift Isabel "off her feet" and even to "force open her set teeth" (4: 434). Goodwood's sexual aggressiveness and "hard manhood" (4: 436) are most famously demonstrated, of course, at the end of the novel, when he gives Isabel the "white lightning" kiss that is the hottest in James's fiction (4: 436). I shall come back to Goodwood's role at the end of the novel, and particularly to the triangle he forms with Isabel and Osmond, because that role in effect exceeds the bounds of his rather stereotypical character. Osmond's prominence in *The Portrait of a Lady*—relegating Goodwood to a second-string role—suggests that James wished to explore alternatives to the "American business-man," before whom he had felt "absolutely and irredeemably helpless" and "fatally incompetent" (*Art of the Novel* 193). The feckless Osmond seems more a cross between the spectatorial Rowland Mallet and the passively aggressive Morris Townsend of *Washington Square* (1880).

While Caspar Goodwood occupies one extreme in James's gallery of gentlemanly portraits, Ralph Touchett occupies another. With Ralph, too, James turned his attention to different possibilities of manhood from those he explored in Newman or Goodwood. Ralph in particular embodies a flaccid and feminized masculinity and thus offers James something of a "cover" for his other portraits of male alternatives to Goodwood and other Masculine Achievers. Resembling Rowland Mallet in *Roderick Hudson* and Tom Tristram in *The American*, Ralph is an "alienated American," according to Henrietta Stackpole, a "gentleman of leisure," according to Isabel (90), the "idlest man living," according to his own assessment (91). Madame Merle claims, in fact, that without his consumption, Ralph would signify "absolutely nothing" (203), whereas consumption gives him "something to do." "His consumption is his career" (202). Merle puns on the word "consumption," designating Ralph's diseased lungs, hinting at his materialism. James himself would later term Ralph one of his "secondary physical weaklings and failures," or "accessory invalids" (*Art of the Novel* 290), and would claim that the reason his character produced a "happy effect" "could never in the world have been his fact of sex; since men, among the mortally afflicted, suffer on the whole more overtly and more grossly than women, and resist with a ruder, an inferior strategy" (*Art of the Novel* 290). James's comment occurs in his preface to *The Wings of the Dove*, and certainly in comparison to Milly Theale's melodramatic malady, Ralph's appears inferior. James underestimates his achievement in this retrospective aside, however, especially insofar as the "fact" of Ralph's "sex" comes into play in *The Portrait of a Lady*.

Ralph's malady does not unify him as a subject, but splits him in much the same way that Christopher Newman split in two in *The American*. Robert K. Martin argues that Ralph "is of the character and physical type that constituted the male homosexual as he was constructed in the years surrounding the novel" ("Failed Heterosexuality" 88), but insofar as James explores Ralph's homoeroticism, he does so intra-psychically rather than in relation to other men.[4] Relegated to an essentially narcissistic mode of self-understanding, Ralph feels split into subject and object. When forced to give up the "high stool" he occupied in his father's bank so that he can take care of himself (39), Ralph initially feels "greatly disgusted," because "it appeared to him that it was not himself in the least that he was taking care of, but an uninteresting and uninterested person with whom he had nothing in common" (39). Examining this second self from the vantage point of the first—arguably, a subject position inscribed by the culture of investment capitalism in which he has had his place—Ralph experiences himself as a disgusting stranger, as someone other than a successful businessman like his father (or other economically successful characters, such as Newman, Goodwood, and Warburton).[5] "This person, however, improved on acquaintance," James notes, "and Ralph grew at last to have a certain grudging tolerance, and even undemonstrative respect, for him" (39). Ralph's increasing identification with his second, sickly self is also James's, or his narrator's, as this narcissistic splitting of the male self generates a closed circuit of male-to-male desire, as if Ralph's increasing desire for that second self breeds desire in the narrator. "Misfortune makes strange bed-fellows," the narrator observes, "and our young man, feeling that he had something at stake in the matter—it usually seemed to him to be his reputation for common sense—devoted to his unattractive *protégé* an amount of attention of which note was duly taken, and which had at least the effect of keeping the poor fellow alive" (39).

Having constituted a double self within Ralph's character, James triangulates that selfhood by exploring Ralph's relations to various others. Given the essential narcissism of Ralph's subjectivity, however, it is not surprising that those relations tend to be consumptive. For the aggressive action—the physical and sexual consumption—that characterizes Caspar Goodwood, Ralph substitutes voyeurism, or specular consumption of beautiful objects such as Isabel. The "conscious observation of a lovely woman" strikes him as the "finest entertainment that the world now had to offer him" (41).[6] For the patronage that characterizes Mallet's relationship to Hudson, or Newman's to Valentin de Bellegarde, however, Ralph must rely upon his father, who "patronizes" Isabel for him—by transferring some of his inheritance to her. Ralph even identifies himself at secondhand, referring Isabel to a "small Watteau," which "represented a gentleman in a pink doublet and hose and a ruff, leaning against the pedestal of the statue of a nymph in a garden, and playing the guitar to two ladies seated on the grass." "That's my ideal of a regular occupation," he explains (91).

Despite this portrait of a "pink" gentleman, however, James does not liberate Ralph's character or his masculinity from a phallocentric embodiment. Even though Ralph considers Isabel a work of art—indeed "finer than the finest work of art" (64)—he does not simply appreciate her from a distance. He objectifies and penetrates her visually. "The key of a beautiful edifice is thrust into my hand," he says to himself, "and I am told to walk in and admire" (64). Ralph admires the "edifice" greatly from the outside; "he looked in at the windows, and received an impression of proportions equally fair. But he felt that he saw it only by glimpses, and that he had not yet stood under the roof." Indeed, Ralph's voyeurism, James implies, stems directly from his feelings of physical or sexual inadequacy. Like Newman's experience with Claire de Bellegarde, the "door" to Isabel's "edifice" is fastened, Ralph thinks to himself, "and though he had keys in his pocket he had a conviction that none of them would fit" (64).[7] Drained of desire as a subject and of desirability as an object, Ralph regards Isabel dispassionately—hardly enjoying a relation at all and thus suffering no challenge to his manhood.[8] He resembles Christopher Newman in his most flexible mode. Ralph, James notes, "indulged in a boundless liberty of appreciation" precisely because, he implies, he forms no relation or only a casual relation with things: "nothing long imposed itself" on his mind (38).

Ralph's character needs to be understood, furthermore, in terms of his relation to Warburton and also to the triangle that he, Isabel and Osmond form. While it is accurate to note that Ralph depends upon vicarious pleasure, that pleasure is complex—rooted in the tension that triangulated relationships allow in both heterosexual and homosexual registers, while settling in neither subject position. Ralph's situation dramatizes another aspect of Jamesian suspense—the suspension of the male subject between desires and genders. Himself a delegate (of his father's) in his original relation to Isabel, Ralph deploys her for his own psychosexual purposes, delegating desire to her and to the men who desire her—investing a diversified desire in the various triangles that Isabel's performance of a female subject-as-object entails. Feminizing desire in the process, Ralph covers homoerotic desire by heterosexualizing it. He recreates himself fantasmatically as a transgendered subject—masculine and feminine, homosexual and heterosexual at the same time.

James describes Ralph's relation to Isabel in artistic language in order to emphasize the relevance of character relations to the aesthetic issues he raises in the novel. Whereas most women, in Ralph's view, wait "gracefully passive, for a man to come that way and furnish them with a destiny," Isabel's "originality," he thinks, "was that she gave one the impression of having intentions of her own (64–65)." *His* stance will be the passive one; he wants only to be present to "see" what Isabel will do (59). Recalling the ideal James defined in his preface to *The Princess Casamassima*, Ralph "appreciates" Isabel by foregoing rather than forging an "intimate" relationship (*Art of the Novel* 65–66). As he admits to Henrietta Stackpole, where Isabel is concerned, he has been "absolutely passive" (124), and, as in Christopher Newman's case, such renunciation prevents the possibility of discovering a new heterosexual male self-in-relation. In making it possible for Isabel to live independently, as well as in encouraging her to let her life assume a form largely dictated by feeling (what she "likes"), Ralph abdicates all responsibility for her in favor of watching the eroticized spectacle of desire she provokes in other men. Capitalizing Isabel with his inheritance, Ralph projects upon this female stand-in the second self he had rescued from the bank and nurtured into a boon companion. Sending that second self out into the world and the market economy of sexual relations, Ralph cross-dresses as a woman and thus invests in a doubly gendered subject position. Specular in the extreme, he resigns himself to a posture of voyeuristic and masturbatory phallicism—to a spermatic economy, as it were, of no erotic investment and continually compounding "interest." Reporting on the spectacle "as if he had been dancing a jig," he enjoys the "succession of gentlemen going down on their knees to her," and he "looked forward to a fourth and a fifth *soupirant*; he had no conviction that she would stop at a third. She would keep the gate ajar and open a parley; she would certainly not allow number three to come in" (283). Doubly invested in the triangle that his desire makes possible, Ralph can enjoy the prospect of gentlemen going down on their knees from both positions—a benefit of the "pink" manhood that his character performs.

One of the reasons that Ralph feels so disappointed by Isabel's announcement that she will marry Osmond is that her decision limits his enjoyment of secondhand desire. "It hurts me," said Ralph audaciously, "as if I had fallen myself!" (356). Unfocused, polymorphous, the desire Ralph has invested in Isabel comes to rest on Osmond. Ralph does not like Osmond, he makes clear to Isabel, and insofar as Isabel enacts Ralph's desires, she thwarts his desire to soar "far up in the blue—to be sailing in the bright light, over the heads of men" (356). In effect, Isabel has killed the suspense into which Ralph had cast his manhood, denying him the fantasmatic pleasure afforded by the image of a "succession of gentlemen going down on their knees." Part of that image's appeal is that none of the men in that succession need be imagined as successful. As long as Isabel's womanhood remained in a state of suspense—"over the heads of men"— Ralph's manhood, to the extent he invested it in her, remained in suspense, too.

Isabel's choice of Osmond, or James's choice of Osmond for her, has puzzled many of James's readers. Virginia Fowler points out, however, that the "attractiveness of a man like Gilbert Osmond resides in his not resembling at all the masculine figures of power and energy [Isabel] has previously known" (77), and Robert White notes that Osmond charms Isabel "because he is so unlike her other wooers, because his appeal is seemingly non-assertive, non-aggressive, almost, it would seem, non-masculine" (66). James's characterization of masculine extremes in Caspar Goodwood and Ralph Touchett makes Isabel's preference for Gilbert Osmond more understandable than most critics recognize. To some extent the differences Fowler and White infer simply disguise Osmond's passive-aggressive use of power, but in deploying Osmond as he does—especially in targeting him as the object of Isabel's desire and thereby confirming his victory in the homosocial marriage market—James seems as determined to explore alternative possibilities for his character as he was with Christopher Newman's.[9] Placing Osmond next to Newman proves particularly useful, illustrating the scope of what I am calling James's experiments in manhood. Face-to-face—and on their faces, as it were—it is difficult to think of two more radically different men. Osmond is "not in business," Isabel boasts to Goodwood. "He is not rich." He is only a "very good man" (340)—although probably not as "good-natured" as Newman at the end of *The American* and not made of the same "good wood" as Caspar.

While nothing so simple as a synthesis of active and passive masculinity or a happy medium between Masculine Achiever and Christian Gentleman, Osmond and his relation with Isabel can be illuminated by the context those masculine roles provide. A variation on the manhood Ralph himself performs, Osmond makes gentleman-hood a virtual profession, as if performing the gentleman—and making that performance pay—were a signal masculine achievement. In that respect, he represents a version of the Victorian dandy, as James Eli Adams defines the type—repudiating self-interest, at least in principle, and "claiming instead devotion to a rigorous and impersonal code of duty" (54).[10] One nineteenth-century reviewer, Edgar Fawcett, termed Osmond a "frigid self-worshipper, a creature whose blood is ichor, whose creed is an adoration of *les usages*, whose honor is a brittle veneer of decorum, beneath which beats a heart as formally regular as the strokes of a well-regulated clock" (Gard 145), and another admitted that "our flesh creeps and our gorge rises as if our eye detected across the path we were to tread the tortuous and slimy track of a noisome snake" (Hayes 124). Twentieth-century critics have eagerly entered the competition of assailing Osmond's character. For the majority, Osmond qualifies as the archetypal misogynist in James's rogues' gallery. In Elizabeth Allen's view, for example,

Osmond simply epitomizes a "masculine culture where the appropriators are male and the signs of value to be acquired or disposed of are female" (59). Dennis O'Connor cites his "diabolic egotism, serpentine, heavy-lidded indolence, and parodic phallic aggressiveness displaced into the semblance of consummate knowledge" (28). Dorothy van Ghent goes so far as to convict him of aesthetic murder: "Morally dead himself, incapable of reverence for the human quality in others, Osmond necessarily tries to duplicate his death in them, for it is by killing their volition that he can make them useful; dead, they are alone 'beautiful'" (269). Jonathan Freedman calls him "so spectacularly pestiferous as to have defined the lineaments of the aesthete for the next 50 years" (145). Robert Weisbuch, an Osmond-basher par excellence, turns the screw of disdain perhaps the final notch. "There are few creepier beings in the history of literature," he maintains (284). Osmond is "egotistical, competitive, envious, small, and materialistic, self-proclaimed convention in its emptiest form and dishonest even in that. This man's life," he says, "is as much a work of art as a stuffed bat" (289).[11]

When first mentioned by Serena Merle, Osmond is most notable for what he is *not*. As a man with "no career, no name, no position, no fortune, no past, no future, no anything" (203), Osmond suggests an anti-type of manhood, a self-made Masculine Failure. Although the "desire to succeed greatly—in something or other—had been the dream of his youth," as the "years went on, the conditions attached to success became so various and repulsive that the idea of making an effort gradually lost its charm" (313). Osmond has therefore become, as Merle says, the "worst case," a man significant for his insignificance—for what he lacks—and therein attractive to Isabel, who later defends him to Ralph in precisely these same terms as a man with "no property, no title, no honours, no houses, nor lands, nor position, nor reputation, nor brilliant belongings of any sort. It is the total absence of all these things," she maintains, "that pleases me. Mr. Osmond is simply a man—he is not a proprietor!" (359-60).

Isabel, of course, proves critically wrong about Osmond, who does establish a proprietary interest in her, but her litany of negatives, like Madame Merle's, makes clear James's desire to explore a non-traditional or even anti-traditional masculinity from a woman's point of view—to explore what it means to be "simply a man," as in *The American* he had explored what it meant for Newman to be "simply" himself. It is as if James wished to evacuate conventional male qualities from the site of Osmond's character, creating almost a genderless and sexless *tabula rasa* on which a new man could be erected. This is a very different tack from the one he had taken with Christopher Newman, who presented the challenge of reeducating or reconstructing a traditional manhood. Osmond is "so indolent," Madame Merle says, "that it amounts to a sort of position" (182). Whereas the Masculine Achiever sublimates sexual energy in success-oriented projects (in war or business, in the cases of Christopher Newman and Caspar Goodwood, or social advancement and political power, in the case of Lord Warburton), Osmond seems hardly to invest his energy at all or to invest it only in aesthetic appreciation or observation. Michael T. Gilmore points out that Ralph and Osmond "share the same vocation of doing nothing whatever" (65), but Osmond does nothing with better taste than Ralph does. Doing nothing well becomes the ultimate form of doing something. If, in Jane Gallop's terms, the "rule of the Phallus is the reign of the One, of Unicity," if men "arrested" in that phase are "obsessively trying to tame otherness in a mirror-image of sameness," James's gentlemen—Ralph Touchett and Gilbert Osmond, especially—seem marked by their lack of such desire, by the absence of such phallocentrism. According to his mother, Ralph is "not in the least addicted to looking after number one" (216). And as I mentioned, in thinking of Isabel as a house, or "edifice," he has the conviction that none of the keys in his pocket would fit her fastened door. Osmond says much the same thing. Characterizing his dilettantish life in Italy, he calls himself "as rusty as a key that has no lock to fit it" (266). I am playing here with James's imagery, emphasizing its phallogocentricity in order to establish James's desire to open and to destabilize male phallocentrism—the identification of manhood with phallic power, with "number one." In that regard, Osmond's characterization of himself as a rusty key that has no lock to fit it differs subtly from Ralph's conviction that he has no key to fit Isabel's lock. If Ralph's manhood is signified by the absence of a "key," Osmond's is marked differently by its disuse, by the absence of an "other," a lock, that his key will turn. Isabel, obviously, represents that lock, and her presence therefore poses a special challenge to Osmond's passionless and passive manhood. How to be a man and not a man at the same time? That is the question. One obvious answer: let a woman be a man for you. As Beth Sharon Ash tracks Isabel's psychic development, Osmond in fact figures provocatively as a maternal object, a "feminized patriarch" who "possesses many of the distinctive traits of the omnipotent phallic mother" ("Frail Vessels" 150). Ash goes on to argue that Isabel becomes "Osmond's phallus" and thereby becomes an "empty function in another's (the husband's, the mother's) system of desire" (153). Ash's insight makes sense from Osmond's point of view, as well. Particularly in his desire to cede power to his wife, as in his thought that "she would do the thing for him," Osmond signals his desire to repossess a lost signifier of his manhood through a kind of gender and sexual inversion—a homoerotic heterosexual marriage. Osmond feels energized as a man by enjoying the absence of traditional power. As he tells Isabel, "It polishes me up a little to talk with you—not that I venture to pretend I can turn that very complicated lock I suspect your intellect of being" (266). The key to Osmond's power, so to speak, depends on Isabel's ability to turn her own "lock"—to do the manly work for him.

In marked contrast to Caspar Goodwood, who seems in his "hard manhood" akin to Melville's mincer in *Moby-Dick*, dressed up in the whale's foreskin (in "The Cassock" chapter), Osmond attracts Isabel and James, I would argue, for his intellectual or imaginative phallicism—for his sublimation of erotic energy in the exercise of his "taste." "There was such a fine intellectual intention in what he said," Isabel thinks to herself, "and the movement of his wit was like that of a quick-flashing blade" (286).[12] Isabel, of course, will feel the cutting power of that wit before the novel is over. Indeed, as he contemplates her willfulness and high temper, Osmond thinks that "the defect might be managed with comparative ease; for had one not a will of one's own that one had been keeping for years in the best condition—as pure and keen as a sword protected by its sheath" (314). Osmond's key may be rusty, but he has other, more lethal weapons at his disposal.

Although he deleted the above passage for the New York Edition, James's obvious delight in such phallic imagery—especially evident in the context that this study affords—carries subtle modulations even as it suggests his failure or unwillingness in the 1881 edition to decenter the Phallus as the sign of manhood. Even in creating anti-types of conventional masculine achievement, he has metaphorized the Phallus more than destabilized it—translated it, literally, by saying the "One" thing in terms of an "other." Osmond enjoys what James calls his "recovered singleness" (314), but even in making the "generous sacrifice" and marrying he will continue to signify himself with his sword in the most enjoyable and gentlemanly way possible—by rarely removing it from its sheath. Like Newman contemplating his revenge, he thinks of success in terms of making "himself felt; that was the only success to which he could now pretend." He may envision a less public display of power than Newman's almost apocalyptic fantasy of bringing the Bellegardes "down, down, down," but his "line" is still "to impress himself not largely but deeply; a distinction of the most private sort. A single character might offer the whole measure of it; the clear and sensitive nature of a generous girl would make space for the record" (315). There is no question, in other words, of Osmond's desire to see himself reflected and represented in Isabel, to employ *her* as a sign of manly presence and power—paying her for the work, of course, with her own (that is, Ralph's) money. Indeed, while Osmond has not thought very seriously of marrying, he recognizes the opportunity Isabel presents to make himself felt—"like a gentleman" (315). What that means, James suggests, is that Osmond wishes Isabel to transcribe his "style" onto herself, to be impressed, as it were, with his character rather than simply to be inscribed by him. This is a passive-aggressive phallicism—different from Ralph's absolute passivity, as well as from Goodwood's more active force. "Let it not . . . be supposed," James insists, "that he was guilty of the error of believing that Isabel's character was of that passive sort which offers a free field for domination. He was sure that she would constantly act—act in the sense of enthusiastic concession" (315).

In the long passage (in chapter 29) he deleted for the New York Edition (the passage that ends with the just-quoted sentences and precedes Osmond's declaration that he is "thoroughly in love" with Isabel), James provides an extended definition of Osmond's "new manhood." But instead of discovering a non-phallic masculinity that might inscribe a new fiction, he has largely disguised the phallocentrism at the center of this paradoxically non-phallic phallicism. With each of Isabel's suitors, in fact, James emphasizes and tests manly self-control, a sheathed or sublimated masculinity. Even his most forceful male characters in *The Portrait of a Lady*—Lord Warburton and Caspar Goodwood—suppress aggressive or phallic impulses. In a wonderful little image, James describes Lord Warburton's retreat after Isabel rejects his proposal of marriage. He was "evidently very nervous," James observes, and he walks rapidly away "shaking his hunting-whip with little quick strokes" (114).[13] Goodwood, too, despite epitomizing conventionally aggressive male behavior, is capable of exercising "remarkable self-control" in Isabel's presence—a quality that Isabel resents even as this "manly staying of his hand" makes her heart "beat faster" (342). James, in other words, seems to experiment with a range of male characters, each of whom can stay his hand in a "manly" fashion, especially if that suppression of energy can energize someone else. In the best example—a climactic example, in fact—James describes Osmond's "love" for Isabel in almost oxymoronic terms. He was "not demonstrative," James says;

the consciousness of success, which must now have flamed high within him, emitted very little smoke for so brilliant a blaze. Contentment, on his part, never took a vulgar form; excitement, in the most self-conscious of men, was a kind of ecstasy of self-control. This disposition, however, made him an admirable lover; it gave him a constant view of the amorous character. He never forgot himself, as I say; and so he never forgot to be graceful and tender, to wear the appearance of devoted intention. (362)

In Rosenberg's "gentlemanly" terms, Osmond qualifies as a gold-medal "athlete" of continence. Indeed, he has found a way to turn nineteenth-century emphasis on spermatic economy on its head. If continence or chastity were designed to serve masculine achievement by redirecting energy toward business and other forms of manly endeavor, Osmond finds a way to beat continence at its own game. Eschewing traditional forms of male achievement, he makes continence itself his profession—experiencing ecstasy in self-control.

I should like to return at this point to the final major scene of *The Portrait of a Lady*—the scene of the notorious "white lightning" kiss that Caspar Goodwood plants on Isabel just before she returns to Rome. Authorial intentions are risky to reconstruct, but revisions encourage inferences of purpose—and James revised key passages in *The Portrait*'s concluding scene. Two examples will help me make my point that James's efforts to revise definitions of manhood seem to founder, so to speak, on the rocks of the conventional—that is, on Goodwood, the phallic male, "as firm as a rock" (608). The first passage describes Isabel's reaction to Goodwood's question—the same in both editions: "Why should you go back—why should you go through that ghastly form?" In both versions Isabel answers, "To get away from you," and in both versions James observes that "this expressed only a little of what she felt. The rest was that she had never been loved before." What follows by way of explanation, however, differs markedly in the New York Edition. Originally James commented simply, "It [this feeling] wrapped her about; it lifted her off her feet" (607). But in his revised version he went further: "She had believed it [that she had been loved], but this was different; this was the hot wind of the desert, at the approach of which the others dropped dead, like mere sweet airs of the garden. It wrapped her about; it lifted her off her feet, while the very taste of it, as of something potent, acrid and strange, forced open her set teeth" (4: 488). The significance of these changes in the context of this study are only too obvious—as is the sexual and textual pleasure of forcing Goodwood's "hard" manhood upon a heroine who has recently flouted her husband's will. It might be argued, in fact, that Goodwood offers not so much an alternative to Osmond as a service—as an Overseer or fugitive female catcher who disciplines a woman and makes her appreciate the comparative attraction of her "master."[14] To be sure, in letting himself be left at home to await Isabel's return, Osmond seems to occupy a traditionally feminine position. But that is the trick, if you will, of Osmond's pose—being the opposite of what he appears: the most active when he appears the most passive, the most masculine when he appears the most feminine. Employing Goodwood, so to speak, without incurring the obligation to pay him for his performance, Osmond can simply wait for Isabel to finish her dutiful errands in England before she returns to Rome—with Goodwood's potent taste, so to speak, still fresh in her mouth, still capable of increasing her value.

The second revised passage—describing the kiss itself—helps to confirm Goodwood's coincidentally cooperative role. James's first version is relatively tame, although Goodwood's aggression and hostility are obvious enough: "He glared at her a moment through the dusk, and the next instant she felt his arms about her, and his lips on her own lips. His kiss was like a flash of lightning; when it was dark again she was free" (609). Simple enough—a kiss like a "flash of lighting," recalling the "flashing blade" of Osmond's wit, a quick kiss whose impression leaves with Goodwood. But in the New York Edition the kiss comes, as it were, with a vengeance:

He glared at her a moment through the dusk, and the next instant she felt his arms about her and his lips on her own lips. His kiss was like white lightning, a flash that spread, and spread again, and stayed; and it was extraordinarily as if, while she took it, she felt each thing in his hard manhood that had least pleased her, each aggressive fact of his face, his figure, his presence, justified of its intense identity and made one with this act of possession. So had she heard of those wrecked and under water following a train of images before they sink. But when darkness returned she was free. (4: 489)

Difficult as it is to think of another literary kiss as overdetermined as this one, James's extended description is even more remarkable as a revision—as an example of writerly pleasure in masculine identification with the intimate process of phallic possessiveness and possession. Tenuously grafted onto Isabel's subjective experience, James's description enables him (technically, his narrator) to occupy both positions—for example, to comment that Isabel "feels the full force" of Goodwood's "devotion" (*Complete Notebooks* 15). In Silverman's Oedipal paradigm, the narrator enjoys both positive and negative identifications—with the man and with the woman. In the context of this study, it seems to me, the narrator's subjectivity covers two male positions—one through the screen of female subjectivity, the other through direct, homoerotic identification with phallic pride of place.

The ending that follows, with Isabel heading back to her husband in Rome, has perplexed many readers, and James himself anticipated such responses in his Notebooks. "The obvious criticism," he noted, "will be that it is not finished—that I have not seen the heroine to the end of her situation—that I have left her *en l'air*" (*Complete Notebooks* 15). James is being a bit disingenuous. Given his relatively infrequent appearances in the novel, it has always bothered me that James should bring Goodwood back for this climactic scene. With Ralph dead and immortalized in Isabel's imagination in the safe role of "brother" (596) and Lord Warburton rescued from incipient pedophilia (with Pansy) and married off to Lady Flora or Felicia (590), only Goodwood remains to place Osmond in bold relief (in absentia).[15] In resurrecting his most aggressive male character, the phallic male resplendent in all of his "hard manhood," James makes Isabel's preference for Osmond a lot more plausible. Faced with a choice between Masculine Achiever and Christian Gentleman, Isabel makes the obvious choice, the choice James himself has made in the differences between *The American* and *The Portrait of a Lady*. Except for one thing: Isabel's choice is truly a Hobson's choice. Osmond's sword may be sheathed, whereas Goodwood's, in the kiss of "white lightning," is obviously unsheathed, but Osmond's sword is no less deadly. It may be sheathed, but it's obviously ready for battle. Despite his efforts to reform or reconstruct masculinity by liberating his male characters from an ideology of Masculine Achievement, James ends up in both *The American* and *The Portrait of a Lady* reinscribing a phallocentric masculinity—a sublimated or "sheathed" masculinity, camouflaged in a feminine position, but a masculinity still as "keen" as a "quick-flashing blade."

In that respect *The Portrait of a Lady* seems to feature the restoration of phallic authority, despite James's efforts to explore an alternative, gentlemanly masculinity. The situation is more complicated than that, however, and I would like to take another look at Gilbert Osmond from a different point of view. Like Ralph Touchett, Osmond has often been identified with James's own authorship. Michael T. Gilmore claims that Osmond has the "most James-like imagination of the book's characters" because he "fully shares his creator's penchant for reducing or equating people with valuable pieces of art" (54). Carren Kaston argues that Osmond "corresponds to the part of James that wants, tyrannically, to discipline the subject in the house of fiction or to possess it from a window of the house" (43).[16] James identified his own creative impulses with Osmond and used his relationship with Isabel to test the limits of his own aesthetic and moral values, to explore the elasticity—the capacity for what he called "appreciation"—of an imagination whose first impulse is to objectify people as things.

In exploring his own relations with his characters in the preface to *The Princess Casamassima*, James described "appreciation" as an open, sympathetic state of mind that produced a feeling of "intimacy." "As soon as I begin to appreciate," he comments,

> simplification is imperilled: the sharply distinguished parts of any adventure, any case of endurance, melt together as an appeal. I then see their "doing," that of the persons just mentioned, as, immensely, their feeling, their feeling as their doing; since I can have none of the conveyed sense and taste of their situation without becoming intimate with them. . . . Intimacy with a man's specific behaviour, with his given case, is desperately certain to make us see it as a whole—in which event arbitrary limitations of our vision lose whatever beauty they may on occasion have pretended to. (*Art of the Novel* 65–66)

Dependent upon intimacy, or identification, appreciation means feeling *with* characters and thus seeing them "as a whole." In short, imaginative forms become elastic, more conducive to the complexity of relations. As much as possible, the artist resists the temptation to frame his characters or to limit their autonomy within his imagination, their power to express themselves.

Although Gilbert Osmond might seem an unlikely exponent of such values, his relationship with Isabel offers a kind of test case, or "worst case" (in Madame Merle's phrase), of the tension James described in the preface. Rather than viewing Isabel simply as a collectible object, for example, Osmond feels attracted to her in the first place by *her* desire to make her life a work of art (317) and thus by the prospect of discovering creative power through her. Rather than using her as *his* "material," he regards himself as material for her artistic talents. She will be the artistic self he has never been and the medium through which he will express himself. In the New York Edition James explicitly compares *Osmond* to a portrait or picture that Isabel, playing female Pygmalion to his male Galatea, contemplates and thereby brings to life. "If an anonymous drawing on a museum wall had been conscious and watchful," Osmond thinks, "it might have known this peculiar pleasure of being at last and all of a sudden identified—as from the hand of a great master—by the so high and so unnoticed fact of style. His 'style' was what the girl had discovered with a little help; and now, beside herself enjoying it, she should publish it to the world without his having any of the trouble. She should do the thing *for* him, and he would not have waited in vain" (4: 12).

Rather than simply appropriating and exploiting Isabel's emerging selfhood, Osmond would invest his own limited creative "capital" in her expressive power. Isabel herself notes his desire not to suppress her powers of self-expression but to engage them. "He didn't wish her to be stupid," she recognizes. "On the contrary, it was because she was clever that she had pleased him. But he expected her intelligence to operate altogether in his favour, and so far from desiring her mind to be a blank, he had flattered himself that it would be richly receptive. He had expected his wife to feel with him and for him, to enter into his opinions, his ambitions, his preferences" (446). Anticipating James's description of "appreciation" in *The Princess Casamassima* preface, Osmond expects Isabel to *appreciate* him through intimacy, to penetrate his body and mind and to "feel with him" and then to become his voice and to "publish" his style. If we fault him for his belief (anticipating Basil Ransom's in *The Bostonians*) that a "woman's natural mission is to be where she is most appreciated" (244)—that is, to metamorphose into a portrait—it is because his concept of "appreciation" is not as open as James's. But Osmond still places the burden of activity on Isabel, as she seems to recognize in agreeing that the "point is to find out where that is" (272).

James marks out a fine line on this question, walking a tightrope between intimacy and possessiveness, openness and control, but he seems intent upon positioning Osmond in a passive position. A major problem for readers of *The Portrait of a Lady*, in fact, is Isabel's apparent willingness to conform to Osmond's intentions—the ease, as it were, of her portrait's self-composition. Isabel herself even accepts a share of the blame, recognizing that unintentionally she had "deceived" her husband: "She had effaced herself, when he first knew her; she had made herself small, pretending there was less of her than there really was" (440). Of course, observing Isabel's willingness to become an object—to objectify herself—merely shifts the charge of objectification from Osmond to James. And in fact James's description of his imaginative relationship to his heroine clearly links him with his hero.

Stephanie Smith provocatively discusses James's possessive and proprietary attitude toward his heroine. According to her female Gothic and neo-Freudian reading of family romance in the novel, "James can, through the ownership of Isabel's virginal (daughterly) consciousness, appropriate the power of 'conception' and . . . self-conception, entirely to himself or to the (supposedly) invisible artist's eye." Most importantly, such appropriation, in Smith's view, enables the stabilization of a secure gender identity for the author. "The (male) artist with a (female) consciousness can then gestate and bring to term a perfect Portrait," she argues, "without risking either a threatening involvement with the taboo mother or a homosexually tainted brush with the feminized—without himself risking the gender confusion that marks all the artistic male characters in the novel" (604).[17] Smith's brilliant reading of *The Portrait of a Lady* oversimplifies the androcentric implications of the story. Rather than stabilizing manly authorship through proprietorship, for example, I think that James places masculinity in jeopardy. Much of what happens in the text occurs precisely because of men's "brush with the feminized." James's account of writing *The Portrait of a Lady* reveals the same tension between fluidity and form that he attributes to Osmond, and he seems initially to place himself, as he does Osmond, in a feminine or maternal position. The germ itself was Isabel, and even in retrospect James feels intrigued by the spontaneous way her portrait evolved. "These are the fascinations of the fabulist's art," he observes, "these lurking forces of expansion, these necessities of upspringing in the seed, these beautiful determinations, on the part of the idea entertained, to grow as tall as possible, to push into the light and the air and quickly flower there" (*Art of the Novel* 42). In describing the novel's growth as an example of intimacy and appreciation, James resorts to another metaphor that suggests the opposite of spontaneity and imaginative openness. Most famous, of course, is the figure of the "house of fiction" with its potentially infinite number of windows, but James develops a much smaller figure to describe how *The Portrait of a*

Lady attained form. He recalls having had the idea, his "grasp of a single character," in mind longer than he cares to reveal, and he equates the development of his "acquisition," his "vivid individual," with "the history of the growth of one's imagination." Isabel's character, its being "in motion" and "bent upon its fate," is thus identified with his own imaginative development (*Art of the Novel* 47). Even at this point, of course, James's choice of terms suggests Isabel's objectification, but he goes on in even more explicit terms to describe the specially "constituted, animated figure or form" that her image assumed. Her figure, he says, has been

placed in the imagination that detains it, preserves, protects, enjoys it, conscious of its presence in the dusky, crowded, heterogeneous back-shop of the mind very much as a wary dealer in precious odds and ends, competent to make an "advance" on rare objects confided to him, is conscious of the rare little "piece" left in deposit by the reduced, mysterious lady of title or the speculative amateur, and which is already there to disclose its merit afresh as soon as the key shall have clicked in a cupboard door. (*Art of the Novel* 47–48)

James himself acknowledged that his analogy may have been "superfine" for the particular "value" he identifies—that is, for the "young feminine nature" that he had "for so considerable a time all curiously at [his] disposal"—but he finally decides that the figure "appears to fond memory quite to fit the fact" (*Art of the Novel* 48). And he clearly identifies himself with the shopkeeper who has kept Isabel (a "rare little 'piece'") in his "back-shop." "I quite remind myself," he admits, "of the dealer resigned not to 'realise,' resigned to keeping the precious object locked up indefinitely rather than commit it, at no matter what price, to vulgar hands" (*Art of the Novel* 48). The movement of James's thought contradicts his ostensible intention, however. As he purports to describe the forces of expansion by which Isabel's portrait grew, the imagery he employs becomes more and more contracted. The house of fiction with its innumerable windows becomes the little back-shop of the mind, an enclosure within an enclosure. In equating his idea of Isabel, despite its residual power to "disclose its merit afresh," with an object that he can physically and imaginatively possess and save for the right occasion, James clearly identifies himself with Osmond and with the transition from feminine to masculine power. Isabel may have germinated from the "piece" left by a "reduced" lady—constructed out of the discourse of "ladies and gentlemen"—but she lies latent until activated by a male imagination that, like Osmond, possesses the "key" to unlock the cupboard door and disclose her merit. Phallic authority, therefore, depends upon an almost fairy-tale like awakening of a woman's being. However, as he implicates the authorial imagination in the marketplace of shops and publication, James posits an authorial (arguably spermatic) economy that requires not realizing or spending inspiration—that is, requires a man to "stay his hand," to be a different kind of man, a gentle man.

In resisting the temptation to end *The Portrait of a Lady* definitively, James was able to "end" it in a state of suspense that dramatizes the aesthetic, as well as moral, issues he had treated. Although Isabel wants to live an "uncircumstanced" life at the beginning of the novel, the lesson James would have her learn during the second half is that she must live within the self-imposed frame of her portrait. But this is not to say that integrity of self is necessarily surrendered when given form, or that the artist's integrity of vision is compromised by the aesthetic form it necessarily assumes. James can have Isabel act decisively and still choose to act within the form—the "magnificent form"—of her marriage (555). If her character possesses any consistency, she will exert as much pressure as possible upon that form. In the aesthetic terms James defines, she will seek as much creative freedom—as much appreciation—as the inevitable limits of that form make possible. In his preface to *The Wings of the Dove,* James suggests that appreciation is "greatest, it is delightfully, divinely great, when we feel the surface, like the thick ice of the skater's pond, bear without cracking the strongest pressure we throw on it" (*Art of the Novel* 304–5). In the relation he establishes between Isabel and Osmond, it seems to me, James anticipates and tests that ideal. The ending of *The Portrait of a Lady* enacts the tension between form and energy that proved so central to James's aesthetic. Depicting Osmond and Isabel as separate, independent individuals, each with intentions of his or her own, James dramatizes the limits of authorial intentions. Truly to appreciate a literary character means to allow that character a certain freedom. In short, at the end of the novel James finds himself as author in much the same position as Osmond finds himself—in a state of suspense in which he waits to see what Isabel will do, waits in his relation to her to see what kind of gentleman he will become.

Chapter 4
Reconstructing Masculinity in *The Bostonians*

In a brutal scene from his 1845 *Narrative* Frederick Douglass describes his Aunt Hester being whipped by the overseer Aaron Anthony. "It was the blood-stained gate," Douglass says, "the entrance to the hell of slavery, through which I was about to pass" (51). Indeed, as he hides in a closet, afraid to "venture out till long after the bloody transaction was over" (52), Douglass has a revolutionary primal scene experience in which he identifies himself as a slave for the first time. But as Jenny Franchot and Eric Sundquist have argued, the scene also registers confusion in Douglass's gendered and racial self—the "chilling bifurcation" of his "double racial identity" (Sundquist 100).[1] That is, if Douglass identifies with Aunt Hester as a slave, he identifies as a woman. Being a slave means being inverted, or feminized—taking a woman's place as the object of male sado-erotic violence. If Douglass identifies with Mr. Anthony as a man, on the other hand, he identifies with a sadistic, misogynistic—and white—manhood. Being a man means being the subject rather than object of the same sado-erotic violence. In this chapter I want to put James's Basil Ransom in the closet with Douglass, so to speak, because Douglass's precarious position between races and genders presents a paradigm that can illuminate other male subjectivities.

Not surprisingly, during a period in which many structures of Southern power were destabilized, political and social reversals translate as racial and sexual inversions. But in novels such as *The Bostonians* (or, as we shall see, *Adventures of Huckleberry Finn* and Thomas Dixon's racist jeremiad *The Leopard's Spots*) a reconstructed male subjectivity depends upon the reversal of reversal—the re-inversion of inversion. Like Douglass rebelling against the thought of being in Aunt Hester's position, male characters struggle for power positions within a homosocial economy that often entails putting other men in a woman's place.

Most graphically, such power struggles involve cross-dressing. In *Black and White Strangers*, for example, Kenneth Warren refers to *The Leopard's Spots*, in which Harriet Beecher Stowe's Simon Legree reappears as Speaker of the North Carolina House of Representatives. But Thomas Dixon signals Legree's moral and political turpitude by observing that he saved himself from capture during the war by dressing as a German emigrant woman, passing "for a sister," and doing housework (85). Transposing the pervasive rumors that Jefferson Davis had donned drag to evade his Union pursuers, Dixon rehearses postbellum attempts to emasculate Southern men.[2] Taking a woman's place, dressing like a woman, leading a black and white coalition—in *The Leopard's Spots* all signify the inversion of true manhood. As *Adventures of Huckleberry Finn* demonstrates, furthermore, male power struggles can involve making another man wear drag. When Jim dresses Huck in women's clothing early in the novel, his power to do so coincides with the manhood he displays in plotting his own escape from slavery and planning to ransom his wife and children. Huck and Tom reverse Jim's power late in the novel, however, and the Kemble illustrations (in which Jim appears in drag as a stereotypical "darkie") graphically demonstrate Jim's humiliation. His feminization coincides with his re-enslavement and reinforces his racial emasculation.[3] Vern and Bonnie Bullough note that the "association of cross dressing with blacks reflects nineteenth-century racist beliefs that blacks were lower on the evolutionary scale and therefore more likely to engage in sexual perversions" (192), and Jim's prolonged feminization in *Adventures of Huckleberry Finn* partakes overtly in such gendered and racist discourse, as transgendering signifies positions in a racial hierarchy.

More subtly than *The Leopard's Spots* or even *Huckleberry Finn*, *The Bostonians* also conflates gender and racial identity, suggesting the transposition of gender for race through a complex process of subject positioning. Whereas Mark Twain reinforces racism with sexism by cross-dressing Jim, James supplements gender subordination with racial connotations—adding a kind of blackface to gender inversion. James himself encourages us to read race through the medium of gender, as if marking the shift (after the Emancipation Proclamation and the Civil War) from abolitionism to women's rights and, for a Southern male like Ransom, the imaginative shift from fearing racial reversal to fearing gender inversion. As Olive Chancellor observes, in citing Ransom's plan for imaginative compensation, he "desired to treat women with the lash and manacles, as he and his people had formerly treated the wretched coloured race" (172). Placing Ransom in the middle of a northern women's movement that originally fought slavery neatly triangulates race and gender through an embattled male subject position, as James repeatedly ironizes the dominating subject position about which Olive speculates. Ransom himself recognizes how the women's movement represents a reincarnation of abolitionism. "And as for our four fearful years of slaughter," he observes to Verena, "of course, you won't deny that there the ladies were the great motive power. The Abolitionists brought it on, and were not the Abolitionists principally females?" (111). In Louis Althusser's term, James "interpellates" Ransom's manhood with several discordant subjectivities from a Reconstruction-era culture rife with gender, race, and class conflicts. Never appearing in black face or drag, Ransom nonetheless finds himself occupying triangulated positions with others that force him to inhabit "other" subject positions. Ransom responds to such subjection by reconstructing an archaic, phallogocentric male self—becoming the subject of the Subject (Althusser 180)—but James persistently subverts that construct of male identity.[4] The result is a Reconstruction novel of unreconstructed manhood and constant imaginative tension for its male protagonist as he seeks to control the constitutive process of his own subjectivity.

Although Warren discusses *The Bostonians* as a representative Reconstruction-era text, the novel reveals little obvious interest in race. From the viewpoint of Southern men like Ransom or Dixon's narrator, however, political polarities reversed during the War and Reconstruction, and men like Douglass and Legree gained power, as well as manhood. And when Ransom first sees Selah Tarrant, he finds himself uncannily occupying a position like Douglass's—in the closet of racial and gender instability. "There was nothing ambiguous" about Verena's father, James writes. "Ransom simply loathed him, from the moment he opened his mouth; he was intensely familiar—that is, his type was; he was simply the detested carpetbagger. He was false, cunning, vulgar, ignoble; the cheapest kind of human product" (81–82). Ransom's spontaneous loathing of Selah Tarrant, like the narrator's hatred of Simon Legree in *The Leopard's Spots* or Pap Finn's tirade against a "govment" that lets Negroes vote in *Huckleberry Finn* (34), masks intense personal insecurities.

The Civil War and Reconstruction threatened a revolution in southern manhood—a male role reversal in which the master experienced the abject position of the slave, liable to be beaten by another man. As Joel Williamson puts it, the "organic society of the Old South found an important part of its strength in the dichotomous nature of western civilization. Opposites were held in tight tension in the organic society—slavery was set against freedom, white against black, and men were strenuously balanced by women. Increasingly, the South grew intolerant of anything that was not distinctly slave or free, black or white, male or female" (74). Bertram Wyatt-Brown argues, in fact, that the Civil War was "reduced to a simple test of manhood" for Southern men (168–69). Douglass's climactic fight with Edward Covey shows such tests crossing racial lines, as Douglass reverses his own brutalization and rehearses the process by which "a slave was made a man" (107). More bluntly, Dixon's Legree assures his black listeners, "Your old masters are to dig in the fields and you are to sit under the shade and be gentlemen" (86). James subtly confuses Basil Ransom's racial identity early in *The Bostonians*, noting "something sultry and vast, something almost African," in the "rich, basking tone" of his voice—"something that suggested the teeming expanse of the cotton-field" (36)—but Ransom rebels against the reversals that Douglass and Legree promote and prides himself in resisting reconstruction and reconstructors like Tarrant. "He had seen Tarrant, or his equivalent, often before, James writes; "he had 'whipped' him, as he believed, controversially, again and again, at political meetings in blighted Southern towns, during the horrible period of reconstruction" (82).

Although James reconfigures Ransom's "whipping" of such carpetbaggers more in gendered than in racial terms, his battle for Verena Tarrant and his struggle to restore gendered order both carry racial markings. As his daughter's Pygmalion-like manipulator, for example, Selah Tarrant resembles a slave master.[5] Ransom's reaction to him registers the fear of finding himself in the feminine position that Verena occupies—the object of a master's "whipping" that inverts him in racial as well as gendered terms. Indeed, Ransom grows "impatient" at Tarrant's "grotesque manipulations, which he resented as much as if he himself had felt their touch." "They made him nervous, they made him angry," James notes, "and it was only afterwards that he asked himself wherein they concerned him, and whether even a carpet-bagger hadn't a right to do what he pleased with his daughter" (83). Claire Kahane rightly notes that "James points to Ransom's identification with Verena and flirts with the pleasure as well as the fear of being handled" (293), but Ransom also resists identification with Verena and, to prevent such repositioning, imagines taking Selah's place with her. His nervousness and anger register ambivalence, the sort of double identification that Kaja Silverman describes in *Male Subjectivity at the Margins*—an identification with both Verena and her father that recalls Douglass's double identification with Aunt Hester and Aaron Anthony: being in Verena's position and feeling Selah's "touch," being in Selah's place and doing what he pleases with Verena. The latter fantasy, furthermore, resembles Douglass's role reversal in his 1848 letter to Thomas Auld, in which he threatened to kidnap his old master's daughter Amanda, "whip her on the naked back," and "annihilate" the "graces that adorn the character of virtuous womanhood" (*Life and Writings* 1: 343). As Sundquist argues in Douglass's case, whipping and enslavement by another man are rewritten as mastery of the master's daughter. Racial subordination is reinscribed as gender superiority—a reinscription in which *The Bostonians* is deeply rooted.

James further complicates gender and racial issues in *The Bostonians* by interpolating another set of binaries—a third possibility of "inversion." He thwarts Ransom's masculinist reconstruction strategies by blurring the boundaries not only between racial and gender identities but also between heterosexual and homosexual desires. *The Bostonians* appeared at a watershed moment in the history of male sexuality—just before, through the medium of the Oscar Wilde trial in 1895, deviant male gender and sexuality shifted, as it were, from inversion to perversion. Deviant male identity became figured through sexual practices rather than through a wider range of (effeminate) behaviors that may not have included homosexuality.[6] James began writing *The Bostonians*, as Leon Edel points out, only a few weeks after composing "The Author of Beltraffio," a "subtle and poisonous narrative of Mark Ambient's struggle with his wife for possession—body and soul—of their exquisite little boy" (Edel, *Henry James* 313), whom Mrs. Ambient allows to die rather than be contaminated by her husband's homosexuality.[7] *The Bostonians* seems informed by James's sensitivity to such a sexual paradigm shift, as well as by his awareness of American racial and gender politics. Each power position that Ransom imagines reverses upon itself, implicating him in heterosexual and homoerotic economies of exchange and subjecting him to socially constructed feminine as well as masculine identifications that often carry racial implications. In the passage describing his instant hatred of Selah Tarrant, for example, Ransom tries to convert a homosocial relationship (with Selah) into a heterosexual one (with Verena), but the patriarchal position into which he projects himself carries its own complications, especially after the Tarrants transfer Verena to Olive Chancellor.[8] Although Ransom had offered to change his "position" for Olive's "any day" (53), Verena's transfer from a patriarchal, heterosexual relation to a gynocentric, homosexual one confuses his own gendered position even as it opens up a range of relational possibilities.[9] If Ransom thinks he can escape feminization and/or homoerotization by imagining himself in Selah's place with Verena, seeing that subject position covered by Olive implicates him all over again in a homoerotic matrix of desire. Since Olive works within a homoerotic economy, taking her place with Verena will subject Ransom (from either direction) not simply to homoerotic but to female homoerotic desire of the sort James discovered in the career of George Sand.[10] Ransom as male lesbian, in Thaïs Morgan's term—male heterosexuality bleeds, as it were, into female homosexuality, although not quite into male homoeroticism. The northern "haunts of men" for which Ransom longs become truly haunted with the ghosts of intermediate sexes and indeterminate gender possibilities—a deconstructed more than reconstructed world.[11]

In a study of three of James's contemporaries (Courbet, Baudelaire, and Swinburne), Morgan analyzes the phenomenon of "male lesbianism," a "fantasized activity" between men "who have temporarily adopted female body drag" and "may be, as well, ventriloquizing the female voice." As a "discursive strategy situated within mid-nineteenth-century sexual politics," she argues, "male lesbianism may be seen as an attempt on the part of an all-male avant-garde to explore an enlarged range of pleasures and subjectivities without forfeiting the sociocultural privileges long accorded to a masculinity faithful to the hegemonic model for men's gender and sexuality established by the hetero-patriarchy" (41). Discussing Marcel Proust, Silverman also analyzes male lesbianism. "'Same-sex'" can mean "two morphological men," she points out; "a gay man and a lesbian woman, both of whom occupy a masculine psychic position; or a lesbian woman and a gay man, both of whom occupy a feminine psychic position" (381). Although Ransom appears to be one of the most masculine of James's heroes, a Southern version of Christopher Newman and Caspar Goodwood, James deftly immerses him in a world of women and feminists. Furthermore, his efforts to seduce Verena Tarrant and to steal her away from Olive Chancellor—taking Olive's place with her—put him in a conventionally male subject position that women have taken over. Ransom's desire to silence Verena's public speaking and to conscript her and her voice into his own private service resembles the ventriloquism that Morgan points out, as if Ransom wants to adopt or interpolate her voice. Possessing Verena in the way that Ransom intends comes very close to wanting to be Verena—making Ransom the subject and object of lesbian desire. Male lesbianism is not the goal of James's representation of Ransom's subjectivity, however. As he had done with the other male characters I have examined, James seems more interested in varying the subject positions and male subjectivities that Ransom experiences. Wherever Ransom tries to position himself imaginatively, he finds himself looking into a kind of magic mirror, subject to an unsettled and unsettling gaze of his own that reflects him to himself as if he were masculine and feminine, hetero- and homosexual, even white and black.

Since Judith Fetterley's resisting reading of *The Bostonians* in 1978, in which she scored "phallic critics" for their misogynistic and homophobic readings of the novel, critics have been refocusing attention to James's own feminism and especially to Olive Chancellor and her relationship with Verena Tarrant.[12] Fetterley wants to rescue Olive, Verena, and their friendship from the clutches of critics who translate them into conventional heterosexual discourse, but in the process she and other feminist critics beg the question of Basil Ransom's masculinity. To Michael Kimmel, Ransom epitomizes the anti-feminist backlash of the Reconstruction period (118), but in my view *The Bostonians* critiques such anti-feminism and interrogates the male subjectivity that sponsors it. Although Elaine Showalter claims that "men's resistance to problematizing male subjectivity is likely to be even greater than their resistance to studying women's writing" (183), the "defamiliarization" of masculinity, as she terms it (182), is precisely what James, Ransom, and the male or female reader face in *The Bostonians*.[13] James foregrounds a phallocentric, heterosexual economy in the novel and clearly opposes it to a gynocentric, homoerotic economy, but many leakages occur. If James does not represent a confluence of gendered economies, he does succeed, it seems to me, in "problematizing male subjectivity" and in representing a "male subjectivity at the margins."

Basil Ransom, of course, fiercely resists marginalization. Struggling with Olive over Verena, he means to reverse his loss of personal power in the war and Reconstruction. James notes that Ransom "seemed at moments to be inhabited by some transmitted spirit of a robust but narrow ancestor, some broad-faced wig-wearer or sword-bearer, with a more primitive manhood than our modern temperament appears to require" (199), and that spirit of manhood, adapted to northern conditions, forms an ideal that Ransom pursues for the entire novel. Megalomaniacally, he thinks that "wresting" Verena from the "mighty multitude" (413) will strike a blow for the re-masculinization of American society. For as James notes in a famous passage, Ransom believes that the "whole generation is womanized; the masculine tone is passing out of the world; it's a feminine, a nervous, hysterical, chattering, canting age." The antidote for this "damnable feminization," Ransom argues, is a strong dose of the "masculine character, the ability to dare and endure" (327). Ransom's rhetoric pales beside Dixon's paranoid ranting about attempts to "reverse the order of nature, turn society upside down, and make a thick-lipped, flat-nosed negro but yesterday taken from the jungle, the ruler of the proudest and strongest race of men evolved in two thousand years of history" (97), but only because Ransom covers racial markers with sexual ones. Selah Tarrant's manipulations of his daughter would encode for a southerner like Ransom the racist sexual threats explicitly formulated in Dixon's novel. As part of the larger cultural conversation about embattled white Southern manhood that would include Dixon's jeremiad and Douglass's letter to Thomas Auld, Ransom's response to the threat of "womanization" depends upon a paradigm of inversion—and re-inversion—of bipolar hierarchies.[14] Substituting carpetbagger for black man as scapegoat for his emasculation, Ransom would resurrect his manhood within a similar Reconstruction triangle in which gender can be substituted for racial mastery. Miss Birdseye, in Ransom's view, has shifted her attention from "negroes" to women, the "other slaves," and as a "resisting male," as James calls him, Ransom seems determined to transfer the masterful feeling he misses from one object to the "other." James's own project, on the other hand, seems dedicated to the proposition that re-masculinization, the reconstruction of an archaic masculinity, raises more questions than it answers.

James's conception of Ransom reflects the embattled situation of a postbellum Southern male who feels as if he has lost his manhood. Ransom has "surrendered the remnants of his patrimony to his mother and sisters," James observes, and he longs for "some work which would transport him to the haunts of men" (43). Southern men were raised to equate physical aggressiveness with virility, according to Wyatt-Brown, although "conventional opinion blamed the women for feminizing the young men and giving them wrongheaded notions of reality" (169). The antidote for such feminization, like Ransom's prescription for "womanization," requires reinscribing patriarchal authority. "If only fathers would assert their rightful authority," Wyatt-Brown says, "Southern manhood would yet revive to meet the challenges of a world gone mad for innovation and venality" (169).

In moving Ransom from the South to the North, James invokes the terms of a different type of manhood, reinscribing gender in a fiscal rather than sexual economy. Compensating himself for the lost stature he associates with feminization and homosocial subordination, this Cavalier Yankee, to conflate William Taylor's terms, aspires to be a "Masculine Achiever," a male ideal characterized by "accomplishment, autonomy and aggression—all in the service of an intense competition for success in the market-place" (Rotundo, "Learning About Manhood" 37).[15] Ransom "was not of a mercenary spirit, but he had an immense desire for success," James notes, "and he had more than once reflected that a moderate capital was an aid to achievement" (46). Reacting against the historical "fiasco" he witnessed (46) and the emasculation of his home, Ransom seeks the "haunts of men" and conventional masculine values in which to ground his personal manhood. He "fashions an idealized self-image of the heroic, upwardly mobile man of dignity and power," a description that David Leverenz actually applies to Frederick Douglass (131). More than Douglass, however, Ransom defines his male self in opposition to women and therefore works hard to avoid being repositioned in a woman's place.

For example, early in the novel when Ransom accompanies Olive to Dr. Mary Prance's, he becomes the object of a collective female gaze, and this scopic vulnerability threatens his sense of manhood. The "knowledge of his secret heresy" (his anti-feminism) lurks in all the women's faces he encounters. "He was conscious of all these middle-aged feminine eyes," he worries that Mrs. Farrinder herself will "defy him to combat," and he wonders whether he could "pull himself together" enough to "do honour to such a challenge" (74). Lynn Wardley considers this scene one of the several moments "encoded with gender confusion" that Ransom faces (649), and pulling himself together, reconstructing himself in the presence of women, is precisely the challenge James poses for him. However, because James liberates women in the novel from traditional gendered positions, he seriously complicates Ransom's efforts to define himself as a man against women—and womanization.

The obvious compensations for Ransom's felt impotence are economic achievement and marriage—traditional signs of manly success—but despite his diligence and ambition, this "young Mississippian," James notes, "had not made his profession very lucrative" (196). He even considers returning to the South, but he recognizes that doing so would undermine his profession of manhood. He "had been on the point of giving it up," James writes, "and returning to the home of his ancestors, where, as he heard from his mother, there was still just a sufficient supply of hot corn-cake to support existence" (197). Identified with the feminine in Ransom's mind, the South still represents a world of traditional mothers who rob men of their independent, adult masculinity in the very process of supporting their existence. Despite promising the "haunts of men," however, the North also offers Ransom confusing alternatives—with carpetbaggers like Selah Tarrant or women like Olive Chancellor already occupying the "masculine" positions to which he aspires. In that respect, James seems to deconstruct all constructs of masculinity, leaving Ransom suspended in an indeterminately gendered state, forced to reconstruct himself always in "other" terms.

Ransom's problems are also James's, however. In defining Ransom's manhood relationally, James briefly explores the possibility and implications of erotic attraction between Basil and the Chancellor sisters, Olive and Adeline (Luna), but the effort is awkward and suggests authorial complicity in a reactionary re-formation of manhood. James seems to believe that a Boston feminist who has lost two brothers in the Civil War and considers Ransom an "offshoot of the old slave-holding oligarchy" cannot "defend herself against a rich admiration—a kind of tenderness of envy"—for this former Southern soldier (43). As if by natural force, James implies, this unconventional woman admires a man in a conventional masculine posture (gallant soldier); if a man will only act like a man, even the most resistant woman will "envy" his masculine power. In making Ransom even potentially the object of Olive's desire, however, James raises several questions for his hero's male identity. Olive works within a homosocial and homosexual matrix of women, and her love for Verena obviously eroticizes her womanhood. If she feels desire for Ransom, does that desire feminize and homoeroticize him? Ransom's reaction to her suggests both gynophobia and homophobia, for even as he enjoys a "whimsical vision," contemplating Olive's singleness and wealth, of "becoming a partner in so flourishing a firm," one evening with her makes him conclude "that nothing would induce him to make love to such a type as that" (47). In Ransom's revulsion, James anticipates the use he will make of Balzac in managing desire for George Sand. "Women attract, and she repels," he will write in a 1902 essay; "and, as I [Balzac] am much of a man, if this is the effect she produces on me she must produce it on men who are like me" ("George Sand" 772). Equating gender with economic success in a world where women are economically successful, Ransom risks feminization in the very terms he himself has chosen. Olive threatens him because her wealth gives her power to put him in a woman's place—outside the "firm." Defensively, therefore, Ransom determines to take Olive's place and reclaim the masculine prerogatives—the power to "make love" and to forge economic partnerships—he feels he has lost.

The turning point in that process of masculine reconstruction occurs during Ransom's visit to Mrs. Luna's New York apartment (Chapter 22). Reeling from his failures in the North, Ransom considers an alternative profession—marriage—even as he recognizes that it is "not so elevated nor so manly" (204). He imagines himself Mrs. Luna's literary protégé, writing and publishing at her expense. "Images of leisure played before him," James observes, "leisure in which he saw himself covering foolscap paper with his views on several subjects, and with favourable illustrations of Southern eloquence" (205). Ransom almost persuades himself "that the moral law commanded him to marry Mrs. Luna" (206), but doing so would put him in a paradoxical position—celebrating the masculine from a feminine position—not exactly enslaved, not exactly cross-dressed as "Aunt Basil," but similarly subordinate: a kept man. Not surprisingly, Ransom repudiates such a reversal. He "would have despised himself," James notes, "if he had been capable of confessing to a woman that he couldn't make a living" (209). Nina Silber has shown how postbellum reconstructions of northern and southern masculinity differentiated southern "idleness and dissipation" from northern "hard work and self-improvement" (616). In imagining himself "Mr. Luna," Ransom understands the distinction, and in those terms he finds himself on the verge of switching genders, becoming a southernized northern gentleman and "despising" himself for the feminization and dissipation that position entails.

Ransom may feel safer in Mrs. Luna's presence, even as he risks self-hatred, because he escapes the homoerotic economy in which he imagined changing places with Olive. Like Lambert Strether at the theater or after the scene in the French countryside, Ransom finds that despising himself as a "woman" within a heterosexual relationship seems preferable to the anxious feelings engendered by Olive's "other" kind. Almost immediately, however, Ransom discovers the means to combat both threats to his manhood. When Mrs. Luna teases him about Verena's running off with "some lion-tamer" and speculates that Verena will thereby "give Olive the greatest cut she has ever had in her life" (213), she gives Ransom new terms for reconstructing his embattled masculinity. Repositioning himself imaginatively within a new triangle—rewriting "lion-tamer" as "woman-tamer"—Ransom "chuckled" at the "idea that he should be avenged (for it would avenge him to know it) upon the wanton young woman [Olive] who had invited him to come and see her in order simply to slap his face" (213). Shifting his attention to Verena and Olive enables Ransom to escape the feminized position to which Mrs. Luna subjects him—to become a fugitive (feminized) male—and to turn the tables upon Olive. Moreover, in revenging himself upon her in his newfound character of "lion-tamer," presumably with whip in hand, he repossesses the subject position from which he had fantasized "whipping" Selah Tarrant. Mrs. Luna's "slave" rewrites himself as Olive's master. Instead of being slapped in the face by Olive, he will now "cut" her.

As he leaves Mrs. Luna's apartment, escaping marriage and the patronized position it portended, Ransom exhales an "involuntary expression of relief, such as a man might utter who had seen himself on the point of being run over and yet felt that he was whole" (216). In enabling him to remember that he was a "man of ability" (216) by projecting himself into a relationship with Verena, James seems to indulge Ransom's nostalgic longing to recover the archaic, ante-bellum manhood—that "transmitted spirit of a robust but narrow ancestor" (199)—which the War and Reconstruction took from him. Actually, however, James does not let Ransom off so easily, for the triangulated relations he describes vitiate Ransom's manhood no matter where he stands. Even as Ransom seems to foreclose upon the risks of gender inversion, by entering the cage with the abolitionist-turned-feminist Olive (through the costume, as it were, of the lion tamer) Ransom opens himself not only to racial reversal but also to sexual inversion. In that respect, James positions Ransom on the cusp of the cultural moment I mentioned earlier—as a potential object lesson in the metamorphosis of effeminacy into homosexuality.

Reconstructing his masculinity by refocusing his desire upon Verena becomes a doubly vexed proposition for Ransom, therefore, because of Olive. His remembered masculinity depends upon collapsing the triangle that includes Olive and Verena and establishing a relation with Verena alone, because Olive's presence makes the possibility of a female masculinity—a masculinity not under men's control—a reality.[16] Given Olive's attraction to Verena, even imagining her being attracted to him puts Ransom in Verena's place, forced to see himself as the object of Olive's "masculine" and/or lesbian gaze. Ransom's solution to this problem is to project his gynophobic and homophobic feelings upon Olive, investing an exchange of subjectivity for objectivity in the possibility of a new, self-reliant subject position from which he can exclude Olive. He will not visit her in Boston, he reasons, to spare her feelings—because *she* finds *him* "odious." He would feel "indelicate," James observes, "to inflict on her a presence which he had no reason to suppose the lapse of time had made less offensive." Reimagining himself phallocentrically as an object, Ransom fantasizes about the "fit the sight of his long Mississippian person would give her" (218). His masculine empowerment, a neat reversal of James's feelings about Sand through the agency of Balzac, depends upon Olive's finding him "odious"—upon his not being an object of her desire, not a man attractive to such a "type" as that. If he were to consider himself attractive to Olive, he would be in Verena's position, identified with her as a love-object. By taking Olive's place with Verena he can confirm his manly position, but this strategy is vexed as well, for that "masculine" position is already occupied by a woman, leaving Ransom, it would seem, with no place to be a man.

Ransom's visit with Verena to Harvard's Memorial Hall reinforces the nostalgic reconstruction exercise he had begun at Mrs. Luna's and occurs, as if in imaginative compensation, immediately following Verena's participation in the summer's Woman's Convention. Eclipsing regional with sexual politics, Ransom responds to the Memorial in pointedly masculinist terms, as if it commemorated a desirable type of manhood more than a Union victory. It speaks to him of "duty and honour, it speaks of sacrifice and example," and it seems to him "a kind of temple to youth, manhood, generosity" (246). Referring to his past war experience in the context of his present imaginative need, "he forgot, now, the whole question of sides and parties; the simple emotion of the old fighting-time came back to him, and the monument around him seemed an embodiment of that memory; it arched over friends as well as enemies, the victims of defeat as well as the sons of triumph" (246). Repossessing an old identification as a warrior, Ransom re-empowers himself by affiliating with Union soldiers, eliding the causes of the War (including slavery), and transferring his new self-possession to his relationship with Verena. He recognizes with some relish that he and Verena have become "more intimate" (247) and also that his clandestine visit has put her in his power, because she will keep the secret from Olive. "In playing with the subject this way," James observes, "in enjoying her visible hesitation, he was slightly conscious of a man's brutality—of being pushed by an impulse to test her good-nature, which seemed to have no limit" (248). Ironically, Ransom thus aligns himself by default with the "brutal, blood-stained, ravening race" from which Olive would deliver her "sisters." Reconstructing Verena as a "touching, ingenuous victim, unconscious of the pernicious forces which were hurrying her to her ruin" (251), the man who could imagine himself being whipped by Selah Tarrant, patronized by Mrs. Luna, and slapped in the face by Olive Chancellor re-empowers himself as a kind of fugitive-female catcher—a woman-breaker. As if emerging from the closet he shared with Frederick Douglass, through his own "blood-stained gate" of emasculation, Ransom repossesses a "man's brutality" and enlists in a civil war of the sexes that upstages the "other" war that Harvard's Hall memorializes.

As he pursues the psychological dynamics of Ransom's masculine reconstruction, however, James illustrates the genesis of a false empowerment—the deconstruction, so to speak, of "brutal" manhood through the always already inverted positions to which any male identification can be subject. James's ironization of Ransom's reempowerment develops slowly, to be sure, as the plot movement from the end of Book Two to the end of Book Three seems to represent the sort of re-masculinization about which Ransom had fantasized. By showing Ransom hardening, as it were, into a single male posture, investing himself in the construct or costume of a "man's brutality," James sets him up, like Jefferson Davis in the hands of northern illustrators, to become a caricature of himself.

Recognizing that he is economically and even verbally less powerful than Verena, for example, Ransom shifts his terms of power from the fiscal to the sexual. His admission that he would like to be President in order to "breathe forth" his anti-feminist views in "glowing messages" to a "palpitating Senate" (323) prompts Verena to wonder how far he has advanced toward that goal and thus projects "rather an ironical light" on his "present beggarly condition" (324). Where he had earlier committed himself to economic achievement—thereby identifying, in Silber's terms, with a northern, self-reliant manhood—economic failure prompts Ransom to shift his ground. Risking the reinslavement he escaped at Mrs. Luna's, he contemplates a partnership with the fiscally superior Verena, eclipsing her feminism with sexual desire for him. In effect, this phallocentric re-empowerment stages a secession of the phallus from the complex, emasculating union of racial and gender subordination and its reincorporation as the central (sexual) signifier of male identity. Verena was "profoundly unconscious" of her love for him, Ransom thinks, "and another ideal, crude and thin and artificial, had interposed itself; but in the presence of a man she should really care for, this false, flimsy structure would rattle to her feet" (324). Initially, Verena resists what amounts to conscription into Ransom's phallogocentric fantasy. She asserts a feminist ideal which, to his thinking, replaces sexual with political desire. Indeed, she repeats her earlier question, "Aren't you getting on quite well in this city?" (324), rhetorically emphasizing his financial failure. In effect, Ransom feels beaten. He hears "such a subtly mocking, defiant, unconsciously injurious quality, that the only answer he could make to it seemed to him for the moment to be an outstretched arm, which, passing round her waist, should draw her so close to him as to enable him to give her a concise account of his situation in the form of a deliberate kiss" (324–25). Ransom's fantasy kiss seems purely political, a demonstration of rapacious power, as Judith Sensibar points out (66), at a moment when rational discourse has failed him. In this, he resembles both Christopher Newman and Caspar Goodwood, who kiss Claire de Cintré and Isabel Archer aggressively at moments when they feel most rejected. Recognizing his "beggarly condition," the impotence of his purse, Ransom feels his manhood rendered counterfeit, so he resorts imaginatively to a different currency (physical and sexual power, or brutality) to validate his manliness.

Ransom's trip to Cape Cod, where Verena has cloistered herself to prepare for her important Boston speech, at the beginning of Book Three certainly represents a rescue mission in his own mind, as it also enables him to join his new manly mettle in a battle of the sexes. Reincarnated as his soldierly self, he considers himself on the "attack," and he wants "to take possession of" Verena as if she were a Union stronghold (342). Supporting Anthony Rotundo's conclusion that the "bodily ideal of manhood" became the "dominant ideal" in the second half of the nineteenth century ("Body and Soul" 26), James resorts to metaphors of embodiment—many of them manifestly phallic—to stress Ransom's physical strength and size. He marvels, for example, that "the tread of a tall Mississippian made the staircase groan and the windows rattle in their frames" of the little hotel on Cape Cod where Ransom stays (339), and he repeatedly filters such descriptions through the point of view of his female characters, whom he uses as passive reflectors of Ransom's inflating power. In the war of the sexes, James stages a reversal of power—Ransom's manly triumph over Olive Chancellor, in particular—that depends upon coerced female homage to the phallus. Not only does Ransom force his way into Olive's household but he revels in his powerful purpose. "He didn't care a straw, in truth, how he was judged or how he might offend; he had a purpose which swallowed up such inanities as that, and he was so full of it that it kept him firm, balanced him, gave him an assurance that might easily have been confounded with a cold detachment" (357). James's language could certainly be ironic—a portrait of an overly cocky male—but the women's reactions to Ransom's reappearance seem to validate that cockiness. Olive, for example, stares at him "in sudden horror," "her self-possession completely deserted her" (355), and Ransom enjoys her passivity as brutally as he had enjoyed Verena's. There is nothing to say, he thinks; he "could only let her take it in, let her divine that, this time, he was not to be got rid of" (355). He enjoys similar power over Verena. As her look of desperation deepens, "a quick sense of elation and success began to throb in his heart," for it revealed that "she was afraid of him, that she had ceased to trust herself, that the way he had read her nature was the right way (she was tremendously open to attack, she was meant for love, she was meant for him)" (358). Ransom's reconstruction of his masculinity requires a confusion of sex and power, a triumph over women and women's friendship and over the homosocial economy in which he himself has been implicated. Substituting Olive for Selah Tarrant, the feminist for the carpetbagger, enables Ransom to rewrite the primal scene he shared with Frederick Douglass and to reconstruct his masculinity on the backs, so to speak, of two women—to master the mistress and the mistress's mistress. By the end of the scene in which Ransom proposes to Verena, she and Olive both feel "whipped"—reduced, much like Douglass's Aunt Hester, to tears and desperation. Moaning and shuddering, Olive throws herself on "her friend's bosom" and begs Verena not to "desert" her, while Verena implores Olive to help her resist Ransom (364). Feminism and homosocial solidarity—both collapse as defenses against a phallocentric masculinity and the heterosexual economy it enforces. Gauging Ransom's power by his effect upon these two formerly powerful women, James seems to validate Ransom's reconstruction of his manhood in conventional masculine terms, to applaud his reconstitution of the destabilized hierarchies—sexual and racial—that the Civil War destroyed. As Olive bluntly tells Verena, Ransom has become "one of his own slave-drivers" (363).

Ransom's sudden success with his writing helps confirm his reappropriation of gendered discourse. The *Rational Review* has accepted his article, and that acceptance, coupled with the sense of power he felt in the Central Park scene with Verena, has spurred his attack on Marmion. Ransom conjoins his formerly opposed career tracks and reinforces sexual with verbal power. Phallocentrism becomes phallogocentrism through the power of pen and tongue. The words he had spoken to Verena in New York finally have an effect, Ransom recognizes: "these words, the most effective and penetrating he had uttered, had sunk into her soul and worked and fermented there" (374). Indeed, in the radical shift that occurs in Verena's thinking, the phallus, as signifier of authority and power, changes hands, and Ransom's words impregnate her with an alien alter ego. Verena stands amazed at the "magic touch" that has caused such a "cataclysm" in her feelings. She feels surprise that Ransom "had been deputed by fate to exercise this spell," particularly because she "had flattered herself that she had a wizard's wand in her own pocket" (375). Not only does James transfer this magical wand from Verena to Ransom, but he seems to make its use a function of gender determinism, as if both characters are fated to assume their naturally gendered roles. That is, Verena's reversion to a submissive feminine role enables Ransom's recovery of an aggressive masculine role and thus reverses the "womanization" he had decried.

In her study of eighteenth-century works in which male writers adopt a female point of view, Nancy K. Miller argues that a primary motive of such authorial cross-dressing is "narcissistic gain implicitly achieved by occupying the place of the desired object in the syntax of the Other" (51). The "erotics erected by female impersonation," she says, "is a mirroring not of female desire but of phallic pride of place, a wish-fulfillment that ultimately translates into structures of masculine dominance and authority"

120   Chapter 4

(54). James uses Verena in a similar way, making Ransom an object of female desire that he as male author attributes to her. James goes a step further, in fact, because he uses Verena not only to confirm Ransom's erotic value as love object but to validate the phallocentric terms of his suddenly self-inflating value.[17] As she approaches him before one of their long walks on Cape Cod, for example, Verena subjects Ransom to an extended female gaze, but instead of measuring him from a feminist point of view, she sees him as he would want to be seen, supplanting her feminist subjectivity with a male-oriented abjectivity. She "felt that his tall, watching figure, with the low horizon behind, represented well the importance, the towering eminence he had in her mind—the fact that he was just now, to her vision, the most definite and upright, the most incomparable, object in the world. If he had not been at his post when she expected him she would have had to stop and lean against something, for weakness; her whole being would have throbbed more painfully than it throbbed at present, though finding him there made her nervous enough" (375).

Having achieved such phallocentric power over Verena, Ransom also seems ready to wage civil war with Olive over the phallic authority, the "tremendous big gun" of rhetoric (381), that Verena carries. As if still playing the "lion-tamer," he wants "to take up again a line of behaviour which he had forsworn," and he wonders what "consideration" he owes Olive during his campaign. Resisting reinscription as a Southern gentleman in the Northern rhetoric of emasculation, he decides that Olive deserves no consideration, because in wartime chivalry is only for the weak, whereas Olive "was a fighting woman, and she would fight him to the death, giving him not an inch of odds" (381).

Given the threat that Verena's power poses for his manhood, moreover, Ransom becomes obsessed with preventing her lecture at the Boston Music Hall. Not only does he level many "shafts" at her plans, but "to 'squelch' all that, at a stroke, was the dearest wish of his heart" (382). When Verena repulses Ransom and hides in Boston while she prepares for her Music Hall address, his manhood is thrown in jeopardy—so dependent on subjugating women that, without Verena's passive presence, his feelings of "agitation and suspense" are "tremendously acute" (412). To recover the masculine character that Verena has stolen, Ransom must rescue her from the "jump into the abyss" of feminism, because such a jump would cast his own gender identity into a similarly indeterminate, abysmal state. Intervening against Verena's jump means preventing his own. "The vision of wresting her from the multitude set him off again," James writes, "to stride through the population that would fight for her. It was not too late, for he felt strong; it would not be too late even if she should already stand there before thousands of converging eyes" (413).

Ransom's success in this final scene suggests the efficiency of the sexual economy James has created. Consistently, James has represented Ransom's manhood as erected upon a prostrate femininity, and Ransom's final re-empowerment in the masculine does depend upon a reversal of power designed to confirm his recuperation of his lost Southern manhood. John Carlos Rowe argues that Ransom's "destiny is to repeat the 'romance' of the Old South and all its corruptions. Basil's defensive projection is the displacement of his cultural authority over the black slave to domination of the New England woman, herself a token of the abolitionist movement" (*Theoretical Dimensions* 95). This nostalgic reinscription, the cost by default of his resistance to the several "other" positions he faces in the novel, also consists with his sudden literary success, itself apparently an inscription of archaic ideas and values. In effect, Ransom has written himself into being as his old self. He feels "pure pity" for Verena's agony, as she struggles with her dilemma, but he also flushes with a sense of power: "he saw that he could do what he wanted, that she begged him, with all her being, to spare her, but that so long as he should protest she was submissive, helpless" (425).

Feeling that the whole scene "flamed before him and challenged all his manhood," Ransom feels himself soaring above the Boston audience (425) and especially above Olive Chancellor: "To his astonishment, the eyes that looked at him out of her scared, haggard face were, like Verena's, eyes of tremendous entreaty. There was a moment during which she would have been ready to go down on her knees to him, in order that the lecture should go on" (426). James's imagery effectively marries racial and sexual power. Forcing Olive—a phallic woman—to "go down on her knees" recalls and reverses Ransom's first imaginative encounter with Selah Tarrant. Although she reminds him of "some feminine firebrand of Paris revolutions, erect on a barricade" (432), Olive has been metaphorically castrated, whipped and rendered impotent in her rigidity—and left in Verena's place—so that Ransom can reclaim phallic power for himself, wrenching Verena away from the others "by muscular force" (432) and hurrying her away, "palpitating with his victory" (433). Read "straight," as Ransom himself intends it, this climactic gesture stages a victory for the "masculine character" over the "feminine" age—a reactionary re-construction of an archaic, antebellum manhood.

To read the scene otherwise, to argue as I have been doing that James subverts each subject position that Ransom constructs, requires ingenuity that challenges my own readerly position, because it requires a subtle teasing out of "other" meaning from James's language that lurks deep in the jungle of his discourse. In Dixon's *The Leopard's Spots* a group of white men actually kill a young white woman rather than see her—they assume—raped by the black soldiers who have kidnapped her on her wedding day.

Tom Camp, Annie's father, could be speaking for Thomas Auld, responding to Frederick Douglass's threat against his daughter Amanda, as he thanks God that she was "saved from them brutes" because, in the notorious phrase, "There are things worse than death!" (125). The incident forms an object lesson for the North Carolina community, a rallying point for restoring racial and sexual order. "A few things like this will be the trumpet of the God our Father," says the Reverend John Durham, "that will call the sleeping manhood of the Anglo-Saxon race to life again" (127). Although Basil Ransom's climactic kidnapping-rescue of Verena Tarrant at the end of *The Bostonians* seems devoid of such explicit racism, it is grounded in similar motives. Ransom's action recapitulates even as it reverses traditional captivity narratives—saving a woman from a fate worse than death—in this case, from sexual inversion rather than racial perversion. Reclaiming Verena for a heterosexual and patriarchal economy, rescuing her from a homosocial and homoerotic relationship, Ransom—slave-driver and woman-breaker—seemingly blows the trumpet that calls his own sleeping manhood to life again.

Eve Sedgwick has provocatively argued that at the end of "The Beast in the Jungle" John Marcher becomes "not the finally all-knowing man who is capable of heterosexual love, but the irredeemably self-ignorant man who embodies and enforces heterosexual compulsion" (*Epistemology* 210). Although the "muscular force" with which Ransom abducts Verena seems radically different from Marcher's abject passivity toward May Bartram, Ransom's "palpitating victory" can be subjected to a similar reading. Through a complex series of identity exchanges Ransom can be linked, if only in contrast, with the cross-dressed Jefferson Davis, whose wife *Varina* (according to his own account) threw a shawl over his shoulders just before Union soldiers arrested him.[18] In *The Bostonians*, of course, Ransom thrusts the hood of Verena's long cloak over her head as he spirits her away from *her* Union "captors." The resemblance of names (Varina-Verena) and gestures, performed under similar circumstances, suggests James's deliberate interpolation of well-known material. Ironically, this interpellation of subject position for Ransom rehearses previous transpositions he has experienced and puts him back in the closet of gender indeterminacy. Not unlike the closeted Frederick Douglass or his own earlier specular self (when he watched Selah Tarrant's "grotesque manipulations" of Verena), Ransom finds himself transgendered no matter which position he occupies. For if his gesture with the cloak reverses the gender inversion of the original event by placing Verena in the cross-dressed Jefferson Davis's position, it also inscribes Ransom himself in Varina Davis's role. Earlier in the novel, moreover, Ransom had told Verena that he wanted to be President of the United States so that he could "breathe forth" his views to a "palpitating Senate" (323). Such a grandiose fantasy, especially if Ransom is linked with Davis, would have provoked ridicule in the North; a Currier and Ives lithograph entitled *A "So Called President" in Petticoats*, for example, mocked Davis's presidential pretensions (Neely 86).

In another respect, too, Ransom's "palpitating" fantasy unsettles the gendered identity his muscular gesture constructs. In transferring male palpitations from the Senate to Ransom, James ironically implicates him in the homoerotic economy of exchange that his words and actions are designed to deny. In other words, taking the place of the "palpitating" male Senators, before whose collective male gaze he had imagined himself starring, ironically reenacts the exchange of positions Ransom had projected with Selah Tarrant.[19] Reconstructing his masculinity by taking Tarrant's patriarchal place with Verena, it turns out, subjects Ransom to the same gender indeterminacy he had tried to escape when he left the South. He may palpitate with his victory, but he flaunts his muscularity and his manhood to a group of gawking men.

Chapter 5
Deploying Homo-Aesthetic Desire in the Tales of Writers and Artists

> *It is the common belief that all subjects from inverted instinct carry their lusts written in their faces; that they are pale, languid, scented, effeminate, painted, timid, oblique in expression. This vulgar error rests upon imperfect observation.*
>
> —John Addington Symonds, Sexual Inversion *107*

"You bewilder me a little," says the narrator of "The Death of the Lion" to Lady Augusta Minch, "in the age we live in one gets lost among the genders and the pronouns" (296). The occasion for this provocative confession is the anticipated arrival at Mrs. Wimbush's country estate of Guy Walsingham, the "pretty little girl" author (298) of the novel "Obsessions," and Dora Forbes, the red-mustachioed, "indubitable male" (274) author of "The Other Way Round." The narrator's bewilderment offers a cryptic point of entry for this essay, because it so efficiently links—and problematizes—the issues of gender, sexuality, and writing that loom large, I argue, in James's stories of writers and artists. Typically, these tales feature the close relationship between an older male writer and a young male admirer, who devotes himself to the older man as "the friend, the lover, the knower, the protector" (*Complete Notebooks*, 87). That core male relationship is complicated in various ways—by a wife or fiancée, by other admirers (male or female), by the marketplace that James repeatedly decries. Writing and reading between men—the interplay of male desire among "the genders and the pronouns"—I would like to explore what Eve Sedgwick calls the "asymmetries of gendered desire" (*Epistemology* 197) in four of James's stories of writers and artists: "The Author of Beltraffio" (1884), "The Lesson of the Master" (1888), "The Middle Years" (1893), and "The Death of the Lion" (1894).[1]

In this chapter I am not concerned simply with James's homosexuality or representation of homosexuality, but with his poetics of male desire—the deployment of male desire in acts of writing and reading between men. In a section of *The History of Sexuality* entitled "The Deployment of Sexuality," Foucault argues that the "appearance in nineteenth-century psychiatry, jurisprudence, and literature of a whole series of discourses on the species and subspecies of homosexuality, inversion, pederasty, and 'psychic hermaphroditism' made possible a strong advance of social controls into this area of 'perversity.'" He goes on, however, to note that "it also made possible the formation of a 'reverse' discourse: homosexuality began to speak in its own behalf, to demand that its legitimacy or 'naturality' be acknowledged, often in the same vocabulary, using the same categories by which it was medically disqualified" (101). Writers such as Oscar Wilde and John Addington Symonds clearly enlisted in the ranks of those who wrote a "reverse" discourse, but the extent of James's participation presents a trickier matter. They key question, I think, is what form James's participation took. As the epigraph from Symonds's "A Problem in Modern Ethics" suggests, reading homosexuality is an "imperfect" process because homosexual men do not necessarily "carry their lusts written in their faces" where they may be easily read. James's stories of writers and artists play with writer-reader relationships and with the difficulty of reading gender and sexuality, as well as other figures in the authorial carpet. Rather than simply revealing the homoerotic subtext in these stories, however, I would like to examine the various paths of desire that James himself interrogates and, more importantly, the variously gendered subjectivities that differently encoded desires construct. Homosexuality does not simply figure in these stories as a hidden figure in James's carpet, covered by a layer of culturally enforced, or "compulsory" heterosexuality. Instead, I think, James experiments with several forms of male desire and explores the subjective consequences, as it were, of various object choices—supporting Richard Dellamora's argument that "there is no unitary 'gay subject' just as there are no unitary 'masculine' or 'feminine' subjects" (4). Homoerotic desire figures as a vexed idea in these tales because it, too, takes several forms—sometimes represented as a virtual physicality, sometimes mediated by women (positioned "between men," in Sedgwick's phrase), sometimes mediated homo-aesthetically through works of art, and sometimes circulated narcissistically through another man as a self-creating, autoerotic force.

In some intense instances, James transgenders desire, cross-dressing its object in a woman's body. In "The Aspern Papers" (1888), for example, the first-person narrator must go through two women (Juliana and Tina Bordereau) in order to gain access to the deceased Jeffrey Aspern, whom he idealizes and has fetishized in the "papers" he tries to retrieve. Through their relationships to Aspern, the two women physically mediate the narrator's relationship with the poet. Touching them means touching what Aspern himself touched. They offer the narrator the imaginative experience of taking Aspern's place, the power to "look into a single pair of eyes into which his had looked or to feel a transmitted contact in any aged hand that his had touched" (8). Like his counterpart in "The Author of Beltraffio," the narrator feels intense emotion as he gets nearer to Aspern—that is, to an Aspern embodied in a woman: Juliana's "presence seemed somehow to contain and express his own, and I felt nearer to him at that first moment of seeing her than I ever had been before or ever have been since" (23).

As James examines the relation between male authors and their audience in other tales, he consistently imagines enabling and empowering male readers, who enjoy an intimate, closeted relationship with the Master writers whose work they admire. Brooke Horvath has wryly noted the almost postmodernist, circular relationship between these two characters. The master, he notes, "as his greatest creation, produces the perfect protégé, who in turn invents the masterfulness of his master" (102), but such narcissistic interdependency, or intersubjectivity, has erotic as well as aesthetic dimensions. James configures these homo-aesthetic bonds in both phallogocentric and dominant-subordinate terms, while making the Master more often the object than the subject of male desire. Deploying homoerotic desire uni-directionally in this manner makes it a function of a male reader's response more than of the writing or the writer, but homoerotic desire nonetheless emerges as the product of an intersubjective, homosocial transaction. Typically, however, James destabilizes these utopic male bonds by dispersing male desire among several gendered objects and, through the investment of homoerotic, heterosexual, and autoerotic desire, he thus diversifies the male subjectivity that those different object choices reflect.

In the whirlwind of changing relationships and substitutions he includes in "The Figure in the Carpet" (1896) James circulates homo-aesthetic desire through a series of male and female characters (George Corvick, Gwendolen Corvick, Drayton Deane) and so provides multiple screens for the narrator's desire. "I was young enough for a flutter at meeting a man of his renown," the narrator says early in the story (358), and in an interesting twist, he worries about the effect his own writing will have on the Master—the effect it "would have on Vereker up there by his bedroom fire" (362). Vereker "fires" him as he has "never been fired" (367), and he admits that he "had taken to the man" more than he "had ever taken to the books" (378). He considers marrying Gwendolen after Corvick's death in order to get what he wants, but he finds himself at the end of the story re-inverted and confronting another man, Drayton Deane, who in marrying Gwendolen himself is "now exactly in the position" (395) that the narrator covets—in position to see Vereker's "idol unveiled" in a "private ceremony for a palpitating audience of one" (389). "It was therefore from her husband [Deane] I could never remove my eyes," the narrator admits; "I beset him in a manner that might have made him uneasy. I went even so far as to engage him in conversation. Didn't he know [Hugh Vereker's secret], hadn't he come into it as a matter of course?—that question hummed in my brain. Of course he knew; otherwise he wouldn't return my stare so queerly. His wife had told him what I wanted and he was amiably amused at my impotence" (396–97). Much as he endlessly defers revelation of Vereker's secret "figure," James disperses desire so polymorphously in the story that he effectively deconstructs any subject position that directed desire might entail. That dispersion of desire, however, remains centered in the story's core relationship between male writer and male reader.

Originating in an anecdote from Edmund Gosse about John Addington Symonds (*Complete Notebooks* 25), "The Author of Beltraffio," in Fred Kaplan's words, "dramatizes James's attraction to, and fear of, the horrible consequences of homoerotic love" (303).[2] But the tale also explores the basis of a homoerotic poetics—the connection between what Jonathan Dollimore calls "transgressive desire" and a "transgressive aesthetic." Dollimore notes the widespread fear of "cross-over between discursive and sexual perversion, politics and pathology" in the Oscar Wilde case, for example (67). "Wilde's transgressive aesthetic subverted the dominant categories of subjectivity which kept desire in subjection," he argues, and "subverted the essentialist categories of identity which kept morality in place" (68). James plays on the line between aesthetics and erotics, it seems to me. He enjoys the leakage that occurs between the two through the connotations of his exotic and erotic language. Throughout "Beltraffio" he conflates sexual and aesthetic concerns. Ambient's allegedly perverse writing threatens his marriage, but it also clearly attracts the narrator to him. The young narrator feels marked curiosity about the "mysteries of Mark Ambient's hearth and home" (65) and even more intense desire when he imagines his first meeting with Ambient in the flesh. The "pleasure, if it should occur—for I could scarcely believe it was near at hand—would be so great that I wished to think of it in advance," he confesses, "to feel it there against my breast, not to mix it with satisfactions more superficial and usual" (57). When he does finally see Ambient's "handsome face," his heart "beat very fast" (59), and he feels "altogether happy and rosy, in fact quite transported," when Ambient lays his hand on his shoulder (60). Later, he subjects Ambient to an extended male gaze that anatomizes even as it enjoys his features. He emphasizes the play of Ambient's expression, for example, and the way "innumerable things" "chased each other in and out of his face" (60). Such fascination with the author's face quickly transfers to the author's writing—the site where James prefers to liberate male desire for the sort of close reading that faces, as in the Symonds passage, can resist. Texts, too, can become transparent or at least subject to the projection of various readerly desires, as in the Oscar Wilde case. In *The Picture of Dorian Gray* (1891), Wilde himself offers a cautionary note about close reading when Basil Hallward explains to Dorian why he has not exhibited his portrait. "One day, a fatal day I sometimes think, I determined to paint a wonderful portrait of you as you actually are, not in the costume of dead ages, but in your own dress, and in your own time." Clearly, however, painting Dorian as he "actually" is creates the same quandary that Hugh Merrow faces in James's later unfinished story. Painting Dorian as he "actually" is—presumably gay—means painting him as Basil sees him. The artist is both reader and painter. "I know that as I worked at it, every flake and film of colour seemed to me to reveal my secret. I grew afraid that others would know of my idolatry. I felt, Dorian, that I had told too much, that I had put too much of myself into it. Then it was that I resolved never to allow the picture to be exhibited" (149). Hallward's anxieties about representing desire and especially about having that desire interpreted or read certainly resemble the anxieties James explores in his tales of writers and artists. Hallward's decision to keep his canvas from view, moreover, uncannily resembles the situation in "The Author of Beltraffio," where Mark Ambient's manuscript-in-progress is closeted for similar reasons—the volatile, even fatal, consequences that reading it may entail.

Like Wilde, James does not grant his narrator unmediated access to Mark Ambient as he "actually" is. The narrator's budding relationship with Ambient is doubly or even triply mediated—by Ambient's wife Beatrice, by their son Dolcino, and by the scandalous text (Beltraffio") which the narrator has read five times. As he explores relationships in "The Author of Beltraffio" and especially the subjectivities or subject positions each of them entails, James employs a complex series of screens and substitutions.[3] He triangulates the narrator's relationship with Ambient, for example, by confronting him with Beatrice—and thus with the "problem" of Ambient's heterosexuality. Although the narrator assesses Beatrice as "quite such a wife as I should have expected him to have; slim and fair, with a long neck and pretty eyes and an air of good breeding" (63), he also wonders whether she is "worthy of the author of a work so distinguished as 'Beltraffio'" (63–64). He goes on, in fact, to describe Mrs. Ambient in catty terms—noting her "coldness," her lack of attention to her husband (63), her "slightly too osseous hands" (65), her frigid amusement (68)—and he emphasizes her lack of passion, as if to elide the erotic basis of her marriage. "In looking for some explanation of [Ambient's] original surrender to her," the narrator later observes, "I saw more than before that she was, physically speaking, a wonderfully cultivated human plant—that he might well have owed her a brief poetic inspiration. It was impossible to be more propped and pencilled, more delicately tinted and petalled" (93). In particular, he feels considerable relief when he concludes that Beatrice has "no great intellectual sympathy with the author of 'Beltraffio,'" because that conclusion emboldens him to imagine substituting his own sympathy and taking her place. He thinks her lack of sympathy "strange," he comments, "but somehow, in the glow of my own enthusiasm, didn't think it important: it only made me wish rather to emphasise that homage" (67). Thus, when he has the chance to spend an evening with Ambient in the latter's study, the narrator relishes even the "longish pauses" in their "communion," because they make him feel that they have "advanced in intimacy" and reinforce his conclusion that his friend's "personal situation" is "by no means the happiest possible" (81–82).

James further complicates this homosocial relationship when he introduces the Ambients' child. Ambient's son and his writing double for one another throughout the story as transposable objects of exchange through which desire circulates. Where the boy evidences the procreative power of heterosexual practice, Ambient's writing (at least to the adoring narrator) represents the creative or recreative potential of homoerotic desire. The narrator describes Dolcino as "some perfect little work of art" (71), and the boy's affiliation with the feminine seems clinched by his mother's constant vigilance and by the presence of his miniature portrait, which she wears around her neck. Beatrice's contempt for her husband's arguably homoerotic writing and her determination to keep that writing from her son, therefore, give the narrator the opening he needs to insinuate himself into a literary relationship with Ambient. For him, Ambient's writing figures as a kind of surrogate child, the product or construct of a homo-aesthetic writing-reading transaction.[4] In a confrontation with Beatrice in Ambient's study, for example, the narrator, with admitted "perversity," flaunts the "precious proof sheets" of the work in progress Ambient has given him—which, James observes, he "nursed" under his arm. "They're the opening chapters of his new book," the narrator gushes. "Fancy my satisfaction at being allowed to carry them to my room!" (82). In Eric Savoy's useful formulation, Ambient's work-in-progress "cruises" its reader, whose ecstatic response to this "homotext" helps seal his sublimated, homo-aesthetic relationship to Ambient himself. As Savoy comments, the "subtle play of glances *through* the mask of repression is the essential mode of the homotext, the operation by which the writer may be said to cruise the reader and thus to construct his receptive community" ("Hypocrite Lecteur" 20).

Whatever Ambient has written—whatever his text "actually" is—the narrator of course brings his own subjectivity to the reading. Since the narrator's desire for Ambient and Ambient's writing appears largely phallocentric, he constructs himself as a reader in a largely passive, receptive position. The phallically empowered Ambient assumes a dominant posture. The narrator describes Ambient's "artistic ego," for example, as "erect and active" (86), while Ambient himself describes his own work-in-progress, the same work that the narrator covetously nurses under his arm, as a "golden vessel, filled with the purest distillation of the actual," which he has "hammered" into shape. "I have to hammer it so fine, so smooth; I don't do more than an inch or two a day. And all the while I have to be so careful not to let a drop of the liquor escape" (87). In this iconic and spermatically economical view of art, Ambient and the narrator relate to one another across the sign of this phallus-in-progress and thereby mark off the bounds of an all-male literary. Hyper-masculine more than hyper-aesthetic, this male poetics features mimetic accuracy, the "distillation of the actual," more than an epistemological or sexual uncertainty. Carefully guarded against spillage, or any excess of creative energy, Ambient's writing does not seem to represent a "transgressive aesthetic," in Dollimore's term, although its phallogocentrism does establish his assertive (or insertive) masculinity and writing. In contrast to "Life herself, the brazen hussy," Ambient characterizes himself as a "poor reproducer," but he still wields the power of an aesthetic and autogenetic patriarch. "To sink your shaft deep and polish the plate through which people look into it—that's what your work consists of," the narrator remembers his saying (88). Ironically, however, Ambient's desire to assert the hyper-masculinity of his writing does not preclude the interpellation of deviant sexuality. He and his writing remain open to the deployment of "transgressive desire" through the intersubjective relationship he and the narrator enjoy in the writing-reading process. Writerly gender performance does not necessarily determine the writerly "face" and subjectivity that a reader may discover in the text.

If this complicated homoerotic economy of literary exchange governs the first part of "The Author of Beltraffio," the second part of the story moves toward the restoration of a heterosexual economy. Priscilla Walton argues that the tale re-establishes "the need for patriarchal order" by pushing women to the "margins of the text" (71), but another sort of exchange occurs as well. The narrator abdicates his privileged position as male reader in favor of Beatrice, whom he successfully encourages to take up her husband's new manuscript. "I'm sure [those pages will] convert you," he assures her (101), although in fact Beatrice's reading converts Ambient by re-inverting him, so to speak—that is, by heterosexualizing him. In being passed from male to female reader, in short, Ambient's writing becomes subject to the inscription of diversified desires and thus to the possibility of reconstruction, or conversion.

Restoration of heterosexual relationships and desires proves vexed, however, because the narrator's sudden determination to reconcile the Ambients and to end the "ugly difference" (100) between them derives from his response to Dolcino and from his acutely sensitive reading of the boy's pathetic condition. Recuperating the heterosexual through the boy, then, reinvokes the homoerotic. Whenever he sees Dolcino, the narrator responds extravagantly to the child's extraordinary beauty. He emphasizes the intensity of the child's gaze, for example, which he says "attached itself to my face as if among all the small incipient things of his nature throbbed a desire to say something to me," and he regrets that he did not "even for a moment hold Dolcino in my arms" (98). The child's pleading look does gradually "kindle" a spark of inspiration in the narrator and also rehabilitates Beatrice as a sympathetic (and heterosexual) reader. The "plea I speak of," he says, "which issued from the child's eyes," seemed to "make him say: 'The mother who bore me and who presses me here to her bosom . . . has really the kind of sensibility she has been represented to you as lacking, if you only look for it patiently and respectfully. . . . I'm my great father's child, but I'm also my beautiful mother's, and I'm sorry for the difference between them!'" (99–100). That difference between the parents becomes manifest in their relationship to him, so that in being removed from the triangle his presence forms, Dolcino re-establishes the original and originating difference—the heterosexual difference—between the two of them. In that respect, he and the narrator work together to facilitate a conversion, or re-inversion, of Ambient's writing and, apparently, of Ambient himself.

I want to suggest, by way of explaining the narrator's sudden turnabout, that he denies his own pedophiliac desire for Dolcino by repressing all homoerotic desire, that he enlists in the service of the compulsory heterosexuality Eve Sedgwick describes in "The Beast in the Jungle." "I was aware that I differed from [Beatrice Ambient] inexpressibly," the narrator admits, but I think he refuses to explore the full implications of that difference by sacrificing Dolcino, the sign of Ambient's heterosexuality, to his mother's homophobia. She "has a dread of my brother's influence on the child," Gwendolen Ambient tells the narrator. "It's as if it were a subtle poison or a contagion—something that would rub off on his tender sensibility when his father kisses him or holds him on his knee. If she could she'd prevent Mark from even so much as touching him" (84). Gwendolen's extravagant imagery of physicality and disease certainly suggests more than the danger of aesthetic or intellectual corruption. The "poison" from which Beatrice Ambient wants to save her son would be communicated physically through his father's touches and kisses, while the boy sits in his father's lap. Reading her husband's new book—holding Dolcino's hand in one of hers and the proof-sheets in the other—she determines to let the boy die, "to prevent him from ever being touched" (110). The narrator admits somewhat ruefully that the child's death converts her. She not only reads the new book over again upon its publication, but she "even dipped into the black 'Beltraffio'" (112), which she apparently reclaims and rehabilitates for readerly consumption. In the process, of course, she takes the narrator's place in the triangle he had established with her husband. The narrator has subvented this exchange and has thus subverted his own desire for the author of "Beltraffio."

Whether or not we take Henry St. George at his word, critics typically cite "The Lesson of the Master" as exemplifying James's view that marriage threatens male artistic integrity. Leon Edel, characterizing the Master's lesson, argues that the "artist must choose. He can either marry and cheapen his art—and be a success—or take a celibate course, and produce the masterpieces which the world will not understand and which alone justify dedication and self-denial" (*Henry James* 347).[5] James himself certainly lends credence to this view of the tale. In his notebook he records a conversation with the British journalist Theodore Child "about the effect of marriage on the artist." It "occurred to me," he writes, "that a very interesting situation would be that of an elder artist or writer, who has been ruined (in his own sight) by his marriage and its forcing him to produce promiscuously and cheaply—his position in regard to a younger *confrere* whom he sees on the brink of the same disaster and whom he endeavors to save, to rescue, by some act of bold interference—breaking off the marriage, annihilating the wife, making trouble between the parties" (*Complete Notebooks* 43–44). "The Lesson of the Master" does more than elaborate this pat moral lesson, however. In fact, emphasizing the heterocentric triangle obscures the intensity of the tale's most important relationship—that between Henry St. George and Paul Overt, the master and the disciple. Triangulating and even quadrangulating a false dichotomy of marriage and art, James dramatizes—covertly, if you will—an "other" alternative: a transgressive homo-aestheticism.

At its simplest, "The Lesson of the Master" divides desire along heterosexual and homosexual lines. Midway through the tale, as Paul watches St. George drive off with Marian Fancourt, he experiences an "indefinite envy" (NY 15: 49)—a "feeling addressed alike, strangely enough, to each of the occupants of the hansom. How much he should like to rattle about London with such a girl! How much he should like to go and look at 'types' with St. George!" (15: 50). Divided desire in "The Lesson of the Master," however, gives way to a mediated homoeroticism, as both heterosexuality and heterotextuality screen desire between men. "Do you wish to pass exactly for what she represents you?" Paul Overt asks St. George about the textualized and heterosexualized self-in-relation he becomes in

Marian Fancourt's appreciative discourse (15: 34). But at its emotional center, "Lesson" features an intimate subject-object relation between male writer and reader—a master-disciple relation that Michael Cooper has termed an "erotonomy," a male-male relationship featuring a "mutual desire of the participants for personal interaction with each other and a mutually accepted system of exchanging satisfactions" (66). These homo-aesthetic relationships eroticize male homosocial intimacy *through the act of reading* by creating an exclusive, male-to-male circuit of desire that is not so much overtly written, as it is covertly read. Homoerotic desire therefore remains effectively closeted—subject to being disclosed through the immediate experience of individual reading practices but not subject, as it were, to publication. Put another way, if literary sexuality remains identifiable only in the reading—transactionally—then both writerly and readerly sexuality are left in a state of suspense.

James's text and the challenge it poses for his readers, furthermore, both reflect and enact an "object lesson" from the Master, because James establishes a relationship with his readers that mirrors the one he represents between Paul Overt and Henry St. George. "The Lesson of the Master" cruises male readers in particular, flirting with us, "winking" at us (in James Creech's term), subtly encouraging us to identify with a gay reading practice.[6] Even Henry James "practiced textual cruising for readers who would exchange a look with him, who would wink back" (Creech 97). Not "more than two or three people will notice you don't go straight," St. George tells Paul (15: 66), for example, and he even offers to invert himself—to "turn myself inside out"—to "save" Paul from imitating his own mediocre art (15: 67). To claim, as many Jamesian critics have done, that St. George merely means to "save" Paul from following the "mercenary muse" is of course to ignore the connotations of this language—that is, to refuse to take James at his word, or to read "straight" straight. But insofar as we wink back, recognizing the homoerotic suggestions of the tale, we construct a gay-identified meaning and acknowledge those suggestions by performing a gay reading practice. To write truly, Paul should not "go straight." He should avoid marriage *not* simply because it distracts the artist from his craft, but because heterosexuality in effect belies or closets the homotextuality in which, James suggests, men like Paul and St. George most truly and passionately write about themselves. When Paul asks St. George about the book his wife has made him burn, St. George replies, "it was about myself," and he enjoins Paul to "write it—*you* should do me." "There's a subject, my boy: no end of stuff in it!" (15: 74). Paul seems to accept St. George's challenge, of course, by leaving England for two years and devoting himself to a new novel. He acknowledges that St. George has "inverted" him, too—turned him "upside down that night—by dosing him to that degree, at the most sensitive hour of his life, with the doctrine of renunciation" (15: 83). For James's readers to read truly—with full attention to language—means not going "straight" as well, not reading "renunciation" without reading "upside down." Not going "straight" does not mean reading a gay meaning into the text or even discovering a gay *subtext*. While James does leave gay identification in a state of suspense—suspended between writer and reader (between intentional and affective fallacies) in an indeterminate textual space that awaits sexualization—he does not hide a gay meaning in "The Lesson of the Master." Craig Milliman claims that, "as a skilled writer, St. George manipulates both Marian and Paul by producing ambiguous textual versions of himself which exploit the expectations of his audience" ("Dangers" 83), but I think James leaves writer-reader relations more ambiguous than such a purposeful, exploitive view allows. Encoding is performed by readers who wish at some level of awareness to repress a meaning that, like Poe's purloined letter, is so obvious we do not see it. Despite the many "straight" readings of this tale as a warning to the artist to avoid marriage, it is remarkable that so many critics ignore the implicit invitation to explore the obvious alternative to marriage—not simply art, but homosexuality *and* art. Some of St. George's later books "seem to me of a queerness," Paul tells Marian (15: 23). James's language, it seems to me, could hardly be more overt, or straight.

Like the narrator of "The Artist of Beltraffio," Overt brings his own complex desires for art and relationship to his meeting with his Master. His heart beats faster as he anticipates the prospect of meeting St. George (15: 7), and he quickly insinuates himself into the Master's marriage as fan and reader. He wonders if St. George is "unhappy" in his "relations with his wife," and he jealously assays Mrs. St. George's fitness to be a writer's "second self." "St. George certainly had every right to a charming wife," Paul thinks, "but he himself would never have imagined the important little woman in the aggressively Parisian dress the partner for life, the *alter ego*, of a man of letters" (15: 9). Paul, in fact, seeks to displace St. George's wife as a "second self" by becoming the privileged reader of the Master's writing. Learning that Mrs. St. George has burned one of St. George's books, Paul "saw on the instant how the burnt book—the way she alluded to it!—would have been one of her husband's finest things"(15: 11). Via a kind of inverse economy, Paul's valuation of St. George's writing appreciates in direct proportion to Mrs. St. George's devaluation of it. "Didn't she, as the wife of a rare artist, know what it was to produce *one* perfect work of art? How in the world did she think they were turned off?" (15: 11–12). Fantasmatically occupying Mrs. St. George's subject position, Paul jealously imagines himself a more appreciative, wifely reader.

To be sure, James mediates and thereby covers male desire in "The Lesson of the Master" in several ways. Reading St. George as if he were a text rather than the author of one, Paul reconfigures desire as aesthetic appreciation. Anatomizing St. George through an extended male gaze, Paul concludes that the Master "certainly looked better behind than any foreign man of letters—showed for beautifully correct in his tall black hat and his superior frock coat." And when Paul catches a "glimpse of a regular face, a fresh colour, a brown moustache and a pair of eyes surely never visited by a fine frenzy," he promises himself to "study these denotements on the first occasion" (15: 14). James shifts Paul's gaze between St. George and his wife, however, using his identification with the wife's gaze to mediate his own desire. "Paul's glance, after a moment, travelled back to this lady," James notes, "and he saw how her own had followed her husband as he moved off with Miss Fancourt. Overt permitted himself to wonder a little if she were jealous when another woman took him away. Then he made out that Mrs. St. George wasn't glaring at the indifferent maiden. Her eyes rested but on her husband, and with unmistakeable serenity. That was the way she wanted him to be—she liked his conventional uniform. Overt longed to hear more about the book she had induced him to destroy" (15: 15). Using Mrs. St. George to screen his investment of desire, Paul registers his own jealousy of St. George's interest in Marian, but then he returns, via that same female-mediated gaze, to the Master himself in order to admire his writerly pose. While the wife's gaze can rest serenely on her husband, Paul deflects his own desiring gaze to the Master's book—taking Mrs. St. George's place as sympathetic reader. Homoerotic desire is doubly screened—heterosexualized and aestheticized.

Although he does not discuss "The Lesson of the Master," Michael Cooper notes that in other tales of writers and artists, James textualizes the male authors' bodies in order to make them "capable of being known, interacted with, and mistreated" (69). Moreover, Cooper argues, James "frankly feminizes the author position, making it the passive object of desire" (70). When Paul focuses on St. George, he does textualize the writer's body, making it accessible to his own readerly desire, but he does not exactly "feminize" the Master. Indeed, James suggests that St. George's textualized meaning—which I take to include his gender and sexuality—remains in some suspense. Paul "saw more in St. George's face, which he liked the better for its not having told its whole story in the first three minutes," James writes. "That story came out as one read, in short installments—it was excusable that one's analogies should be somewhat professional—and the text was a style considerably involved, a language not easy to translate at sight. There were shades of meaning in it and a vague perspective of history which receded as you advanced" (15: 17–18). Fred Kaplan speculates that James's desire for young men such as Hendrik Andersen remained largely aesthetic, that "Andersen's work stood in for Andersen himself" (448), and in this passage James certainly cuts male desire with aesthetic tropes. Gazing at another man's body is "excusable" when mediated by "professional" analogies. The meaning—the sexualized meaning—that male homo-aesthetic translation engenders recedes before the male gaze precisely because of the aesthetic metaphors that screen it, and the pleasure of reading increases in direct proportion to the suspense created by a face that—it is tempting to say, flirtatiously—conceals the shades of its full meaning and thereby forces the reader to read it serially in "short installments" in order to get it to "come out."

In the long climax of the tale—the midnight vigil in the Master's private writing room—St. George enjoins Paul to give up everything, especially the thought of marrying Marian, for his writing. That advice, for which the tale is best known and ostensibly titled, masks the intensity of the relation between the two men. We cannot imagine Rowland Mallet giving the same advice to Roderick Hudson, and we should recall that Hudson's sculpture deteriorated when he met Christina Light and started sculpting female figures. Apparently advocating a heterocentric aesthetic, St. George had earlier complimented Paul upon his literary success by telling him that he is "on all men's lips and, what's better, on all women's" (15: 33). Why exactly it is better to be on women's lips, St. George doesn't say, and the tale's central scene suggests to the contrary that—at least within the confines of the Master's study—writer, text, and reader all are subject to homoerotization. This windowless, closeted space—a "good big cage" in which St. George's wife "locks" him up every morning (15: 62)—liberates male desire even as it polices it. "Lord, what good things I should do if I had such a charming place as this to do them in!" Paul exclaims (15: 62). A men's "locker" room of creative empowerment, the closet in which St. George writes his "queer" novels is embedded within the heterotext that circumscribes his life. In entering the closet with St. George, Paul enters a closed circuit of desire that neither man will dare to publish. "The outer world, the world of accident and ugliness," Paul reflects, "was so successfully excluded, and within the rich protecting space, beneath the patronising sky, the dream-figures, the summoned company, could hold their particular revel" (15: 64). A closeted space that male writers can share, this male utopia enables the liberation of a homoerotic imaginary—a space in which dream-figures can cavort in carnival.

As he had in "The Author of Beltraffio" and does in such later tales as "The Death of the Lion," James invests these scenes of writer-reader intimacy with remarkably sensual imagery—sexualizing art where he had previously aestheticized sexuality. As Paul looks up from the sofa at his "erect inquisitor," for example, he feels "partly like a happy little boy when the schoolmaster is gay, and partly like some pilgrim of old who might have consulted a world-famous oracle" (15: 65). And when St. George presses

Paul to devote himself to writing for a select "two or three" readers, Paul feels "locked" for a minute "as in closed throbbing arms" before he flirtatiously replies, "I could do it for one, if you were the one."[7] Here, I think, is James's homo-aesthetic ideal: the ideal readership in which Paul himself seeks membership reverses upon him, as if he and St. George will exchange positions and form a mutually fulfilling circuit of male-to-male communication that does not so much sublimate erotic energy in creative commitment as it eroticizes aesthetic experience. That is, the aesthetic *becomes* rather than screens the erotic.

St. George confesses that he himself has led the "mercenary muse" to the "altar of literature," and he warns Paul not to put his nose "into *that* yoke" because the "awful jade will lead you a life!" (15: 67). James's persistent subversion of the conventional—that is, the heterocentric and heterosexual—clears a space for an alternatively sexualized male aesthetic. Ironically and self-servingly, the "full rich masculine human general life" that St. George has enjoyed has emasculated him as an artist—"taken away" his "power," in his own words (15: 72).[8] Conventionally, of course, this resistance to the married masculine has been interpreted as a brief for the celibate, monkish life of the artist, but James's articulation of an art-for-art's-sake ideology within the framework of an intimate male-male relationship between Master and disciple opens another obvious possibility—a transgressive, homosexual aesthetic whose eroticized excesses are realized in the reading by a hyper-sympathetic other man. As St. George claims that Paul would "put a pistol-ball" into his brain if he had written his books (15: 72), Paul tries to imagine the other text that St. George could write but not publish—"the book Mrs. St. George made you burn—the one she didn't like" (15: 74)—the book that St. George acknowledges is about himself. That "homotext" cruises its reader, thereby constructing Paul as a "receptive community" of one (Savoy, "Hypocrite Lecteur" 20). James's homo-aestheticism works more subtly, it seems to me, with readerly desire cruising and thereby constructing the sexuality of the writer. A "coming-out" of homo-aesthetic response, Paul's ecstatic reaction to St. George's confession and advice signals the power of writing to provoke desire and the power of that desire to reconstruct St. George himself as a homoeroticized writing subject.

[Paul's] impression fairly shook him and he throbbed with the excitement of such deep soundings and such strange confidences. He throbbed indeed with the conflict of his feelings—bewilderment and recognition and alarm, enjoyment and protest and assent, all commingled with tenderness (and a kind of shame in the participation) for the sores and bruises exhibited by so fine a creature, and with a sense of the tragic secret nursed under his trappings. The idea of *his*, Paul Overt's, becoming the occasion of such an act of humility made him flush and pant, at the same time that his consciousness was in certain directions too much alive not to swallow—and not intensely to taste—every offered spoonful of the revelation. It had been his odd fortune to blow upon the deep waters, to make them surge and break in waves of strange eloquence. (15: 73)

A covert homotextuality sexualized only in the reading, St. George's protest could be James's—protest at his entrapment within a heterocentric aesthetic and a heterocentric plot—as he delineates the high stakes for gender, sexuality, and art of this transgressive alternative. James added the oral metaphor (including the words "swallow," "taste," and "spoonful") when he revised the tale for the New York Edition. The original version had read simply: "The idea of his being made the occasion of such an act of humility made him flush and pant, at the same time that his perception, in certain directions, had been too much awakened to conceal from him anything that St. George really meant" (*Complete Tales* 7: 266). Either way, the passage expresses sexual desire, but the revised version, with its oral twist, emphasizes the physical intimacy of reading and calls to mind James's metaphor for expressing his response to French novelists. "The artist—the artist! Isn't he a man all the same?" Paul wants to know. "I mostly think not," St. George replies. "Then you don't allow him the common passions and affections of men?" Paul asks with wonderful ambiguity (15: 76). "What a false position, what a condemnation of the artist, that he's a mere disenfranchised monk and can produce his effect only by giving up personal happiness. What an arraignment of art!" (15: 77). This sudden shift to legal language emphasizes the transgressive power of an art that, masquerading as monkish and asexual, dare not speak its name or celebrate the "common passions and affections of men." I am not suggesting that this exchange cannot be read heterocentrically as a generalized warning about the incompatibility of passion and art, but James's language—especially the legal language—makes more sense, historically considered, if interpreted homosexually. In England in 1888 (or 1909) there was no more "false" or precarious a position for the male writer who wanted to celebrate the "passions of men" than a homosexually-identified position.[9] What an "arraignment" of art indeed. St. George in fact picks up the word "arraignment" in order to suggest the subversive power of "common passions." "Happy the societies in which [this alternative art] hasn't made its appearance," he tells Paul, "for from the moment it comes they have a consuming ache, they have an incurable corruption, in their breast. Most assuredly is the artist in a false position!" (15: 77). James could hardly be clearer about the social, political, and legal dangers of the art St. George advises Paul to write.

The pledge with which Paul ends this conversion scene enables the two men to commit themselves to each other through the medium of high art.

"I *am* an artist—I can't help it!" Paul exclaims. "Ah show it then!" St. George pleads. "Let me see before I die the thing I most want, the thing I yearn for; a life in which the passion—ours—is really intense" (15: 78). Art-for-art's-sake "passion," to be sure, but a passion generated, this climactic scene makes clear, through the eroticized activity of men reading men—throbbing, flushing, panting, swallowing, and tasting every spoonful of revelation, blowing upon the deep waters of male creativity until they surge and break in waves of strange eloquence. What a climax, this lesson of the master!

Whether or not Paul actually writes a novel of "our" passion during his two-year exile in Switzerland and Italy James leaves ambiguous. That hiatus, of course, enables Henry St. George to marry Marian Fancourt, leaving Paul feeling "diabolically sold" (15: 96). Sara Chapman argues that Paul fears the "possibility of an ironic connection between one's sexual life and the requirements of art" (40–41). By "sexual life" Chapman clearly means heterosexual life—hence, Paul's fear that marriage will rejuvenate St. George as an artist. But in view of the powerful and empowering scene in St. George's writing room, I think Paul is doubly "sold"—forsaken not only by Marian but also by the man who promised to form a select readership of one for the novel about "our" passion. In fact, as he finds himself once again triangulated with Marian in his relation to St. George, Paul withdraws his double investment in both characters—judging Marian "almost stupid" in her happiness (15: 90) and seeing St. George as a superannuated failure despite the "ripeness" of a "successful manhood" that "didn't suggest that any of his veins were exhausted" (15: 95). James disjoins gender and sexuality—masculinity and artistic power—in this description. A ripeness of masculinity, converted to heterosexual investment of desire, still produces artistic failure.

In the narrator's comment that Mr. and Mrs. St. George found Paul's book "really magnificent" (15: 96), James hardly suggests the sort of passionate reader response for which St. George had "yearned," nor does he suggest that Paul has written the sort of fiery book that the new Mrs. St. George might burn. James's clichéd conclusion—Paul's recognition "that the Master was essentially right and that Nature had dedicated him to intellectual, not to personal passion" (15: 96)—seems disingenuous. With intellectual and personal passion disjoined, James leaves Paul's sexuality and textuality in a state of suspense, awaiting the male reader who will complete, covertly, the circuit of writerly-readerly desire in a throbbing, panting, surging reading that will climax the object lesson of the Master.

Like "The Author of Beltraffio" and "The Lesson of the Master," "The Middle Years" features a similar triangle, as the aging novelist Dencombe's conflicted feelings about his art and himself come into focus because of the young Dr. Hugh, who enters the story "absorbed" in Dencombe's novel (236) rather than in the two ladies, Miss Vernham and the Countess, whom he trails behind. When he unwraps his own copy of *The Middle Years*, Dencombe suffers a literary blackout. He can remember nothing of the novel's substance: "He couldn't have chanted to himself a single sentence" (237). When he begins to reread his own prose, and especially when Dr. Hugh reads it aloud to him, however, the young man's readerly emotion communicates itself to Dencombe, drawing him out of the depression, or "abyss," into which he had sunk and suddenly making him appreciate himself all the more. This rehabilitation of his creative self through the medium of his own words, in fact, takes him deeply into his own interior mind—as if, "by a siren's hand," he is drawn down to the "dim underworld of fiction, the great glazed tank of art," where "strange silent subjects float" (238). Most important, Dencombe recovers a sense of creative power. Instead of the creative lassitude he had earlier experienced, he now feels confident that "Surely its force wasn't spent—there was life and service in it yet" (238). Indeed, he swells with a sense of autogenetic and phallogocentric power, "as if he had planted his genius, had trusted his method, and they had grown up and flowered with this sweetness" (239). Whereas Dencombe's earlier feeling of alienation promoted verbal and mnemonic impotence, his own writing—especially when read to him by another man—restores him to himself.

Dencombe's creative rejuvenation depends in large part, then, upon the mirroring effect of another man's admiration. Dr. Hugh serves not only as Dencombe's double but also as the subject of a homo-aesthetic desire that renders Dencombe a desirable object. James establishes a cycle of homo-aesthetic "cruising," in Savoy's term, by which Dencombe's text cruises its reader, who then cruises him. Doctor Hugh "grew vivid, in the balmy air, to his companion," James writes, "for whose deep refreshment he seemed to have been sent; and was particularly ingenuous in describing how recently he had become acquainted, and how instantly infatuated, with the only man who had put flesh between the ribs of an art that was starving on superstitions" (244). James's vivid body metaphor, in which Dencombe's art serves both as created object and as fetish, clarifies the homoerotic and autoerotic nature of this infatuation. Through another man's gaze, Dencombe falls in love with the body of his own work. "His visitor's attitude promised him a luxury of intercourse" (244). Dr. Hugh, then, rehabilitates Dencombe as a subject, even as his presence raises questions about what lurks in Dencombe's unconscious and in the "underworld" of his fiction—much as the Archdeans' request that Hugh Merrow paint what comes "naturally" to him causes similar anxiety. Does Dr. Hugh see behind Dencombe's anonymous facade to his "actual" (homoerotic) creative self and thereby recover that self for Dencombe?

Or does Dr. Hugh's reading project and inscribe a new creative self—making Dencombe the subject as well as the object of homo-aesthetic and homoerotic desire? James pushes such questions to the limit even though he finally leaves the answers ambiguous.

Dencombe's "intercourse" with Dr. Hugh proves suddenly problematical when the other man catches him, "passionate correcter" that he is, editing his own writing—"fingering" his own style, as James provocatively puts it. Such fingering exercises, like Dencombe's opening blackout, suggest some degree of alienation from his own writing, as well as a desire to defer closure, but they also suggest an obvious form of verbal self-pleasuring. The "last thing" Dencombe "ever arrived at was a form final for himself," James notes. "His ideal would have been to publish secretly, and then, on the published text, treat himself to the terrified revise" (246). Richard Hocks links Dencombe's creative method with James's own passion for revision (55–56), and Sara Chapman cites the "convergence of imagination between the writer-artist and his audience that James came to believe is necessary to the creation of art" (54), but the issue here is more than aesthetic or editorial, and the relationship that develops spontaneously between Dencombe and Dr. Hugh registers an immediate intensity that aesthetic issues alone cannot account for. Caught red-handed, so to speak, in an act of writerly masturbation, Dencombe experiences such inner turmoil that he changes color, stammers ambiguously, and finally faints dead away. His last impression before losing consciousness is of Doctor Hugh's "mystified eyes" (246). When he awakens, he feels "rueful and sore" at the recognition that his identity is now "ineffaceable," and he feels "as if he had fallen into a hole too deep to descry any little patch of heaven" (246). He finds himself in the abyss he had momentarily escaped through Dr. Hugh and his "deep demonstration of desire" (247).

I have puzzled over this event and this passage—over its metaphors of masturbation and homosexual penetration, its association of masturbation and writing, its use of the male gaze, its extravagant outcome. Why does Dencombe faint? What is there about being subjected to another man's gaze—especially in the act of "fingering" his own writing—that provokes such trauma?

The issue is partly violated privacy, partly the shift of power that being "outed" entails. But sharing his privacy with an admiring younger man who expresses desire for the writing and the writer promotes self-pleasuring, a form of male *jouissance* characterized, in Dencombe's case, by its exemption from the demands of an exchange economy and hence enabling him to postpone closure or any "final" form. In that respect, Dencombe's aesthetic "fingering" can be contrasted with Mark Ambient's creative "hammering." Where Ambient seemed working within a spermatic economy of limited energy, Dencombe's creative and recreative energy seems more alchemical than economical—endlessly pleasurable in a manner similar to what Melville describes in "A Squeeze of the Hand" in *Moby-Dick*. Like Melville, James limns the terms of a homoerotic and autoerotic poetics—an empowering creative circuit of doubled desire that, like some process of fusion (or alchemy), keeps building energy by circulating desire through a piece of writing positioned between men.

Through the obvious homosocial pleasure Dencombe and Dr. Hugh derive from reading *The Middle Years*, moreover, James suggests the benefits of private, closeted literary transactions. Although Priscilla Walton argues that Dencombe's ideal of a text that can be endlessly revised, whose meaning can be endlessly deferred, puts him in the "space of the Feminine" (81), the homosocial transactions that occur in the tale mark out an all-male space, especially on those occasions when Dr. Hugh leaves his female companions in order to meet with Dencombe. "I don't get on with silly women," Dr. Hugh explains at one point (248). Indeed, in the terms that Walton uses, homo-aesthetic exchanges like the one that occurs in "The Middle Years" seem especially well-served by the proto-deconstructive view of texts that James embeds in the story. It is not necessarily that *The Middle Years* encodes a homoerotic subtext in its language, which James of course never shares with the reader. In fact, if Dencombe's fictive speculations within the story are any indication, his imagination runs in paths of heterosexual desire. As he watches Dr. Hugh, Miss Vernham, and the Countess, for example, Dencombe challenges himself as an "approved novelist" to establish the relations among them. He projects a heterosexual family romance in which Dr. Hugh is the Countess's son and the object of Miss Vernham's "secret passion" (236–37).[10] Despite the obviously close relationship between the Countess and Miss Vernham, despite the former's "aggressive amplitude" (236) and Dr. Hugh's physical distance from the female couple, Dencombe does not apparently consider the possibility of a lesbian relationship.

Even if he writes heterosexually, however, Dencombe finds himself the subject and object of homo-aesthetic desire. James implies that homoerotic desire can be generated intersubjectively through the reading process—that autoerotic desire can be appropriated by the homoerotic. Politically considered, of course, this strategy of using a text as a screen upon which proscribed desires can be projected also allows them to be protected from invigilation. Part strategic repression and part male *jouissance*, the deferment of any "final form" promotes a mutually pleasurable play with the text—an exchange of desire between men. "You're a great success!" Dr. Hugh will tell Dencombe at the end of the story, and James's language neatly weds the erotic and aesthetic facets of his admiration, as Dr. Hugh puts "into his young voice the ring of a marriage-bell" (258). Like Basil Hallward's explanation of secrecy to Dorian Gray, Dencombe's fainting spell suggests that such desires between men must be deployed carefully and covertly. As soon as they are acknowledged and identified—as soon as they become "ineffaceable"—they provoke shame, as if the autoerotic has become the homoerotic in an instant of specular exchange.

In the aftermath of his fainting spell, Dencombe becomes even more dependent upon Dr. Hugh, to whom he looks for rehabilitation. "This servant of his altar had all the new learning in science and all the old reverence in faith," he thinks; "wouldn't he therefore put his knowledge at the disposal of his sympathy, his craft at the disposal of his love.... Who would work the miracle for him but the young man who could combine such lucidity with such passion?" (251). Dencombe quickly sacrifices his own needs, however, when Miss Vernham appeals to him to discourage Doctor Hugh, who is jeopardizing his inheritance from the Countess. His plan to force Dr. Hugh's return to the Countess, like the narrator's plan to reunite the Ambients in "The Author of Beltraffio," suggests a "compulsory heterosexuality," because Dencombe smothers his own desire in attempting to thwart Doctor Hugh's. Not surprisingly, in view of Dr. Hugh's tonic effect, Dencombe suffers an immediate relapse when he learns that Dr. Hugh has gone with the Countess, and even the young man's return—with the news that he has given up the Countess ("I gave her up for you," he gushes [257])—cannot save him. "The thing is to have made somebody care," Dencombe concludes (258), as he nears death, and "The Middle Years" does demonstrate the regenerating power of male desire, even as it covers the tracks of that desire in its strategic deployment of the heterosexual.

Neil Paraday also makes a young man care for himself and his writing in "The Death of the Lion" (1894), and the bond that develops between Master and acolyte extends and complicates the connection James explores between homoeroticism and a male homo-aesthetics. Like the narrator of "Beltraffio," this narrator admits that, as a new reviewer assigned to Neil Paraday, he wants to lay his "lean hands" on the reclusive author (261) and wants to "touch" him "under the fifth rib" (262). And when Paraday shares with him the scheme of another book, the narrator positively gushes at the prospect of being such a privileged male reader. Suggesting its aesthetic as well as emotional excess, he observes that Paraday's prospectus "might have passed for a great gossiping eloquent letter—the overflow into talk of an artist's amorous plan" (266–67). As in other cases of male-to-male reading transactions, furthermore, Paraday's already "amorous plan" gains erotic energy through the intersubjective exchange of words between men. Paraday's reading of the "fond epistle," the narrator says, "made me feel as if I were, for the advantage of posterity, in close correspondence with him—were the distinguished person to whom it had been affectionately addressed." Like Mark Ambient's phallic "hammering," although without the same spermatically economical limitations, Paraday's aesthetic potency is complexly phallogocentric. It was "Venus rising from the sea and before the airs had blown upon her," the narrator concludes (in a cross-gendered metaphor). "I had never been so throbbingly present at such an unveiling" (267). Obviously aroused by this privileged moment—a sight of the Master principle unveiled—the narrator seems positioned by Paraday's reading in a problematical male place. That is, he can (barely) avoid the homoerotic connotations of the scene by deploying his masculine desire toward a feminized phallic object.

Like other artists in these tales, Paraday is separated from his wife, and more successfully than the narrator of "The Author of Beltraffio," this narrator "achieves a kind of married intimacy" with the Master (Barry 98). He appoints himself Paraday's guardian and assigns himself the job of protecting him from the public that lionizes him—specifically from the clutches of another man, a Mr. Morrow, who represents a syndicate of thirty-seven journals. Obviously threatened, the narrator compares Morrow to a "policeman" whose glare "suggested the electric headlights of some monstrous modern ship." Like Beatrice Ambient's effect on the narrator of the earlier tale, Morrow's male gaze couples Paraday and the narrator, as if catching them with a policeman's spotlight in some transgressive act. "I felt," the narrator concludes, "as if Paraday and I were tossing terrified under his bows" (271).

Among his other achievements, Morrow has signed up the pseudonymously cross-gendered Guy Walsingham and Dora Forbes. Indeed, as the narrator projects it, Morrow promotes the breakdown of traditional gender categories—the convergence of "transgressive desire" and a "transgressive aesthetic" (in Dollimore's terms). "I was bewildered," the narrator stammers, as Morrow describes his two charges; "it sounded somehow as if there were three sexes" (274). James's interest, however, is not simply in representing the possibility of a third sex. This tale, like the other tales of writers and artists, concerns itself with the relationship between writing and engenderment—with the inscription, or construction, of gender and sexual identity through writing. Dora Forbes and Guy Walsingham take the "ground," Morrow says, "that the larger latitude has simply got to come" (273), and he evidently means by that phrase a more expansive attitude toward sexuality, which their cross-gendered voices pluralize even further.

In *Gaiety Transfigured*, David Bergman notes the importance of reading for gay men as a means of understanding and even recognizing their homosexuality. Homosexuality is a "literary construct for many gay people," he observes, who actually learn to recognize themselves as gay from their reading (6). James, too, explores the constructive power of reading and writing—the power of writing to destabilize conventional gender and sexual categories, as well as to reveal or inscribe gender roles and sexual orientation. "Is this Miss Forbes a gentleman?" the narrator asks Mr. Morrow, who does little to un-confuse him. "It wouldn't be 'Miss,'" he replies, "there's a wife!" "I mean is she a man?" the narrator rejoins. "The wife?" retorts Mr. Morrow, who seems to the narrator "as confused as myself" (274). In contrast to the spirit of this campy byplay between the narrator and Mr. Morrow, Neil Paraday himself appears relatively straight and conservative. Like James calling upon Balzac to solve the "riddle" of the ambiguous George Sand, Morrow wants an "authoritative word" from Paraday on the subject of the "larger latitude," which he assumes would strike a conservative note and thus resolve some of the confusion. But by making the aesthetically conservative Paraday the object of the narrator's idolizing attention, James threatens to confuse Paraday's aestheticism and eroticism—eroticizing the aesthetic, so to speak, and making it transgressive.

As he positions Paraday and his writing between the narrator and Mr. Morrow, James insightfully explores the power of writing to engender and to engender desire in its readers. The narrator, for example, uses Paraday's writing to screen others from the writer himself, enabling him to enjoy an exclusive physical, as well as interpretive, intimacy. He also suggests that Paraday's writing, more overtly than Dencombe's in "The Middle Years," forms a screen behind which his actual self hides. Paraday "pays for his imagination," the narrator comments, "which puts him (I should hate it) in the place of others and makes him feel, even against himself, their feelings, their appetites, their motives. It's indeed inveterately against himself that he makes his imagination act. What a pity he has such a lot of it!" (294). In this intriguing passage James suggests on the one hand the versatility and mobility of Paraday's imagination—his ability to project himself into others and to write what they feel. Writing liberates Paraday's imagination, enabling him to project himself into various characters and thus to experience various subjectivities. On the other hand, the narrator implies that such imaginative fluidity enables Paraday to deny or avoid himself in his writing, to police the border between his writing and his writing self. What he cannot guard against, however, are his readers' responses—the power of his writing to provoke desire and the power of that desire to reconstruct him as a writing subject. Just as the narrator has apparently succeeded in dissuading Morrow from interviewing Paraday, for example, Morrow notices the new manuscript that Paraday has shared with the narrator, and the sight rekindles his desire for the man. "Presently his eyes fell on the manuscript from which Paraday had been reading to me and which still lay on the bench," the narrator observes. "As my own followed them I saw it looked promising, looked pregnant, as if it gently throbbed with the life the reader had given it" (277). In this literary primal scene, the narrator finds himself and Morrow in the position of voyeuristic sons. His own desiring gaze transforms Paraday and text into father and mother and the creative transaction between them into a scene of insemination and conception. In the very process of heterosexualizing Paraday's poetics through the transfiguring power of the narrator's gaze, however, James unsettles gender positions and the paths of male desire in the relationship he establishes between Paraday's two male readers. Positioning the text Paraday has impregnated between the narrator and Morrow, James demonstrates the phallogocentric power of Paraday's prose—and its arousing effect on the privileged male reader who possesses it. For as the narrator grabs the manuscript away from Morrow, he notes that the incident "left Mr. Paraday's two admirers very erect, glaring at each other while one of them held a bundle of papers well behind him" (277). Exchanging covetous looks across this sign of phallogocentric power, a text that throbs with heterosexual and homo-aesthetic desire, the narrator wins the battle for the Master and his writing. In that process, however, he does not simply make off with a text that embodies Paraday's hetero-aesthetic power. He appropriates this heterotext, holding it "well behind him" where, erect and glaring, he tacitly invites Mr. Morrow to seek it.

However conservative the gist of Paraday's prose, then, it remains liable to be charged in the reading with very different desires. As he had in "The Author of Beltraffio" and "The Middle Years," however, James covers the homoerotic desire he represents in the first part of this tale by shifting attention to a heterosexual relationship, as the narrator tries to guard Paraday from a young American woman, Fanny Hurter, who wants his autograph. As threatened by Fanny's desire to see Paraday as he had been by Mr. Morrow's, the narrator determines to keep the Master, so to speak, "well behind him," and away from this desiring woman. When Fanny exclaims that she wants to see Paraday "Because I just love him!" the narrator finds it difficult to recover from the "agitating effect" of her words (283). Preventing a meeting between Paraday and Fanny (the image, like Paraday's writing, is "pregnant" with possibility) enables the narrator to reserve Paraday as an object of homo-aesthetic desire. The narrator is even willing to sacrifice himself for Paraday by pursuing Fanny for himself—dividing his desire between the aesthetic and the erotic. He even conscripts Paraday and his writing into service, inviting him to transcribe into Fanny's album "one of his most characteristic passages" and continually supplying her with information. "We read him together when I could find time," he notes, "and the generous creature's sacrifice was fed by our communion" (287).

In addition to reserving Paraday for himself, the narrator also hopes by keeping Fanny away from Paraday to enable and empower the creative process. It is a "question of reconstituting so far as might be possible the conditions under which he had produced his best work" (288), and appropriative heterosexual desire—Fanny's desire to acquire the man's signature—clearly threatens the composing process. Despite the narrator's best efforts, however, Paraday does become caught up in an increasing social—and heterosocial—world. When he becomes Mrs. Wimbush's guest for a week, for example, he must read his work in public, particularly for the benefit of Mrs. Wimbush's friend, the Princess. Casting Paraday into the unlikely role of writerly Prince Charming, Mrs. Wimbush makes his working manuscript available to her other female guests, whom the narrator comes upon "in attitudes, bending gracefully over the first volume" (292).

The ironic result of the lion's lionization by this houseful of bent-over women is the loss of his manuscript, which he lends to Lady Augusta Minch. In a slapstick comedy of errors, the narrator fruitlessly tracks the manuscript around the country—from man to woman, valet to maid—before acknowledging, after Paraday's death, that it simply cannot be recovered, even though he and Fanny Hurter (now apparently his wife) go on "seeking and hoping together" (303) to find it. Ironically, in view of his desire to deflect Fanny's attention from Paraday to his work, this lost manuscript provides the "firm tie" that unites him with this female Fanny. Far more tangibly than in "The Author of Beltraffio," this narrator covers his homoerotic literary desire with a normative heterosexual "tie" to a woman who shares and thereby mediates his desire for the Master—even though, nominally considered, "Fanny Hurter" suggests the power of dominant-subordinate, homoerotic desire.

In emphasizing Oscar Wilde's "transgressive desire" and "transgressive aesthetic," Jonathan Dollimore points out that the vicious attacks on Wilde consistently linked his deviant desire and his deviant art, suggesting a widespread "fear of cross-over between sexual perversion and intellectual and moral subversion" (240). The result is an aesthetic as well as sexual hierarchy in which Wilde's art is labeled "false," "cheap," "shallow and specious," "nerveless and effeminate" (240). In opposing Neil Paraday to Guy Walsingham and Dora Forbes, James creates a similar binary, but he complicates the issue dramatically with the presence and role of his narrator, who finds himself as it were between writers, between writers' genders, and between desires. Guy Walsingham and Dora Forbes, like Oscar Wilde and George Sand, invert gender identities and subvert conservative art (in Dollimore's terms) by expressing the "larger latitude." But Paraday's sexual and aesthetic conservatism makes it difficult for the narrator to reconcile his own personal and aesthetic desires. His transgressive desire conflicts with his conservative aesthetic; to preserve the latter, he surrenders the former and devotes himself to seeking the manuscript that would presumably foreclose on the discourse of homoerotic desire. In ending with a marriage between the young acolyte and a woman, "The Death of the Lion" seems to end more definitively than the other stories of writers and artists. But Paraday's lost manuscript in "The Death of the Lion," like the other lost or absent texts in these tales, leaves open the possibility of an object tie that would recuperate a repressed homoeroticism. With Paraday dead and his manuscript lost, the narrator may not exactly be "lost among the genders and the pronouns," but he does occupy a position of some suspense, indefinitely deferring the deployment of his divided desire—the homo-aesthetic desire that dare not publish its name.

Chapter 6
The Paradox of Masochistic Manhood in *The Golden Bowl*

The "likeness" of Charlotte Stant's "connexion" to Adam Verver, James comments in a famous passage, "wouldn't have been wrongly figured if he had been thought of as holding in one of his pocketed hands the end of a long silken halter looped round her beautiful neck" (NY 24: 287). The "shriek of a soul in pain" (24: 292) that Charlotte utters in response to such bondage comprises not the only example of violent imagery in *The Golden Bowl*. Fanny Assingham describes Prince Amerigo as a "domesticated lamb tied up with pink ribbon" (23: 161), for instance. Maggie Verver later thinks of him as "straitened and tied" (24: 192) and, like Charlotte, "writhing in his pain" (24: 193). Reversing the lines of power, Maggie herself fantasizes that Amerigo might "some day get drunk and beat her" (23: 165), and then later, as she contemplates Amerigo's sexual power, she recognizes that a "single touch" from him—"any brush of his hand, of his lips, of his voice"—would "hand her over to him bound hand and foot" (24: 142). Although Charlotte distinguishes Amerigo from other men, all of whom she considers "brutes," because he can "check himself before acting on the impulse" (23: 290), these examples of brutality in *The Golden Bowl* suggest that the psychic economy James represents and dissects might usefully be explored for its potential sado-masochism. In particular, Prince Amerigo and the vexed subject position he inhabits suggest James's experimentation with male masochism— his exemplifying and finally challenging a masochistic paradigm.[1]

Although she has not explicitly applied the idea to James, Kaja Silverman explains male masochism in *Male Subjectivity at the Margins* in terms that can be helpful in understanding *The Golden Bowl* and particularly Prince Amerigo's position—subject position, in her terms—within the novel's larger psychic economy. Although I think that James ultimately deviates significantly from the model of male masochism that Silverman derives from Freud, Theodore Reik, Gilles Deleuze, and others, Prince Amerigo, as he appears in "abject" relation to Maggie Verver at the end of *The Golden Bowl* (e.g., 24: 193), can be usefully understood, at least to start, as a "feminine yet heterosexual male subject" (Silverman 212)—that is, as an example of "feminine masochism," which as Silverman points out, is a "specifically *male* pathology, so named because it positions its sufferer as a woman" (189).²

Silverman argues that "feminine masochism" is an "accepted—indeed a requisite—element of 'normal' female subjectivity, providing a crucial mechanism for eroticizing lack and subordination," but the male subject "cannot avow feminine masochism without calling into question his identification with the masculine position" (189–90). In Amerigo's case, I shall argue, James explores the paradox that Silverman's distinction suggests: the case of a "feminine" male masochist who remains identified—strategically identified—with the "masculine position." The passages I quoted at the beginning of this chapter, moreover, alternately represent *both* Amerigo and Maggie (not to mention Charlotte) as bound and tied. Despite this seeming paradox—two objects occupying the same subject position, so to speak—I want to argue that the paradox is more apparent than real. That is, male sadism represents the form that Amerigo's feminine masochism is allowed to take. In turn, Maggie's female masochism masks the masculine sadism she executes with her father's authority. In its paradoxical representation of a radically unstable masculinity, *The Golden Bowl* itself represents one of James's most complex efforts to experiment with a multivalent manhood that does not rest easily in any traditional subject position.

Although Mark Seltzer argues persuasively that *The Golden Bowl*, through Maggie Verver's regulatory agency, works toward the characters' conformity to a normative vision of marriage (65), that normative vision does not inhibit James from exploring a more fluid gendered economy or non-normative gender identifications. As he had in earlier novels, for example, James destabilizes even as he valorizes phallocentric authority and again positions male characters within quadrangular relationships. He transpositions characters, so to speak, making them subjects *and* objects of diversified desires—dividing male desire, for example, among two men and a woman. As he had in *Roderick Hudson* with Rowland Mallet and Roderick, James divides male subjectivity between Prince Amerigo and Adam Verver, making each man the co-dependent of the other. He then splits male subjectivity even further, feminizing it in the process, when he delegates authority to Maggie in the second half of the novel. Put another way, the "hard" labor within James's sado-masochistic economy is divided between Adam and Amerigo along traditional capitalistic lines. Amerigo's potent manhood works for Adam—and for his "fore(wo)man" Maggie—in order to reinforce patriarchal authority, leaving Amerigo to constitute his own male subjectivity, as it were, on his own time. I want to focus most of my attention on Amerigo in this chapter because it seems to me that his character offers the best example of the male psychic econ-

The Paradox of Masochistic Manhood in *The Golden Bowl*   151

omy James explores in the novel. In representing Amerigo as the "hidden hand" of labor, I emphasize the employment of his phallic power within the capitalist economy that Adam and Maggie Verver supervise, but I think Amerigo nevertheless remains more a complex male subject than a passive, feminized male victim. Phallically and seminally empowered through the female subject position delegated by the father (Adam) to his daughter Maggie, Amerigo becomes the hidden third hand of the Ververs' labor.

James anatomizes Adam Verver, on the other hand, in rather traditionally gendered terms within the context of Maggie's marriage to Amerigo, his own marriage to Charlotte Stant, and his continued zeal for looting the treasure troves of European museums and shops in order to amass an art collection. Not only does Adam value everything in the same aesthetic and economic terms—for its collectability—but economic principles of exchange govern his psychology and particularly his relationships with the other principal characters. Seltzer notes "a distribution or dispersion of the political into economic, linguistic, and sexual relations" (67), and Beth Sharon Ash considers Adam's collecting to represent an "assertion of narcissistic mastery," the fulfillment of a "grandiose fantasy of being master of a created world" ("Narcissism" 59).[3] In my view, however, James renders Adam's traditional masculinity more ambiguous. "He put into his one little glass everything he raised to his lips," James says, "and it was as if he had always carried in his pocket, like a tool of his trade, this receptacle, a little glass cut with a fineness of which the art had long since been lost, and kept in an old morocco case stamped in uneffaceable gilt with the arms of a deposed dynasty" (23: 196). Arguably phallogocentric, this "pocket" image cuts several ways, suggesting Adam's specular and ethical rigidity on one hand, his attenuated phallic authority on another, and the feminization of his manhood (the phallus transfigured as receptacle) on a third. Indeed, James goes on to complicate Adam's manhood even further by suggesting a covert, even closeted, dimension to it—something illicit that he must keep under wraps. He had "learnt the lesson of the senses, to the end of his own little book," James concludes, "without having for a day raised the smallest scandal in his economy at large; being in this particular not unlike those fortunate bachelors or other gentlemen of pleasure who so manage their entertainment of compromising company that even the austerest housekeeper, occupied and competent belowstairs, never feels obliged to give warning" (23: 197). Seltzer notes the "*recession* of signs of authority" throughout the novel and claims that Adam "represents power" by "appearing powerless" (68). Resembling Gilbert Osmond in this respect, Adam *husbands* his power, as he does his sexual energy—husbands it in the act of "husbanding," in fact, in a classic illustration of spermatic economy. He husbands his sexual energy by spending it at secondhand—by employing another man to make love to his daughter and his wife.

In much the same way that recent critical emphasis on the Olive Chancellor-Verena Tarrant relationship in *The Bostonians* has obscured interest in Basil Ransom, emphasis on Maggie Verver's controlling role in *The Golden Bowl* obscures one of James's most complex male-to-male relationships. In James's continuing drama of relational selfhood *The Golden Bowl* offers the most startling range of potential relationships represented in any of the major novels. Adam Verver's May-December marriage to Charlotte Stant makes Charlotte Maggie's stepmother and renders her affair with Prince Amerigo at least arguably incestuous. And of course Adam's intimate relationship with Maggie herself seems blatantly incestuous. Without claiming that it is *the* central relationship in the novel, however, I want to examine Adam Verver's relationship to Prince Amerigo for what it can add to my evolving view of James's representation of manhood.

"Nothing might affect us as queerer," observes the narrator of *The Golden Bowl*, describing Adam Verver's collecting project, "than this application of the same measure of value to such different pieces of property as old Persian carpets, say, and new human acquisitions; all the more indeed that the amiable man was not without an inkling on his own side that he was, as a taster of life, economically constructed" (23: 196). As one of the greatest collectors in the world and as one of the most "economically constructed" male characters in James's canon, Adam Verver traces his fictional lineage back to Christopher Newman and Gilbert Osmond. As James positions him relationally, furthermore, he also highlights Verver's resemblance to less traditionally masculine characters as Rowland Mallet and Lambert Strether. In fact, Adam Verver synthesizes the attributes that James distributed among different male characters in his earlier fiction. He represents, we might say, the empowerment of the collector-spectator through his strategic deployment of power, the delegation of authority to a hired second hand. Adam's "greatest inconvenience," James suggests, "was in finding it so taken for granted that as he had money he had force" (23: 130). This universal "attribution of power" proves inconvenient, however, not because Adam wishes to forego the possession of power but because he does not wish to publicize it. He wishes not to exercise power but to invest and capitalize it. "Everyone had need of one's power," he thinks, "whereas one's own need, at the best, would have seemed to be but some trick of not communicating it. The effect of a *reserve* so merely, so meanly defensive would in most cases, beyond question, sufficiently discredit the cause" (23: 131, emphasis added). Adam represents one of James's most extensive investigations of phallocentric power—what Seltzer calls the "continuity between love and power" (94)—but neither his possession nor his use of phallocentric privilege proceeds without complication. Indeed, reflecting the paradoxical desire to have his power and use it, too, Verver represents the lure of husbanded and secondhand power that is, as Ash has so convincingly shown, essentially narcissistic—ideally reserved to a self-enclosed and self-perpetuating psychic economy.

Adam's lips "somehow were closed—and by a spring connected moreover with the action of his eyes themselves," James observes. "The latter showed him what he *had* done, showed him where he had come out; quite at the top of his hill of difficulty, the tall sharp spiral round which he had begun to wind his ascent at the age of twenty, and the apex of which was a platform looking down, if one would, on the kingdoms of the earth and with standing-room for but half a dozen others" (23: 131). Specular, as well as phallic, Adam's imperial power seems firmly embodied, part and parcel of a well-regulated organic system in which sight and speech coordinate to produce pleasure. Phallocentric pleasure in this case involves not immediate but indirect involvement with others—a sublimation of sexuality in collection and observation that requires, it turns out, some "other" agency. Adam devotes himself to the "creation of 'interests' that were the extinction of other interests" (23: 144), because his "real friend, in all the business, was to have been his own mind, with which nobody had put him in relation" (23: 149). He fears marriage—even fears having to make the "supreme effort" and say "no" to remarriage—because he conceives of marriage masochistically as a form of "bondage" and being held "in contempt" (23: 133). One of the services Charlotte performs for him is keeping off the "ravening women" who would otherwise "beset" him— "without being one herself" in the "vulgar way of others" (23: 389). In other words, by not being a "ravening woman," Charlotte will presumably enable Adam not to be a ravenous man—not a man who provokes "vulgar" desires that threaten to bind him in a contemptible form of manhood. In that respect, Charlotte will cover his "other interests."

Adam finally considers remarriage because Maggie has married, as if, like a bite from the apple, she has suddenly made their domestic relationship more self-conscious, not necessarily sexualizing it as introducing the knowledge of sexual experience and so upsetting a delicately balanced relational economy predicated on the conservation and investment of sexual energy in "other interests." Maggie understands that "there's somehow something that used to be right" that she has now made "wrong." "It used to be right that you hadn't married and that you didn't seem to want to," she tells Adam, and it also used to "seem easy for the question not to come up." Adam recognizes that now there is no way to keep the question "down" (23: 171), but in remarrying he seeks a wife who will not tax his own emotional resources or force him out of the closed, narcissistic economy in which his own mind serves as his "real friend." Fanny realizes that he chooses Charlotte because she represents the only woman it is possible to imagine Maggie's accepting (23: 389), but Charlotte "works," as it were, more directly for Adam himself. To feel "good," James comments, Adam simply has to "retrace his immense development" (23: 149), in much the same way that James retraces his own development by rereading his novels for the New York Edition. Adam "would have figured less than anything the stage-manager or the author of the play, who most occupy the foreground," James observes; "he might be at best the financial 'backer,' watching his interests from the wing, but in rather confessed ignorance of the mysteries of mimicry" (23: 169–70). If Maggie has learned how to manage and even exhibit Amerigo's masculinity, Adam obviously "backs" her efforts with moneyed power. Adam equates his manhood with his money—for example, with the "sum" he is able to "name" to Mr. Gutermann-Seuss—that is, with the "huge lump" of money he has "thrust" under Charlotte's "nose" (23: 217), but unlike Amerigo, he does not equate masculinity with sexual expenditure. While Adam feels the responsibility to propose marriage to Charlotte after so displaying his "huge lump," he has externalized himself and his manhood in the act—representing himself at "secondhand" and, like any good capitalist, letting his money work for him. As much as Gilbert Osmond, who appreciates Isabel's marital value because she spurns Lord Warburton, Adam takes a secondhand pleasure in watching other men watch Charlotte: "he felt quite merged in the elated circle formed by the girl's free response to the collective caress of all the shining eyes" (23: 216).

Although Maggie believes at the end of the novel that Adam practically offers himself "as a sacrifice" (24: 269), he returns to America with his male power confirmed and, apparently, endlessly confirmable through Charlotte's ready sacrifice of individuality.[4] Indeed, in the sadistic and masochistic economies with which James flirts in *The Golden Bowl*, Adam maintains the aggressive, arguably sadistic power conferred by his wealth and position—that power made manifest in the "long silken halter" he has "looped" around Charlotte's "beautiful neck" (24: 287) and in the "shriek of a soul in pain" that his leading her by the neck provokes (24: 292). Adam's sadism only masquerades as masochism—or "sacrifice"—while Amerigo's masochism, as we shall see, masquerades as sadism. It may be true that Adam's power and male identity depend upon female construction and confirmation—Maggie and Charlotte's coincidentally cooperative efforts—but in that dependency he retains the capitalist's privileged position of seeing others work in his behalf. When Maggie appraises him at the end of the novel, for example, she seems to discount his patriarchal status by considering him the "perfect little father," but in fact she (and James) valorizes his patriarchal position in a veritable object lesson in hagiography. "The 'successful' beneficent person, the beautiful bountiful original dauntlessly wilful great citizen, the consummate collector and infallible high authority he had been and still was," James apostrophizes—"these things struck her on the spot as making up for him in a wonderful way a character she must take into account in dealing with him either for pity or for envy" (24: 273). Adam's traditional manhood may be constructed, but it does not seem thereby subject to significant destabilization. For as Maggie continues to appraise her father, she continues to appreciate, or inflate, his masculine value. "He positively, under the impression, seemed to loom larger than life for her," she thinks, "so that she saw him during these moments in a light of recognition which had had its brightness for her at many an hour of the past, but which had never been so intense and so admonitory" (24: 273). James's language, carefully and insistently registered in a woman's subjectivity, offers a virtual blueprint for patriarchal manhood—the Law of the Father incarnate, but delegated to his daughter.

As they appear at the end of *The Golden Bowl*, in fact, Adam, Maggie, and Amerigo suggest the masochistic tableau that Deleuze discusses in *Coldness and Cruelty*. As Silverman explains, Deleuze "argues that masochism is entirely an affair between son and mother, or, to be more precise, between the male masochist and a cold, maternal, and severe woman whom he designates the 'oral mother.' Through the dispassionate and highly ritualized transaction that takes place between these two figures, the former is stripped of all virility, and reborn as a 'new, sexless man,' and the latter is invested with the phallus" (Silverman 210–11). James works a variation on this masochistic paradigm in Amerigo's case, but Deleuze's theory of masochism can help account for Adam's banishment to America at the end of the novel and to the installation of Maggie and Amerigo as a new first couple. "A contract is established between the hero and the woman," Deleuze argues, "whereby at a precise point in time and for a determinate period she is given every right over him. By this means the masochist tries to exorcise the danger of the father and to ensure that the temporal order of reality and experience will be in conformity with the symbolic order, in which the father has been abolished for all time" (65–66). In contrast to Freud and others, Deleuze considers sadism and masochism to be separate perversions, and he argues against the existence of sadomasochism as a separate entity. That is, he claims that a woman who appears to be sadistic within the masochistic imaginary is not really sadistic. She "cannot be sadistic precisely because she is *in* the masochistic situation, she is an integral part of it, a realization of the masochistic fantasy." She "belongs in the masochistic world," furthermore, "not in the sense that she has the same tastes as her victim, but because her 'sadism' is of a kind never found in the sadist; it is as it were the double or the reflection of masochism" (41). In effect, Deleuze considers sadism the form of necessary otherness projected from the masochistic imaginary, and that idea can help to explain the peculiar, interdependent relationship that James establishes between Amerigo and Maggie. Essentially masochistic from both positions, I want to argue, that relationship produces sadism at the site of masochism. Sadism represents the mask that Amerigo and Maggie wear for each other. Amerigo gets to play the sadist even as he recognizes that Maggie has commissioned the role. In effect, she plays the sadist by making him play that role. In the capitalistic variation on this masochistic scenario that James establishes in *The Golden Bowl*, moreover, Adam may be banished, but he retains full patriarchal prerogatives in his mastery of the "haltered" Charlotte Stant. The power Maggie arguably wields over Amerigo derives from Adam's still massive fortune and, most importantly, seems dedicated to Amerigo's phallic empowerment. Rather than abolish the father's power, James has incorporated it. Amerigo retains the "use-value," in Lynda Zwinger's term, of his phallic manhood, while Adam and Maggie retain the "exchange-value."

What pleasure does Henry James derive, it seems fair to ask, from Amerigo's masochistic role-playing—his immasculation-through-emasculation? The pleasure, I am tempted to say, of having the phallus and eating it, too—that is, the pleasure of creating and identifying with a phallicly empowered male and, through a feminized authorial agency, "changing" the phallic male into a subordinate position. "I wish I could go to Rome and put my hands on you (oh, how lovingly I should lay them!)," James had written to Hendrik Andersen in 1902, after the unexpected death of Andersen's brother Andreas. Come to England "so that I might take consoling, soothing, infinitely close and tender and affectionately-healing *possession* of you" (*Henry James Amato Ragazzo* 88). Without reducing *The Golden Bowl* to a roman á clef, we can infer a similar authorial pleasure in the position James occupies in relation to Prince Amerigo—both dominant and subordinate at the same time, prizing Amerigo's manly character while controlling it, as he suggested to Andersen, with his "hands."

Although Prince Amerigo seems struck from the same classic masculine mould that produced Christopher Newman and Caspar Goodwood, James complicates his manhood from the beginning by quadrangulating it relationally. The Prince prides himself in his love-making and believes that his "recompense to women" was "more or less to make love to them" (23: 21–22). As if representing a natural manhood, an essential, heterosexual male principle—a "basic passional force," in R. B. J. Wilson's phrase (74)—Amerigo seems more "lady killer" than "ladies' man," but any "straight" deployment of his desire or identification of himself as a lovemaker to women proves difficult as he orients himself in relation to Maggie and Adam.

The novel opens, of course, just as the Prince has engaged himself to Maggie, whom he "had been pursuing for six months as never in his life before," but that pursuit has "unsteadied" rather than settled him in an instrumental masculine role (23: 4). Dale Bauer claims that Amerigo's "self is empty or bankrupt" because he is inscribed by so many different cultural discourses (53), and certainly his commitment to Maggie has made him vulnerable—"sealed" his "fate"—and even threatened to emasculate him, like a "crunched key in the strongest lock that could be made" (23: 5). As "one of the great collectors of the world" (23: 100), Adam Verver possesses that "strongest lock," the lock to his "museum of museums" (23: 145), and in engaging himself to Maggie the Prince does indeed risk being collected, locked away, and emasculated by her father. "You're at any rate part of his collection," Maggie explains. "You're a rarity, an object of beauty, an object of price" (23: 13). Elizabeth Allen argues that Adam marries Amerigo through their exchange of women and thus "attempts to render the Prince feminine, the woman in their marriage," by controlling him as a sign (178). It is more accurate to say, I think, that Prince Amerigo's emasculation or feminization coincides with his immasculation—with his triangulation and deployment as Adam's "secondhand" lover of women.

Prince Amerigo may descend—albeit from the distaff—from the "godfather, or name-father," of the new Continent (23: 78), but in marrying Maggie he subjects himself to Adam's colonization.[5] He may have a "beautiful personal presence, that of a prince in very truth, a ruler, warrior, patron, lighting up brave architecture and diffusing the sense of a function," as Fanny Assingham believes (23: 42), but within the patriarchal capitalist economy that Adam superintends, Prince Amerigo hires himself out. As Cheryl Torsney puts it, male characters in *The Golden Bowl*, "in addition to exchanging females, commodify each other. The man with the past wants the man with the cash, and vice-versa" ("Specula[riza]tion" 142). Marrying Maggie is as much a business decision as a romantic one, a homosocial exchange (of a woman) "between men," in Sedgwick's term, and the Prince negotiates the match using his own intermediary, "his own man of business, poor Calderoni" (23: 5). Adam's economic superiority, however, positions the Prince more in the role of hired hand than in the role of co-investor. Acknowledging that Adam's larger capital and "easy way with his millions" taxes his own capacity to reciprocate in this homosocial exchange and thereby become an equal rather than minority shareholder (23: 5), the Prince examines himself in the mirror that Adam's presence provides. He objectifies and commodifies himself in Adam's gaze. He considers Adam "simply the best man" he has ever seen in his life (23: 6), and motivated by a desire to reconstruct himself relationally, to "*make* something different" of himself and thus "contradict" or write over his "old" history (23: 16), the Prince seeks to incorporate Adam. Comparing himself to a chicken that has been "chopped up and smothered in sauce; cooked down as a *creme de volaille*, with half the parts left out," he admires Adam as the "natural fowl" still running free. "I'm eating your father alive," he tells Maggie—"which is the only way to taste him" (23: 8). Covering Adam's incestuous desire for Maggie on the one hand, Prince Amerigo covers the homosocial and homoerotic desire that his marriage-business transaction with Adam entails on the other hand. James's imagery of fragmentation, castration, and fellatio destabilizes Prince Amerigo's gendered and sexual self. Like Adam, he becomes a "false subject," in Torsney's term, because he functions as an object for the "other's desire" ("Specula[riza]tion," 142). To be or even to be *like* Adam represents a writing over of homoerotic desire with narcissistic longing—redirecting homoerotic desire into emulation. Sexually considered, to "eat" Adam in an act of fellatio means assuming a subordinate posture—being on his knees before the superior man and providing him with pleasure. More primitively considered, to "eat" Adam means destroying him in the act of incorporating him and his power.[6] But in the capitalistic terms that pervade the novel, eating Adam means incorporating him in another sense—forming a corporation, or single body, with him through an arguably "friendly" rather than hostile takeover.

From Adam's point of view, furthermore, to "collect" Amerigo as Maggie's husband-lover also suggests a sublimation of homoerotic desire. He enjoys characterizing Amerigo as a "round" man who offers no impediments to his hand "for rubbing against" (23: 138)—a very different man from the "rough trade" that George Chauncey has discovered in late nineteenth-century culture. Indeed, it is fair to ask which of the partners Adam actually uses. Does he employ Amerigo to make love to Maggie, as Osmond had effectively used Caspar Goodwood to make "hard" love to Isabel, or does he use Maggie to "rub against" Amerigo?[7] Most tangibly, of course, Adam uses Amerigo as a surrogate father—a sperm bank from which to sire the child that he himself can no longer father. Mimi Kairschner notes that Adam's apparent impotence, which Charlotte confirms by claiming that their failure to produce an heir is not her fault (23: 307), requires him to make a deal with the Prince to ensure "the perpetuation of the Verver empire intact" (191). Adam's motives are not simply mercenary, however, for he also covets the secondhand pleasure of displacing Amerigo as father in the triangle the Principio forms with Maggie. Converting the "precious creature into a link between a mamma and a grandpa," Adam renders the Principio a "half-orphan, with the place of the immediate male parent swept bare and open to the next nearest sympathy" (23: 156). In the game of musical subject positions that I see James playing throughout his fiction, Adam finds the capitalist-manager's ideal way of playing father—hiring out the "dirty work," as Zwinger terms it (80), to another man, who becomes an invisible *third* hand in the process.[8]

The question James raises in thus satirizing Adam's entrepreneurial manhood, of course, is whether secondhand experience of masculine prerogatives—considered from either point of view—can provide the same pleasure and thus the same male subjectivity as the real thing. The question he raises for Amerigo is whether he can retain his manly integrity while hiring himself out to another man. In dividing manly labor between capitalist and hired hand, does James decimate male power in a variation on the theory of spermatic economy? Is secondhand manhood as manly for either of the two men who cooperate in its production?

James seems especially fascinated by the tension this cooperative arrangement creates for Amerigo. One of the most attractive and phallicly empowered male characters James ever imagined, Amerigo also faces one of the most severe challenges to his manly power. Dale Bauer argues that Amerigo resists Adam's "finalizing" definition of his role, playing out that resistance in his affair with Charlotte (59). Lynda Zwinger points out, in contrast, that even though Amerigo possesses both of Adam's "daughter-wives," he "usurps use-value only." Exchange-value, the "cornerstone of capitalist economy," remains in Adam's hands (80). Even within his roles as husband and father, Amerigo gets the better of his deal with Adam—both fathering a child and endowing that child handsomely with another man's money. He beats Adam Verver at his own capitalist game—out-fathering his father-in-law.

Looked at another way, however, *The Golden Bowl* shows James getting the sexually potent male character under control—if not exactly taming the masculine, at least harnessing and deploying it. The tacit cooperation between Caspar Goodwood and Gilbert Osmond at the end of *The Portrait of a Lady* anticipates the basis for male homosocial relations and identities in *The Golden Bowl*. Whatever he may have been as a man before his marriage, as a married man Amerigo performs masculinity for pay. Charlotte feels amazed each time she sees him at the "disproportionate intensity" with which he affects her sight, but as James describes it, that intensity proves more constructed than natural. In the relational economy in which Amerigo finds himself embedded, a woman's desire constructs its own ideal male object—at least to the woman's perception. "What did he do when he was away from her," Charlotte wonders, "that made him always come back only looking, as she would have called it, 'more so'?" (23: 248). James emphasizes Amerigo's ability to perform himself—to perform a desirable manhood—by comparing him to an "actor who, between his moments on the stage, revisits his dressing-room, and, before the glass, pressed by his need of effect, retouches his make-up" (23: 248). Indeed, James subverts Amerigo's male self, rendering his manhood as something that exists only in performance—in the "make-up" of male or female drag—and depends even at that upon a female audience to give it vitality.

Fanny Assingham realizes, for example, that Amerigo understands perfectly well the role that Adam and Maggie have hired him to perform: "he after all visibly had on his conscience some sort of return for services rendered" (23: 268). Even though he represents a "huge expense," he "had carried out his idea, carried it out by continuing to lead the life, to breathe the air, very nearly to think the thoughts, that best suited his wife and her father" (23: 268–69). Amerigo's ready cooperation in producing a masculine performance on demand effectively reduces him, in the extended financial metaphor that James prosecutes throughout the novel, to a kind of bank—a sperm bank—of masculinity. Adam himself may be impotent, as Charlotte suggests, and may figure as a "little boy" and "infant king" (23: 324) to Amerigo's perception, but he has found the way to manage Amerigo and the fund of masculine power he possesses. As Amerigo himself recognizes, sitting under Adam's powerful gaze:

> This directed regard rested at its ease, but it neither lingered nor penetrated, and was, to the Prince's fancy, much of the same order as any glance directed, for due attention, from the same quarter, to the figure of a cheque received in the course of business and about to be enclosed to a banker. It made sure of the amount—and just so, from time to time, the amount of the Prince was certified. He was being thus, in renewed installments, perpetually paid in; he already reposed in the bank as value, but subject, in this comfortable way, to repeated, to infinite endorsement. The net result of all of which moreover was that the young man had no wish to see his value diminish. He himself decidedly hadn't fixed it—the "figure" was a conception all of Mr. Verver's own. (23: 324–25)

Impotent on his own account, Adam can fulfill a capitalist and patriarchal fantasy—a form of spermatic alchemy—through the infinitely endorsable Amerigo.

This is not to say that reducing Amerigo to a value—even an infinitely endorsable one—or to a masculine performance that Adam has sponsored enhances Adam's own manhood at Amerigo's expense. In the long passage quoted above, the Prince can take an ironic view of himself as a possession, but he effectively remains Adam's accomplice in producing his own "value" by working not to "diminish" it.[9] The two characters remain interdependently connected—as labor and management—sharing what James calls a "community of interest" (23: 293). Indeed, Amerigo savors the "particular 'treat', at his father-in-law's expense, that he more and more struck himself as enjoying," even as he realizes that Adam relieves him of all "anxiety about his married life in the same manner in which he relieved him on the score of his bank-account" (23: 292). In fact, to Fanny Assingham's perception, the Prince's "pay," so to speak, is Charlotte. That is, Fanny believes that she has procured two women (Maggie and Charlotte) for the Prince—that marrying Charlotte to Adam has prevented her taking some husband with whom Amerigo "wouldn't be able to open, to keep open, so large an account as with his father-in-law" (24: 129). If Fanny is correct, then in effect she implicates Adam himself as an accomplice in his own cuckolding—cuckoldry being the price he has paid for the procreative (and recreative) services Amerigo has provided. Ironically, in their cooperative performance of manhood, neither Amerigo nor Adam appears to be a complete man—not "simply a man," in the terms James had propounded in *The Portrait of a Lady*, and not "simply himself," as James put it in *The American*.[10]

Is there, in fact, an essential Amerigo and in turn an essential manhood? Does Amerigo exist as a man apart from his performance of a masculine part? Is he anything more than a "smoothly-working man," a "lubricated item" in the great social machinery (24: 352)? At Matcham, he realizes that his "body" was "engaged at the front—in shooting, in riding, in golfing, in walking"; it also "bore the brunt of bridge-playing, of breakfasting, lunching, tea-drinking, dining, and of the nightly climax over *bottigliera*, as he called it, of the bristling tray; it met, finally, to the extent of the limited tax on lip, gesture, on wit, most of the current demands of conversation and expression" (23: 327–28). That litany of activities and obligations suggests that Amerigo is all performance. But the Prince also realizes that "something of him" was "left out." This "something" does not necessarily exist independent of all relations. The Prince thinks that "it was much more when he was alone or when he was with his own people—or when he was, say, with Mrs. Verver and nobody else—that he moved, that he talked, that he listened, that he felt, as a congruous whole" (23: 328). Construing a manly self in relation only to Maggie—a purely heterosexual subject-object relation, it would appear—Amerigo can feel himself to be a "congruous whole." Bringing Charlotte into the equation suggests that the Prince seeks to define himself as a "sexual subject," in Bauer's term (61), but James complicates that concept of sexual, or gendered, subjectivity—splitting, objectifying, and attenuating Amerigo's masculinity even within this heterosexual register:

"English society," as he would have said, cut him accordingly in two, and he reminded himself often, in his relations with it, of a man possessed of a shining star, a decoration, an order of some sort, something so ornamental as to make his identity not complete, ideally, without it, yet who, finding no other such object generally worn, should be perpetually and the least but ruefully unpinning it from his breast to transfer it to his pocket. The Prince's shining star may, no doubt, have been nothing more precious than his private subtlety; bit whatever the object he just now fingered it a good deal out of sight—amounting as it mainly did for him to a restless play of memory and a fine embroidery of thought. (23: 328)

In this startling passage, James objectifies Amerigo's individuality, the most important part of him, as an ornamental object—a decoration that signifies nothing but without which his identity is not complete. At the same time, James marginalizes the object that presumably makes him a "congruous whole," shuffling it into his pocket where, phallicized as it is, he can finger it "a good deal." To be a "congruous whole," in these terms, means at best playing with oneself. Amerigo's manhood has been rendered an attenuated, narcissistic "trace" or residue. Not surprisingly, of course, this is not the whole story, nor the end point of Amerigo's manhood.

Within the space of two paragraphs in Book Second (chapter 3), James compares Amerigo to a "domesticated lamb tied up with pink ribbon" and observes that the Prince was "saving up" for some "mysterious purpose" all the "wisdom, all the answers to his questions, all the impressions and generalisations he gathered; putting them away and packing them down because he wanted his great gun to be loaded to the brim on the day he should decide to fire it off" (23: 163). Abjectness has the potential to inspire compensation in the form of a violent unloading of pent-up anger, as Emily Dickinson suggests in "My Life had stood - a Loaded Gun." In Amerigo's case, masochism can turn into sadism. The Prince seems to understand the doubleness that these two extravagant figures describe. "There are two parts of me," he tells Maggie in another context. "One is made up of the history"—things that are "written," "literally in rows of volumes, in libraries"—but "there's another part, very much smaller doubtless, which, such as it is, represents my single self, the unknown, unimportant—unimportant save to *you*—personal quantity" (23: 9). Amerigo struggles throughout the novel to liberate himself from the cultural and familial inscriptions that fix identity instrumentally in terms of role, but in allying himself with the house of Verver he risks a secondary, or secondhand, inscription. He feels himself to be some "old embossed coin, of a purity of gold no longer used, stamped with glorious arms, medieval, wonderful, of which the 'worth' in mere modern change, sovereigns and half-crowns, would be great enough, but as to which, since there were finer ways of using it, such taking to pieces was superfluous" (23: 23). Coming to terms with his own value in a marital exchange market, he recognizes that he is "invested with attributes" and that if Adam and Maggie don't "change" him, "they really wouldn't know—he wouldn't know himself—how many pounds, shillings and pence he had to give" (23: 23). Risking the inscription of a new male identity, Amerigo fears the loss of his "single self," which would be subject to "change" in the exchange economy the Ververs control. Amerigo's challenge involves marketing his manhood without marginalizing it—deploying it without rendering it deplorable (or "contemptible," in Adam's term).

The "personal quantity" in which Amerigo holds such stake resides largely in his sexual subjectivity, and he predicates that subjectivity on relationships with women who afford him opportunities for exercising sexual power. Although Amerigo thus seems to perform a conventional, heterosexual masculine role, he differs significantly from the more aggressive Christopher Newman and Caspar Goodwood. Possessing a more refined and confident—a more "gentlemanly"—manhood, he resembles Gilbert Osmond at the end of *The Portrait of a Lady*, as he waits to see what Isabel will do. Like Osmond, the Prince waits passively—spiderlike—for women to put themselves in his power. As a "man conscious of having known many women, he could assist, as he would have called it, at the recurrent, the predestined phenomenon, the thing always as certain as sunrise or the coming round of saints' days, the doing by the woman of the thing that gave her away" (23: 49). The "silent suspense" in which James casts Prince Amerigo's manhood (23: 50) apparently involves no suspense at all, because it seems to derive from the sort of gender determinism with which James had played in *The Bostonians*. It was a woman's "nature, it was her life, and the man could always expect it without lifting a finger," James archly observes. "This was *his*, the man's, any man's, position and strength—that he had necessarily the advantage, that he only had to wait with a decent patience to be placed, in spite of himself, it might really be said, in the right" (23: 49–50). These are remarkable fantasies—actual experiences, it appears, in the Prince's case—and surely they are James's to the same extent that he can identify with Caspar Goodwood in the act of giving Isabel Archer that "white lightning" kiss. James could participate in the heterosexual imaginary—in these cases, in the form of a "wolf." But such sadistic identifications always veer toward the masochistic, and the "hot" heterosexual scenes that James stages always include a double identification. Imagining the male subjectivity capable of lightning kisses and the sort of patience that Gilbert Osmond and Prince Amerigo possess presupposes an "other"—a woman—who plays the abject object of male desire. Insofar as he imagines "her," James places himself and his readers as recipients, objects who are also subjects, of male sadism—in other words, male masochists.

Much as Adam Verver represents power, in Mark Seltzer's view, "by appearing powerless," James disguises Prince Amerigo's brand of power as a strategic passivity or patience. The Prince's manhood, his recurring subject position as a man, will be constructed reflexively—and sadistically—at the site of women's weakness. Weakness "produced for the man that extraordinary mixture of pity and profit in which his relation with her, when he was not a brute, mainly consisted," James explains; "and gave him in fact his most pertinent ground of being always nice to her, nice about her, nice *for* her. She always dressed her act up, of course, she muffled and disguised and arranged it, showing in fact in these dissimulations a cleverness equal to but one thing in the world, equal to her abjection" (23: 50). I can think of no other passage in James's fiction—not even in *The*

Portrait of a Lady or *The Bostonians*—where he so succinctly anatomizes the internal experience of psychological brutality or the psychic economy of sado-masochistic male-female relations. Male and female subjects cooperate in a carnival of gendered dominance and subordination in which weakness and abjection masquerade as strength. Male brutality, furthermore, exists most blatantly in its calculated absence—as a power held in reserve whose disguised presence in effect coerces women into laboring, or "acting," in a man's behalf. Later, in fact, as Prince Amerigo reviews the "books" of his relations with women, he thinks that "he had after all gained more from women than he had ever lost by them; there appeared so, more and more, on those mystic books that are kept, in connexion with such commerce, even by men of the loosest business habits, a balance in his favour that he could pretty well as a rule take for granted" (23: 350–51). This male psychology, so clearly rooted in a heterosexual economy—indeed, in a compulsive heterosexuality—compensates the Prince for the abjection he feels in Adam Verver's clutches without canceling the "debt," as it were, in Amerigo's homosocially constructed manhood.

Prince Amerigo's power over women appears all the more striking in view of his progressive disempowerment over the course of the novel. Moving him from this naturally empowered male position, denaturalizing his manhood and manly privilege by subjecting him to the Ververs' reconstruction, James suspends him between heterosexual and homosocial economies, as well as between sadistic and masochistic desires and identifications. Clearly subordinate when identified homosocially and masochistically, the Prince feels empowered when he is identified heterosexually and sadistically, even as that sense of power disguises his own feminized abjection. "All men are brutes," Charlotte believes, "but the Prince's distinction was in being one of the few who could check himself before acting on the impulse. This, obviously, was what counted in a man as delicacy" (23: 290). Charlotte attributes will power to Amerigo that he may possess in relation to her, but in relation to Maggie and Adam his sense of empowerment—to be "brutal" or "delicate," as he may choose—seems more delusory than real, because James subjects Amerigo's manhood to a cooperative male and female gaze that neutralizes his power and converts it to use.

The "boundless happy margin" that Prince Amerigo comes to occupy in his marriage has been carefully furnished by his father-in-law and maintained by his wife. When Maggie speculates that he might "some day get drunk and beat her," she feels imaginatively compensated by the projected masochistic thought that he can reduce other women to the "same passive pulp." Indeed, the "spectacle" of Amerigo with "hated rivals would, after no matter what extremity, always, for the sovereign charm of it, charm of it in itself and as an exhibition of him that most deeply moved her, suffice to bring her round" (23: 165). Christopher Newman had felt at the Bellegardes' impromptu ball like a trained bear (280) or "a terrier on his hind legs" (281). Similarly exhibited to Maggie's gaze in a kind of carnival for one, Amerigo finds his masculinity transformed more into a pose than into a self-liberating and transgressive force. Hugh Stevens argues that Maggie's "economic power displaces the strength of the Prince's masculinity" (58), but I think the Prince's phallic masculinity is not so much displaced as deployed. He performs the masculine, as it were, and so retains—indeed, must retain—the phallus, but Maggie's leverage and especially her willingness to play the part of battered wife appropriate in the act of theatricalizing his power. In Ash's words, Maggie "occupies a place of passive, staring victimage, but at the same time surmounts this by scripting Amerigo's role of abuser and, more generally, by enacting this role herself as the scene's stage-director" ("Narcissism" 70). Conversely, of course, the Prince can perform his masculine role as abuser from an inverted position of abject dependency—the position of the male masochist. In effect, he becomes a heterosexual male invert.

Later in the novel, for example, as Maggie contemplates Amerigo's "dazzling person" at the very moment she is writing new roles for herself and the other characters, she thinks that "she had never felt so absorbingly married, so abjectly conscious of a master of her fate. He could do what he would with her" (24: 21). Subjecting herself to Amerigo's desire only apparently empowers him as a sexually dominant subject, however. Indeed, somewhat like Babo in Melville's "Benito Cereno," who parodies the master-slave relationship in the shaving scene he stages for Captain Amasa Delano, Maggie stages her own abjection and in turn the Prince's "mastery." Priscilla Walton reads this passage straightforwardly, as evidence of an abjection to masculine ideology from which Maggie then begins to liberate herself (152), but I think James stages this master-slave symbiosis ironically. By carnivalizing their gender identities as roles or poses, Maggie inscribes them with the reifying power of convention, stiffening both of them into stereotypical figures and neutralizing if not neutering Amerigo's manhood.[11] Amerigo must remain manly—empowered in a sadistic masculine pose—because only then does he remain useful. Thus, when Maggie silently announces her "idea" to rearrange the four characters' relations, Amerigo responds by embracing her—a demonstration, "better than words," designed to "dispose of" her idea for reconfiguring relations and restore their relationship at least to a traditional male-dominant, female-submissive form. Even though he thereby puts her "in his power," as she gives up and lets herself go, tasting the "terror" of her own weakness (24: 28–29), she remains ultimately in control—enjoying the performance of weakness without jeopardizing her possession of strength.

James luxuriates in *The Golden Bowl*, as he does in no other novel, in the exercise of masculine and phallocentric power—as if he were determined to replicate the scene of Caspar Goodwood's "white lightning" kiss again and again, repeatedly registering such male power in a woman's subjective experience. Why does James go to such lengths to stress Amerigo's phallocentric potency when in fact that power is consistently contained and harnessed—employed by Adam as a hired (third) hand in a sexual "manu-factory" and domesticated by Maggie's "labour" within a "steel hoop of an intimacy compared with which artless passion would have been but a beating of the air" (24: 141)? The attraction for James arguably cuts both ways, as it did in *The Portrait of a Lady*, by producing pleasure from both subject positions. He can write an exaggeratedly masculine subject into being and simultaneously become the object, masked as the desiring female subject, of masculine desire.

Such confusion of sexual subjectivity intrigued James as he represented his own authorial subjectivity as writer, reader, and reviser of *The Golden Bowl*. Adam Verver's secondhand fatherhood, for example, mirrors James's as he defines it in his Preface. Initially he observes that the figures he creates amount to "nought from the moment they fail to become more or less visible appearances," but when they do so the result is "charming" for their creator because he can see "such power as he may possess approved and registered by the springing of such fruit from his seed" (23: x). In this progenitive view of literary creativity, James names himself the father of his characters—out-Adaming Adam in the context of *The Golden Bowl*. But James also dismisses himself from the scene of creation, much as he does Adam—surrendering power over the "fruit of his seed" by attributing it to others. "His own garden," he says, "remains one thing, and the garden he has prompted the cultivation of at other hands becomes quite another" (23: x). Literary paternity, he suggests, is often secondhand.

Much as he divides male subjectivity between Adam and Amerigo, furthermore, James's sense of his own authorial secondhandedness takes the form of gender doubling and inversion— splitting an androgynous authorial self into separate personae. As re-reader and reviser of his earlier work, he takes his reader's place, transpositioning himself as it were into *self* and *other* and playing both roles. He thereby closes the writerly circuit, collapsing "difference" through a self-authorizing act of auto-aesthetic intercourse. The "march" of his "present attention" coincides sufficiently with the "march" of his "original expression," he says with some satisfaction:

As the historian of the matter sees and speaks, so my intelligence of it, as a reader, meets him halfway, passive, receptive, appreciative, often even grateful; unconscious, quite blissfully, of any bar to intercourse, any disparity of sense between us.

Into his very footprints the responsive, the imaginative steps of the docile reader that I consentingly become for him all comfortably sink; his vision, superimposed on my own as an image in cut paper is applied to a sharp shadow on a wall, matches, at every point, without excess or deficiency. This truth throws into relief for me the very different dance that the taking in hand of my earlier productions was to lead me. (23: xiii)

Characterizing the arguably erotic pleasure that reading offers, James reconfigures that pleasure autoerotically by doubly gendering himself—masculinizing his original writerly self (the historian, or sower of "seed") and feminizing (and homoeroticizing) his readerly self (the "docile" and "passive" receptor, the one who takes "in hand"), in much the same way he had done in his tales of writers and artists.

James goes on, in fact, to elaborate his own feminization as reviser, characterizing himself as a nursemaid or governess—another form of secondhand parent. Not least among the "creeping superstitions" he experienced, as he kept his finished work "well behind" him, "rioted doubtless the fond fear that any tidying-up of the uncanny brood, any removal of accumulated dust, any washing of wizened faces, or straightening of grizzled locks, or twitching, to a better effect, of superannuated garments, might let one in, as the phrase is, for expensive renovations" (23: xiv). Playing governess to someone else's literary progeny, even when that someone else is oneself, can prove dangerous because of the threatened loss of control—the demands for attention and revision—and the potential destabilization of the author's male self. The "moment a stitch should be taken or a hair-brush applied," he recognizes, "the *principle* of my making my brood more presentable under the nobler illumination would be accepted and established, and it was there complications might await me" (23: xv). What interests me about this imagery is the traditional gendering in which James indulges. In positioning himself as the re-reader and reviser of his texts, he removes himself from the procreative moment, which he figures androcentrically as an autogenetically primal scene. Re-reading and revising, on the other hand, he feminizes as woman's work. Analogously, he thus identifies himself with Maggie Verver in the novel itself; for Maggie revises the Verver "brood" in the process of normalizing relations and making them all more "presentable." But in consenting to become a "docile" reader and then reviser of the relational text, Maggie masks her power in order to leave Amerigo's masked manhood intact. So too, it can be argued, does James play the female—nursing his "brood" through the revising process while he valorizes the creative, procreatively masculine self that authored them in the first place. To turn the screw even one more notch, this passage offers evidence to support Eve Sedgwick's interpretation of James's anal eroticism (*Tendencies* 73–103). Keeping his finished work "well behind" him, he makes it available for the "tidying-up" that his editorial self performs—not exactly the more extravagant "fisting-as-*écriture*" that Sedgwick spots in *The Wings of the Dove*, but still pleasurably, autoerotically, and homoerotically anal. As an author empowered through revision to perform many roles, James keeps the form of gendered and sexual pleasure in a state of suspense.

Similarly, as Maggie contemplates Amerigo's "sovereign personal power" in the context of her own complex plot to revise proper relationships, she recognizes that she has opened herself to the possibility of attack—has subjected herself, in Silverman's terms, to "feminine masochism." Such attack would underline the misogynistic heterosexual configuration of their relationship by placing Amerigo in an exaggerated masculine role such as the ones Caspar Goodwood and Basil Ransom play. "Attack, real attack from him as he would conduct it," she thinks, "was what she above all dreaded; she was so far from sure that under that experience she mightn't drop into some depth of weakness, mightn't show him some shortest way with her that he would know how to use again" (24: 139–40). In her martial view of marriage Maggie translates fear and desire into defensive and offensive strategies, but James goes on and on in this extended passage to probe at her "dread" of weakness, balancing female weakness with male power at the site of his own authorial desire. The weaker Maggie feels, the stronger and more potent the Prince appears. "She loved him too helplessly still to dare to open the door by an inch to his treating her as if either of them had wronged the other," James observes, submerging morality in the politics of desire. The "result of the direct appeal of *any* beauty in him would be her helpless submission to his terms" (24: 140). Indeed, a "single touch from him—oh she should know it in case of its coming!—any brush of his hand, of his lips, of his voice, inspired by recognition of her probable interest as distinct from pity for her virtual gloom, would hand her over to him bound hand and foot" (24: 142). In this caricature of male-female relationship as well as masculine and feminine identification, James both satirizes and interrogates the terms of marriage. Anatomizing Amerigo in a manner usually reserved for female characters in male-authored texts, he emphasizes his masculine instrumentality—the eroticized, desiring actions of his body—and his power to fulfill an arguably feminocentric sado-masochistic fantasy. Hugh Stevens argues that, by assuming agency in the second half of the novel, Maggie upturns "the dynamics of her relationship with the Prince, reversing the interplay of machismo and sadomasochism which earlier in the novel seemed to characterize their relationship" (*Henry James* 57–58), but I think this reversal is more apparent than real. Sadism is simply the form that Amerigo's masochism is allowed to take. The more powerful he can be made, the bigger his "gun," the more enjoyable his domestication as a "lamb." Phallicly empowered in a masterful position within a femininely constructed economy, Amerigo can be heterosexualized through the secondhand power of the female gaze and female desire, even as he becomes homosexualized—at third hand—by Adamic and authorial desire. Playing "rough trade" to Maggie's performance of submissive wife, Amerigo effectively reverses positions and roles off the stage—in the closet that compulsively heterosexual relationships hide from view.

Whereas Amerigo, like Gilbert Osmond, had predicated his male subjectivity on being able to wait patiently and passively for women to "place" him "in the right," the tables seem turned in his relationship with Maggie. In effect, she occupies what James called "the man's, any man's, position and strength," while Amerigo's only choice, like Charlotte's, involves "arranging appearances"—that is, showing in *his* "dissimulations" of male strength a "cleverness equal to but one thing in the world, equal to [his] abjection." Immediately after Fanny Assingham smashes the golden bowl, for example, leaving the stunned Amerigo at Maggie's mercy, Maggie feels almost embarrassed by the power she suddenly wields, and she feels a "strong, sharp wish not to see [Amerigo's] face again till he should have had a minute to arrange it" (24: 181). In dreading her own advantage, Maggie reveals her stake in controlling but not emasculating her husband—in allowing him a margin in which to reconstruct his manhood not just for his own sake, but for hers. Take all the time you need, she wants to say to him; "arrange yourself so as to suffer least, or to be at any rate least distorted and disfigured" (24: 184). Amerigo's manhood has been cast suddenly, violently into a state of suspense. In the metaphorically sado-masochistic dance he performs with Maggie, instead of exercising the power to bind her "hand and foot" with a "single touch" or simple "brush" of his lips, he himself is subject to disfigurement. As I noted, however, Maggie has reason to exercise her power in Amerigo's behalf—at least to the extent of enabling him to recover the appearance or pose of manhood. "Above all," she continues to fantasize, "don't show me, till you've got it well under, the dreadful blur, the ravage of suspense and embarrassment produced, and produced by my doing, in your personal serenity, your incomparable superiority" (24: 184).

With his masculinity in this sort of suspense, Amerigo's protean willingness to perform different parts and occupy different gender positions becomes clear as Maggie's plan unfolds. Part of that plan involves reaffirming her ties with Charlotte and in turn repositioning both Adam and Amerigo in homosocial relation to each other. Just as Maggie's marriage upset the delicately balanced relational economy between herself and her father, restoration of the new married economy requires careful rebalancing, because gender roles and sexual identities are at stake—that is, in suspense. If Maggie spends more time with Charlotte, someone must fill the void Charlotte leaves with Adam. Maggie requires that Amerigo, acting on the "cue" he takes from simply observing "the shade of change in *her* behaviour," take Charlotte's place—sitting with Adam while Maggie goes out with Charlotte or making some display that "would represent the equivalent of her excursions" (24: 39–40). So thoroughly inscribed and inscribable is Amerigo that Maggie can safely rely on his ability to play "sublimely a gentleman," using his "instinct for relations" and fulfilling the mission she has tacitly marked out for him (24: 40). He allows himself to be positioned—indeed, readily positions himself—in Charlotte's place with Adam, feigning desire for Adam's company, letting it seem to Adam that he "suits" him (24: 59), because any desire generated by such dangerous repositioning will be carefully covered through Maggie's mediation. "If I didn't love you, you know, for yourself," she tells him, "I should still love you for *him*" (24: 40). Mediating Maggie's love for her father, Amerigo occupies a doubly feminized position, but James screens off the full homosexual implications of his relation to Adam by emphasizing Amerigo's *performance* of this role under Maggie's direction. He thereby covers homoerotic with filial heterosexual desire.

Here, as elsewhere, Maggie works to ensure Amerigo's retention of masculine prerogatives and power even as she employs his gentled manhood for her own uses. Ironically, in fact, Maggie empowers herself within a heterosexual, marital economy precisely to the extent that she apparently cedes sexual power to Amerigo. When she feels herself "in his exerted grasp," she lies at the same time "in the grasp of her conceived responsibility," and "of the two intensities the second was presently to become the sharper" (24: 56). Amerigo can be "so munificent a lover," she recognizes, at the same time that his munificence "was precisely a part of the character she had never ceased to regard in him as princely" (24: 56–57). She calculates her own role and pose, trusting to Amerigo's quick apprehension of the complementary role and pose—the complementary manhood—her desire constructs for him. "She should have but to lay her head back on his shoulder with a certain movement," she understands, "to make it definite for him that she didn't resist" (24: 57). In fact, however, for one of the few times in the novel, Amerigo resists the role that Maggie inscribes, refusing to speak the lines she prompts him to say. Although "touch by touch she thus dropped into her husband's silence the truth about his good nature and his good manners," he does not speak the "five words" (an invitation to be together, just the two of them) that "would utterly break her down" (24: 59–60).

In resisting his part as aggressively heterosexual male, Amerigo preserves a certain integrity even as he jeopardizes it by opening himself to the implications of Maggie's alternative plan. For in refusing to utter the words that would "break her down" and thereby empower himself in a stereotypically aggressive and brutal male role, Amerigo leaves himself little choice but to substitute for Charlotte with Adam. If he won't go off with Maggie, he will have to go off with Adam—indeed, according to Maggie's project, escape with Adam from their domestic confinement "like a shot." As Maggie tells him, "for the question of going off somewhere, he'd go readily, quite delightedly, with you" (24: 61). While this projected realignment of the couples along same-sex lines exemplifies a carnivalesque and transgendered spirit in the novel—the swapping of positions that James has such fun testing in his strict relational economy—the planned excursion, as well as the female-to-female relationship it would leave behind, seems to founder because both Maggie and Adam need to keep up the pretense that they and their spouses "perfectly rub on together" (24: 89). In this case, then, the normalizing pressure of heterosexual marriage, in Seltzer's term, seems to operate effectively to prevent "other," deviant sexualities or subjectivities from emerging. In fact, heterosexual marriage effectively covers "other" relationships, enabling Amerigo to "rub on" with Adam without jeopardizing his subject position within a heterosexual matrix of desires.

Amerigo's male subjectivity, of course, is sufficiently threatened with instability within that heterosexual matrix. In his analysis of late nineteenth and early twentieth-century New York culture, George Chauncey notes that the "relationship between men and 'fairies' was represented symbolically as a male-female relationship," because "gender behavior rather than homosexual behavior per se was the primary determinant of a man's classification as a fairy." More specifically, Chauncey points out, as long as men "maintained a masculine demeanor and played (or claimed to play) only the 'masculine,' or insertive role in the sexual encounter—so long, that is, as they eschewed the style of the fairy and did not allow their bodies to be sexually penetrated—neither they, the fairies, nor the working-class public considered *them* to be queer" (66). Chauncey's model may illuminate Prince Amerigo's predicament. While *The Golden Bowl* seems to work toward Adam Verver's masculine reempowerment, at least at second or third hand, it seems to work toward Amerigo's emasculation—or immasculation under the sign of the feminine. In his case, as in Adam Verver's, James seems to close off possibilities for plural masculine performances. Both male characters, furthermore, occupy their final positions largely through a woman's agency. If they are not exactly positioned *in* the feminine, they are positioned *by* the feminine. Adam may figure as the capitalist patriarch, in Mimi Kairschner's term, but Maggie plays the role of "fore-woman," whose job is to train and get the work out of Prince Amerigo. As I noted at the beginning of this chapter, James describes Amerigo as "straitened and tied" under the spotlight of Maggie's insistent gaze. His "discomfort" yearns at Maggie "out of his eyes," and so deeply does he feel the suspense into which his manhood has been cast that he seems to move back from his felt condition "as from an open chasm" (24: 192). James represents him as "writhing in his pain," the pain, among other things, of gender inversion—of being, "like his wife, an abjectly simple person" (24: 193). Chauncey's paradigm, like James's, emphasizes the pose or performance associated with maintaining a "masculine" identity. Adam's ability to perform the masculine—it is tempting to say, his ability to "stick it to" Amerigo—seems indisputable, despite his cuckolding by his son-in-law. Amerigo's hold on a masculine position seems much shakier, but James's ingenuity is to rehabilitate Amerigo's masculinity through Maggie's powerful performance of an even more "abject" role as abused wife.

Although Joseph Allen Boone claims that Maggie's marriage to Amerigo is "left suspended, open to question, at text's end" (189), it seems difficult to argue convincingly that the two characters' gender identities end in a state of suspense. Boone posits a second story parallel to Maggie's in which Amerigo and his perspective "refuse assimilation into one univocal pattern" (194), but that second story—presumably a manly male narrative of prolific and transgressive love-making—seems more theoretical than real. At the end of the penultimate chapter, for example, Maggie confronts the Prince's "irresistible, overcharged" presence (24: 351), and like Isabel Archer faced with Caspar Goodwood's "hard manhood," she finally gets herself "off" from the threat (24: 353)—without, however, being subjected to any "white lightning" kiss. The scene certainly tests the proposition that Amerigo retains his power, in Boone's terms, to write his own role and story by writing over the character and plot Maggie has inscribed. Approaching her as she prepares to leave, with her hand on the door knob, Amerigo seems reempowered in the masculine role of "lady-killer" he had played at the beginning of the novel, and he seems to override Maggie's own intentions, leaving her only the "endless power of surrender"—suggestively, the power to yield "inch by inch." Maggie "couldn't for her life with the other hand have pushed him away," James notes (24: 352). Like Goodwood, moreover, Amerigo enforces his authority with his body, which he converts into a kind of weapon more like Gilbert Osmond's sheathed sword, however, than Goodwood's "white lightning" kissing ability. In both cases, however, James registers male phallicism through a female subject position. "He was so near now that she could touch him, taste him, smell him, kiss him, hold him," James notes; "he almost pressed upon her, and the warmth of his face—frowning, smiling, she mightn't know which; only beautiful and strange—was bent upon her with the largeness with which objects loom in dreams" (24: 352). Maggie does finally resist Amerigo's power, as well as her own desire. She puts out her hand, which he holds, and like a policewoman instructs him to "wait" (24: 352). Perhaps Maggie only temporizes, postponing the real confrontation over sexual mastery, but she effectively wins this battle with herself and with her husband in the terms I have already suggested—simultaneously appreciating and controlling his powerful masculine performance and, by leaving him his "reserve," enforcing a spermatic economy. Amerigo's hand may be over her "cast" of the dice in the final scene of the novel, but it seems to me that Maggie remains the one who hires and "commissions" that hand to work.[12] With his hands on her shoulders, his "whole act enclosing her," he plays the part she has written for him—seeing only her, dedicating his complete manhood to her alone, specularly causing feelings of "pity and dread," and therefore enabling her safely to bury her face in his breast (24: 369). She can have her "dread" and eat it, too.

At best, it seems to me, James has established a state of uneasy tension in Amerigo's case between being and performance. By that I mean that the Prince reemerges as a "congruous whole"—a complete man—largely because his performance of that part fulfills the job description under which he was hired in the beginning. The challenge James has set himself involves finding a place within a masculine discourse in which Amerigo can remain a male subject—a way to leave Amerigo's masculinity intact, to leave him not one inch less a man, while simultaneously harnessing and directing his masculine power.

Although Maggie wonders if Amerigo has "recovered himself" and retains "any thought of wounding her" in order to "re-establish a violated order" (24: 220), the Prince appears to have settled himself into the role she has written for him—a male masochist under the aegis of female authority rather than the arguably sadistic "lady-killer" of his earlier incarnation. He received the crisis from her, James notes, "as he might have received a bunch of keys or a list of commissions—attentive to her instructions about them, but only putting them for the time very carefully and safely into his pocket" (24: 219). Earlier, James had represented Adam's acquisitiveness and collecting power as a little glass "receptacle" that he "always carried in his pocket," and he had termed Amerigo's male identity a "shining star" he could transfer to his pocket and "finger" a good deal "out of sight." In returning to such a "pocket" metaphor of male power at the end of the novel, James emphasizes the change that has occurred in Amerigo's sense of himself—the extent to which he now experiences his manhood at secondhand, as a performance that Maggie "commissions."[13] The phallic woman in effect gives or lends the phallus to her husband, enabling him to reconstruct himself according to her "instructions"—to police himself, in Seltzer's terms (*Henry James* 61), by dedicating his manhood to her. Indeed, as she penetrates the depths of Amerigo's eyes, Maggie discovers, or perhaps only projects, the "tacitly-offered sketch of a working arrangement." "Leave me my reserve; don't question it—it's all I have just now," she imagines Amerigo pleading; "if you'll make me the concession of letting me alone with it for as long a time as I require I promise you something or other, grown under cover of it, even though I don't yet make out what, as a return for your patience" (24: 221). Like a debtor pleading for more time to the loan shark's collector, Amerigo effectively begs for his manhood—for the chance, under Maggie's supervisory eye, to "grow" a little "something or other" under the protective "cover" she and their marriage provide. There was "but one way," James writes, "in which a proud man reduced to abjection could hold himself" (24: 228), and to underwrite that "one way," to "make sure of the beauty shining out of the humility and of the humility lurking in all the pride of his presence," Maggie "would have gone the length of paying more yet, paying with difficulties and anxieties compared to which those actually before her might have been as superficial as headaches on rainy days" (24: 228–29). If Charlotte ends up with a silken halter around her neck, Amerigo ends up, at least to Maggie's perception, "caged" and even more under her control than Charlotte is under Adam's—the difference being that Amerigo appears caged "by his own act and his own choice" (24: 338). In assuming such a docile position within the sado-masochistic sexual economy James has established, Amerigo has put the whip and the chair, as well as the third hand of his invisible, or "pocketed," manhood, in Maggie's hand. James thus leaves Amerigo holding himself in the only way an abject male can—by holding Maggie's hand (24: 352, 367) and, as James archly puts it (echoing his comments about his own writing), "leaving the thing behind him, held as in her clasping arms" (24: 359).

Notes

Introduction: Henry James and the Plural Terms of Masculinity

1. Viewed in the terms created by Gilbert and Gubar's emphasis on sexual warfare, Henry James figures as one of many male writers for whom "the rise of the female imagination was a central problem" (156) and one of the many who felt their masculinity to be "embattled" and threatened in an increasingly "feminized" age. The result, in their view, is a masculine backlash, and they emphasize the "virulence with which many of these writers struck out against the women whom they saw as both the sources and the witnesses of their emasculation" (36).

2. "Especially in light of a father whom Henry Jr. sees as effeminated as well as lethal, and in the context of a culture where negation is traditionally gendered [in the feminine], the small boy [James] quite inevitably sees himself not only as an orphan but also as a woman" ("Feminine Orphan" 22–23).

3. David McWhirter cites James's identification with girls in order to launch his provocative analysis of James's masochism. Using Freud's essays "On Moral Masochism" and "A Child Being Beaten," he explains how James repeatedly places himself in an abject, female relation to his brother William, but he also demonstrates how James paradoxically stages and restages a scene of being wounded in order to authorize his writing (476). As McWhirter concludes, "it is precisely this reauthorized 'Master' who emerges from James's masochistic restaging of the hurt" (478).

4. In this respect I agree with Eve Sedgwick, who complains that "Silverman's readiness to hear how very openly sexy James's prefaces are is made possible only by her strange insistence that he couldn't have *known* they were." To the contrary, Sedgwick argues, "When we tune in to James's language on these frequencies, it is not as superior, privileged eavesdroppers on a sexual narrative hidden from himself; rather, it is as an audience offered the privilege of sharing in his exhibitionistic enjoyment and performance of a sexuality organized around shame. Indeed, it is as an audience desired to do so—which is also happily to say, as an audience desired" ("Shame and Performativity" 229).

5. According to Butler's interpretation of Foucault's "model of emancipatory sexual politics, the overthrow of 'sex' results in the release of a primary sexual multiplicity, a notion not so far afield from the psychoanalytic postulation of primary polymorphousness or Marcuse's notion of an original and creative bisexual Eros subsequently repressed by an instrumentalist culture" (96). Foucault seems to be arguing the opposite—"that there is no 'sex' in itself which is not produced by complex interactions of discourse and power"—and Butler finds him contradictory on the question (97). Focusing on literary representations of gender and sexual identity adds an additional layer of discourse between the "text" of gender and sexuality and whatever precedes their representation.

6. Christopher Lane offers a useful cautionary note about the "idea that sexuality has explanatory power," and he remains skeptical of studies that discover Jamesian homosexuality behind the "figures" in his writing's "carpet"—"questioning the rash suggestion that his complex aesthetic formulations are reducible to buried secrets" ("Jamesian Inscrutability" 246, 248). The "open secret" of James's work, he concludes, "is less a form of homoeroticism permitting or thwarting self-knowledge than a void—constitutive of subjectivity—that James augments into experiential difficulty, a beast we fight but can neither define nor control" (249).

7. Graham's intent is to explore James's participation in the "construction of homosexuality" at the turn of the century and to show how his "effeminacy anticipated the majority of late nineteenth-century medical, psychiatric, and legal representations of male homosexuals as psychical hermaphrodites" (9).

8. This extraordinary letters project, under the direction of general editors Peter Walker and Greg Zacharias, is being sponsored by the Center for Henry James Studies at Creighton University. James's letters, of which the editors have currently identified 10,269, will eventually be published by the University of Nebraska Press.

9. It is "objected that inversed sexuality is demoralising to the manhood of a nation," Symonds had written, "that it degrades the dignity of a man, and that it is incapable of moral elevation. Each of these points may be taken separately. They are all of them at once and together contradicted by the history of ancient Greece" *(Sexual Inversion* 177). Edmund Gosse had given James a copy of Symonds's 1891 essay, which James praised (Kaplan 402–3).

10. The erotic potential of James's figure would not be so obvious if we didn't recall one of William James's prescriptions for his brother's constipation. "Electricity *some*times has a wonderful effect, applied not in the piddling way you recollect last winter but by a strong galvanic current from the spine to the abdominal muscles, or if the rectum be paralysed one pole put inside the rectum" (Skrupskelis 113). Eve Sedgwick cites this passage as one of many examples of James's anal eroticism ("Inside" 132).

11. In his study of early twentieth-century American homosexual writing, James Gifford identifies six "models" of male homosexuality: natural, unnatural, domestic, alien, athletic, and aesthetic. He too argues that homosexual desire and gender characteristics float free of one another, even though several of his models (unnatural, alien, aesthetic) seem to reflect early homosexual stereotypes, while the others seem to contradict them. No single construct of homosexual manhood was "coherent or settled," Gifford argues. Gay literature was in a "state of flux. There was, in fact, no single gay literary construct; there were many" (2). Gifford places Henry James in the Domestic category: "James's graceful retreat into the pose of the sexless Victorian bachelor and the telltale fascination in his work with canny, observing, outsider bachelor/surrogates (the apotheosis of which type moves from Rowland Mallet to Lambert Strether) and failed heterosexual marriages suggest the Domestic homosexual" (30).

12. Robert K. Martin, for example, helpfully notes the "impossibility of drawing clear chronological lines in the nineteenth century between conceptions of male friendship. From the 1840s to the 1880s a range of possibilities existed that could run from boyhood 'chums' to an idealized comradeship of 'knights-errant' to an anguished and guilt-ridden projection of the self onto figures of Gothic evil. The very range of these possibilities may suggest the extent to which the categories that we now take for granted, such as an absolute split between homo- and heterosexual based on genital behavior, were nascent and fluid" ("Knights-Errant" 182).

13. James attributes a similar autogenetic power to Balzac: "Portraits shape themselves under his pen as if in obedience to an irresistible force.... The fertility of his imagination in this respect was something marvellous. When we think of the many hundred complete human creatures (he calls the number at least two thousand) which he set in motion, with their sharp differences, their histories, their money-matters, their allotted place in his great machine, we give up the attempt to gauge such a lusty energy of fancy" ("Honoré de Balzac" [1875] 53).

14. Cynthia Ozick has speculated, furthermore, that in presenting Hugh Merrow with such a problem, James "was pressing himself to decide his own sex." "If James did not go on with 'Hugh Merrow,'" she concludes, "it may be that it required him to resolve, once and for all, the enigma of his sexual identity" (54).

15. "'Sexual inversion' referred to a broad range of deviant gender behavior," George Chauncey points out, "of which homosexual desire was only a logical but indistinct aspect, while 'homosexuality' focused on the narrower issue of sexual object choice. The differentiation of homosexual desire from 'deviant' gender behavior at the turn of the century reflects a major reconceptualization of the nature of human sexuality, its relation to gender, and its role in one's social definition" (116).

16. Citing Judith Butler, Hugh Stevens posits a performative theory of James and sexuality. "For James there is no 'being' or 'essence' of sexuality which precedes the existence of sexuality," he asserts; "nor can sexuality be understood in terms of stable categories. Sexuality is rather a dynamic process, a performance, a story, a narrative, in which the unstable play of desire and identifications can erode the boundaries of the perceived self" (1).

17. Quotations from *The Ambassadors*, as from most of James's novels and short stories, are from the New York Edition and will be cited in the text by volume and page number. In a few cases, most notably *The American* and *The Portrait of a Lady*, I shall refer primarily to the first edition of each novel.

18. James commented similarly about Guy de Maupassant in an 1888 essay: "Nothing can exceed the masculine firmness, the quiet force of his own style, in which every phrase is a close sequence, every epithet a paying piece, and the ground is completely cleared of the vague, the ready-made and the second-best. Less than any one to-day does he beat the air; more than any one does he hit out from the shoulder" ("Guy de Maupassant" 534). Employing the language of business ("every epithet a paying piece," the ground cleared of the "ready-made") and even of boxing ("hit out from the shoulder"), James identifies his own writerly ideal with a hyperbolically configured male subjectivity.

19. Despite the criminalization of homosexuality in the 1880s and the linkage between homosexual activity and homosexual identity, identity remains difficult to infer from behavior—precisely the problem George Sand poses for James. George Chauncey observes, for example, that the "determinative criterion in the identification of men as fairies was not the extent of their same-sex desire or activity (their 'sexuality'), but rather the gender persona and status they assumed" (47). He notes, for example that "so long as they maintained a masculine demeanor and played (or claimed to play) only the 'masculine,' or insertive, role in the sexual encounter—so long, that is, as they eschewed the style of the fairy and did not allow their bodies to be sexually penetrated—neither they, the fairies, nor the working-class public considered *them* to be queer" (66). See also Jeffrey Weeks's important essay on male prostitution in England.

20. Eric Haralson argues that *The Ambassadors* "simultaneously reflects and confronts the power of the modern gender system, especially in its prescriptions and

expectations for masculine performance" ("Lambert Strether's Excellent Adventure" 172). Reginald Abbott has analyzed the "reversal of gender roles in the novel" (184), pointing out that the water and floating imagery associated with men, and especially with Strether, derives from nineteenth-century iconographies of idealized women (177–78).

21. Richard Henke notes the "dizzying array of male figures" in *The Ambassadors* and concludes that "as Waymarsh is contrasted with Strether who is contrasted with Chad who is contrasted with Little Bilham who is contrasted with Gloriani, gender remains in constant flux, undermining the possibility of resolving an ideal male identity" ("Embarrassment" 279).

22. Sarotte contends that Chad epitomizes the "virile male" for the "passive, timid" Strether. Citing Strether's attraction to Chad's "pagan" side, Sarotte considers him a "moral masochist" who indulges in a "masochist fantasy" (205) about the younger man.

23. In calling Waymarsh "big and black," James seems to encode him racially, thus emphasizing the variously transgressive potential of Strether's relationship with him. Later in the novel Miss Barrace compares Waymarsh to an Indian chief, suggesting that he functions as a kind of all-purpose American racial figure—what Strether calls a "majestic aboriginal" (NY 21: 206).

24. Later in the novel, just prior to Strether's first encounter with Chad, James includes a passage suggesting that the sexual tension between Strether and Waymarsh has not been put, so to speak, to bed: "He looked across the box at his friend; their eyes met; something queer and stiff, something that bore on the situation but that it was better not to touch, passed in silence between them" (21: 132).

25. In the scene at the London theater, Strether feels startled at how much more romantic even this first "date" with Maria Gostrey feels than his usual nights out with Mrs. Newsome. He notes the "pink lights," the "whiff of vague sweetness," the way the red velvet band around her throat enhances her smile and complexion and lips, teeth, and eyes, and especially Maria's "cut-down" dress (21: 50–51). He even toys with the idea of tracing the "ramifications" of the "effect of the ribbon from which Miss Gostrey's trinket depended" (21: 50)—in other words, of looking down her "cut-down" dress. Whatever desire and identification Strether may feel when he sees Chad, in this scene he feels obvious attraction to a woman. Indeed, he feels positioned between women.

Chapter 1. Configuring Male Desire and Identity in Roderick Hudson

1. Richard Henke de-emphasizes the "homoerotics of attraction" between Rowland and Roderick in favor of analyzing the "economy of masculine identification whereby one male must compensate for his fragmentary sense of identity through another" ("Embarrassment" 272).

2. Edel goes on to read the novel as a battle between James's two projected selves. In the end, he maintains, "James was sufficiently a Rowland to realize that he could never be a Roderick. Instead of acting out his passions he could invest his characters with them. In the novel the feeling self had to die. It was too great a threat to the rational self" (*Henry James* 170). Manfred Mackenzie also analyzes Roderick and Rowland as two halves of a single personality and considers their relationship a "compensatory one based upon a sense of insufficiency" on both their parts (59–60). In the process of impersonating one another, the two characters "deplete" as well as "complete" each other.

3. Richard Ellmann draws a different conclusion about homosexuality in *Roderick Hudson*, viewing the novel as James's "counterstatement" to both the aestheticism and homosexuality he found in Walter Pater's *Studies in the History of the Renaissance*. For Ellmann, James "took alarm" at Pater's covert celebration of homosexuality, and wishing to "inscribe himself as neither aesthetic nor homosexual," yet wanting to "portray homosexuals," he accomplished both purposes by "representing them [homosexuals] negatively under the guise of aesthetes" (211).

4. I disagree in this respect with Wendy Graham, who argues that even though "Rowland steadfastly maintains a distance from the means of production and from commercial institutions, he still thinks like a capitalist." "Malletian connoisseurship is a *refinement* of rank consumerism" (107).

5. Wendy Graham believes that James and Mallet fail in this effort, that Rowland "appropriates Roderick's capacity and work like a true capitalist" and "conceives of the younger man as an amanuensis or, more accurately, a prosthesis" (109). I take a more generous view of Rowland's character and of James's efforts to educate it, but I certainly agree with Graham in her pinpointing of the challenge James faces.

6. Although Schmitz devotes more attention to Mark Twain's *The Gilded Age* than to *Roderick Hudson*, he offers an insightful analysis of James's rejection of masculine egotism and the narcissistic "songs of myself" characteristic of Jacksonian America. The hyperbolic Jacksonian style, he argues, exists in James's fiction after *Roderick Hudson* "only as comic relief, as American bluster, American brag" (156).

7. This Whitmanesque male character type continued to appeal to James. George Flack in *The Reverberator* (1888), for example, boasts to Francie Dosson about his plans to improve the newspaper for which he works: "It's a big proposition as it stands, but I mean to make it bigger: the most universal society-paper the world has seen. That's where the future lies, and the man who sees it first is the man who'll make his pile" (NY 13: 62).

8. Gregory Woods offers a subtle and intriguing interpretation of the *Thirst* statuette by noting that "it is not quite his body that prevails in the statuette, but rather 'the perfection of an attitude.'" "It may even be," he suggests, "that, naked as he is, his very masculinity is attitudinal" (70).

9. Moon, 34–35. See also my essay, "Falling into Heterosexuality" (126–27).

10. Moon also cites Pater's essay on Winckelmann for its influence on James's formation of taste for viewing sculptures of male nudes (32–33).

11. Citing James's admission to Andersen that he had "struck up a tremendous intimacy with dear little Conte Alberto," who is the "first object that greets my eyes in the morning, and the last at night" (*Letters* 4: 113), Kaplan asserts that "Andersen's work stood in for Andersen himself, the part for the whole, a combination of phallic synecdoche and marital displacement" (448). Daniel Murtaugh shows that James's revisions of *Roderick Hudson* for the New York Edition "closely parallel in diction and intensity the erotically- charged and emotionally engaged language of his letters to the young men with whom he had fallen in love during the years shortly preceding the revision process" (184).

12. For a contrasting view of Striker and his role, see Craig Milliman, who argues that Striker "serves as a model by which Roderick, if he truly learned from all that he saw, might well have profited. As a self-made man, Striker realizes the importance of self-reliance, independence, and determination" ("The Fiction of Art" 232–33).

13. Nomi Sofer offers a different interpretation of this passage, citing Mary Garland's integral role in mediating the relationship between the two men and James's recognition that he is "writing within a specific social and literary tradi-

tion" in which "homosocial bonds between men always 'walk hand in hand' with heterosexual relationships on which patriarchal social structures are based" (187).

14. Gregory Woods insightfully observes that in this scene with Rowland, Roderick "is able to enjoy two aspects of desirable masculinity at once: the spiritual and the physical. And by unexpectedly combining them in a moment of aesthetic decisiveness, he is inspired with a vision of a new work of art, a representation of physicality so imposing as to transcend the mere body and attain a spiritual perfection which both the gondolier's chest and Rowland's intelligence can only point towards" (75).

15. Although many critics consider Christina a stereotypical femme fatale, William Veeder shows how James combines several popular character types in Christina's portrait, thus enabling him to suggest ambiguities in her character (*Henry James* 116).

16. As part of his case that Christina loves Rowland, Ronald Emerick argues that, in preventing Roderick's foolhardy gesture, Rowland fulfills Christina's dream of finding a strong man (360). It is more likely, I think, in view of Christina's request to be shown the way "out of this horrible place" (1: 266) that Rowland has simply revealed the fatuity of Roderick's gesture.

17. Although she focuses on James's World War I era writings, Susan M. Griffin examines how James uses wounds and scars to "represent, and sometimes substitute for, masculine interiority" (62).

18. See Susan Bordo, especially pp. 283–87, for a relevant discussion of the "homosexual gaze" and its power to strip "orthodox heterosexuality" of its "armor."

19. Christopher Lane has also briefly examined the role of homoerotic desire in *Roderick Hudson* and its effect upon the ending. Comparing that novel to the later *Tragic Muse* (1890), he explores the "complex erotic configuration" that governs character relations, while arguing that those relations and the desire that sponsors the same-sex relations exceed James's narrative ability to contain them. Although Lane mistakenly observes that Rowland marries Mary, he still makes the good point that the "heterosexual imperative" governing their relationship "marks and even scars the end of this novel," because it "seems to obscure Rowland's rivalry with Mary for Roderick" and because Rowland's "conventional (that is, 'homosocial') rivalry with Roderick for Mary only partly subsumes his 'homosexual' interest in the younger man" (747).

20. In a 1906 letter James praised Andersen's sculpture of two lovers embracing: "There is more flesh and *pulp* in it, more life of *surface* and of blood-flow *under* the surface, than you have hitherto, in your powerful simplifications, gone in for." James went on in extravagant terms to encourage Andersen to "keep at *that*—at the flesh and the devil and the rest of it; make the creatures palpitate, and their flesh tingle and flush, and their internal economy proceed, and their bellies ache and their bladders fill—all in the mystery of your art!" (*Henry James Amato Ragazzo* 154).

21. Since my interest in this study is in male characters, I have not examined the important relationship between Christina Light and Mary Garland. Infrequent though their meetings are, each of them can be considered something of a female "model of grandeur" for the other. Christina's break with the Prince results from her meeting with Mary, from her awareness that Mary would "never marry Gennaro" and from her hating the idea of "being worse than she" (1: 405). Similarly, Mary's rather surprising openness to Roman culture can be attributed at least in part to a desire to model herself after European women, such as Christina.

Chapter 2. Nursing the Thunderbolt of Manhood in The American

1. James's anxieties as an author echo his anxieties as a man. Retrospectively in *A Small Boy and Others* he recalls: "Not to have been immediately launched in business of a rigorous sort was to *be* exposed—in the absence I mean of some fairly abnormal predisposition to virtue; since it was a world so simply constituted that whatever wasn't business, or exactly an office or a 'store,' places in which people sat close and made money, was just simply pleasure, sought, and sought only, in places in which people got tipsy" (*Autobiography* 30).

2. Reading a review of André Chevrillon's *La Vie Américaine* inspired James to "do something more with the American character. Another man—not a Newman, but more completely civilized, large, rich, complete, but strongly characterised, but essentially a *product*" (*Complete Notebooks* 70). The result was Adam Verver in *The Golden Bowl.*

3. Martha Banta, in fact, examines Newman as a case of post-Civil-War Traumatic Stress Syndrome by connecting comments James made in both *Notes of a Son and Brother* and *The American Scene* about emasculation during the Civil War and Newman's vengefulness toward the Bellegardes. Once Newman, "the hard-edged man of the North, experiences defeat," she says, "he finds himself emotionally emasculated like the defanged lion of James's *The American Scene*; like the young Virginian, he is made capable of murderous acts by the rancors in his heart" (360).

4. Unless otherwise noted, references to *The American* are to the first English edition (1879).

5. Lewis O. Saum argues that "almost relentlessly, James calls attention to Newman's identification with the West" (2), and he even notes his "half-horse-half-alligator antics" in the novel (3).

6. Mark Seltzer uses the phrase "physical capital" to launch his argument that *The American*, like other realistic novels, interrogates the "status of subjects" and the "status of material things" (132) and illustrates a pervasive uncertainty about distinctions between subjects and objects. What *The American* reveals, he argues, "is the way in which the Jamesian values of freedom and autonomy (the values of romance) forward and are forwarded by the very (novelistic) economizing of relations they seem to oppose" (145).

7. For a contrasting and very negative view of Newman, see K. G. Probert, who emphasizes Newman's acquisitive character, his "simplistic, manipulative romancing imagination" (207), his "dangerous" tendency to conform people to "preconceived patterns" (209), his "absolutist sensibility" (212) and "aesthetic vampirism" (214). See also Cheryl B. Torsney, who argues that at the "heart" of *The American* is Newman's imperial "narrative of himself as a successful American translator with a birthright to raid the resources and markets of the Old World in his desire to extend his empire of self" ("Translation" 41).

8. In *The Daughter's Seduction* Jane Gallop characterizes Jacques Lacan as a "Ladies' Man," or at least as a man who performs the "Ladies' Man." Lacan "derives a phallic enjoyment from his lectures," she observes, "where everyone adoringly takes down his every word as if it were The Word, the Logos which has a phallic fullness, self-sufficiency." At the same time, Lacan "would talk from the audience, 'with the women,' in an attempt to get at the other enjoyment, that which responds to the phallic" (34). As he switches Christopher Newman's subject positions, James tries to move him away from the phallic order, to make him a "ladies' man" not merely so he can enjoy himself from a lady's point of view, but so he can experience "other" pleasures. As we shall see, however, Newman does

not stray far from the subject position from which he can experience, if not enjoy, a "phallic fullness."

9. Porter astutely observes that the "pose" in which Newman first "comes into view for us as readers" identifies him not only with "'weak-kneed lovers of the fine arts' but also with what those arts themselves would have displayed as a feminine pose. A man looking at a painting of a woman, Newman is simultaneously a man posed as a woman" (123–24).

10. As an American male who can no longer claim to be his "own master" (48) because he has surrendered authority and responsibility to his wife, the expatriated Tom Tristram serves a cautionary function for Newman. A "loafer" who lives off his wife's money (54) while she despises him for it (62), Tristram is "shamefully idle, spiritless, sensual, snobbish" (65)—"a very light weight" (65), in Newman's own terms.

11. Robert K. Martin's analysis of *Moby-Dick* and Melville's other sea novels can prove useful here. By eliminating women from these novels, Martin claims, Melville "can focus on the conflict between two erotic forces: a democratic eros strikingly similar to that of Whitman, finding its highest expression in male friendship and manifested in a masturbatory sexuality reflecting the celebration of a generalized seminal power not directed toward control or production; and a hierarchical eros expressed in social forms of male power as different as whaling, factory-owning, military conquest, and heterosexual marriage as it was largely practiced in the nineteenth century, all of which indicate the transformation of primal, unformed (oceanic) sexuality into a world of pure copulation" (*Hero, Captain* 4).

12. In John Carlos Rowe's Freudian reading of the novel, Newman tends to repress unpleasant things (such as Benjamin Babcock's criticism) and especially refuses to recognize himself in others ("The Politics of the Uncanny" 86). For example, he does not recognize how Valentin's duel with M. Kapp doubles his own "duel" with the Bellegardes, nor does he recognize how his own possessive attitude toward Claire doubles her family's.

13. Nomi Sofer emphasizes the positive aspects of Newman's offer to Valentin: "The older man is offering his prospective brother-in-law a different kind of homosocial relationship, one in which male bonds of desire and power are solidified through the exchange of male intelligence and affection, not female bodies. In a sense, Newman is offering himself to Valentin in place of Noémie Nioche as the object of exchange in a transaction that will solidify the bonds of desire between the two men, while circumventing the requirement of heterosexuality" (201).

14. Martha Banta argues that the "new man (Newman) and the old man (Urbain), the democrat and the autocrat, are in outward contention. These two types are also in conflict within Newman himself, a duality that prevents him from being at peace until he can come to terms with each of these categorical forms" (364).

15. Although Lee Clark Mitchell approaches *The American* in very different terms, he sees a similar change in Newman's character: "the novel can be seen as a gradual progression in Newman himself, who turns from a relatively open, flexible reading of experience to an increasingly rigid one. The transition is represented best, moreover, in terms not of his actions but of his language, in the shift away from a preference for oxymorons toward sharp binary oppositions" (14).

16. In planning the play, James commented, Newman will still do the "characteristically magnanimous thing—the characteristically good-natured thing"—and let the Bellegardes off—"but get his wife" (*Complete Notebooks* 53).

17. Robert Secor emphasizes the negative turn Newman's character takes over the last part of the novel. "In his compulsion to revenge and the exhilaration he feels at its prospect . . . Newman's psychology enters the disturbed passages of

Poe's sadistic narrators" (149). Secor compares Newman to Montresor and even to Hawthorne's Chillingworth (149).

18. Characterizing Newman as a "modern-day Orlando Furioso reborn from the wild-man of the forests into a man who has no harm in him," Banta asks the right questions about what it means for Newman to be "himself" again. "Is he *new*—different from what he has ever been," she wonders, "or simply restored to what he had been? Which man gains ascendancy on the book's final page: the man who finds his greatest pleasure in comfort or the man who takes pleasure in pain—his own and others?" (371). Banta goes on to argue that the different endings to the 1877 and 1907 editions of *The American* enable James to have it both ways.

Chapter 3. Sheathing the Sword of Gentle Manhood in The Portrait of a Lady

1. See also Veeder's essay, "The Portrait of a Lack," in which he observes, "That emasculate men inhabit the condition of the feminine is confirmed in the opening description of the tea drinkers" (106). In a very insightful recent essay Dana Luciano takes issue with Veeder's simplification of the "novel's proliferation of erotic and affective possibilities" (205), and she offers a compelling interpretation of Ralph Touchett's character as an example, not of failed manhood, but of the "third sex" model of sexual deviance. Unless otherwise noted, references to *The Portrait of a Lady* are to the 1881 edition.

2. In Robert K. Martin's terms the novel "juxtaposes a social world in which heterosexuality is the norm with a set of characters who have failed to live up to that norm, and the failed relationships are situated in a world increasingly questioning gender and sexuality" ("Failed Heterosexuality" 87). David Lubin notes additional gender inversion in *The Portrait of a Lady*—Henrietta Stackpole, Ralph Touchett, and even Caspar Goodwood, who "plays the more traditionally woman's role of waiting years for a desired marriage partner to have done with adventuring about and settle down into a domestic arrangement" (148). Provocatively identifying James himself with Henrietta Stackpole, Elise Miller calls Henrietta a "James in woman's clothing" who "crosses sexual boundaries and functions as a marriage of both sexes" (25).

3. As James Eli Adams notes, "Increasingly, middle-class professionals (including male writers) legitimated their masculinity by identifying it with that of the gentleman" (6). The gentleman was "compatible with a masculinity understood as a strenuous psychic regimen, which could be affirmed outside the economic arena, but nonetheless would be embodied as a charismatic self-mastery akin to that of the daring yet disciplined entrepreneur" (7). James, I think, diversifies the meaning of the term "gentleman" in *The Portrait of a Lady*, but he is no less interested in discovering an alternative masculinity in gentle manhood.

4. Alfred Habegger discovers Ralph's origin in James's homoeroticism and conflicted relationship to his father and brother: "This strange man, who bears a special nonerotic love for [Isabel] and dies slowly from a lingering illness during the four years the novel covers, surely reflects in some devious way the author's own private state" (*Henry James* 166–67). Dana Luciano points out that almost all readings of Ralph derive from "heteronormative" assumptions about his interest in Isabel, and in arguing that Ralph offers a "third-sex" alternative to prevailing gender and sexual norms, she observes that Ralph "refuses to choose between identification [with Isabel] and desire [for her] and thus moves in a different direction than heteronormative desire" (204).

5. In citing this same passage, Luciano notes that Ralph's "recuperation itself

becomes split": "The convalescing Ralph is not quite himself, but only seems able to become himself again—to become—that is, that earlier self, a well-educated and wealthy young man who hasn't actually done much of anything yet" (203).

6. Jonathan Freedman considers Ralph to be infected by Osmond's virulent brand of aestheticism: "Despite his own desire to do otherwise, Ralph is forced by the very structure of his perception to reify and then aestheticize Isabel, to treat her with the detached but appreciative vision of the discerning connoisseur" (154). Luciano, on the other hand, reads Ralph's "scopophilic" tendencies more positively—as an "erotics of survival" (207).

7. James stages a similar scene in his first novel, *Watch and Ward* (1871), as Roger Lawrence's young ward, Nora, asks to use his watch-key. When Lawrence's key "proved a complete misfit," she has "recourse" to his cousin Hubert's. "It hung on the watch-chain which depended from his waistcoat," James archly observes, "and some rather intimate fumbling was needed to adjust it to Nora's diminutive timepiece" (109). See Henke ("Embarrassment" 265–72) for a provocative analysis of *Watch and Ward*, including this passage.

8. Stephanie Smith offers an especially provocative perspective on Ralph's (and James's) homosocial bond with Osmond. Using Sedgwick's "bachelor taxonomy," she sees both characters as "bound together by their concern with Isabel," who is "between" and thus joins them. "In effect, Isabel separates and connects the two men. There is a wedge of hatred between Gilbert Osmond and Ralph Touchett, yet their opposition, projected onto Isabel, glues them together, Janus-faced. She is their common desire; they both want possession of her" (602).

9. In a well-known passage James makes clear the market economy in which Osmond appreciates Isabel's potential marital value. When he realizes that Isabel has rejected Lord Warburton's suit, Osmond "perceived a new attraction in the idea of taking to himself a young lady who had qualified herself to figure in his collection of choice objects by rejecting the splendid offer of a British aristocrat" (311). Robert White notes that Osmond's "phallic personality" becomes increasingly apparent as the novel goes along (68).

10. Versions of the Carlylean hero, the dandy and professional men prove successful, Adams argues, by virtue of a "charismatic authority that would displace the influence of wealth and inherited rank" (192). "Like the Paterian aesthete, the professional defines himself through the possession of a knowledge or talent in some degree arcane, the value of which depends not on the market, but on the professional's power of persuasion, which tends to be charismatic" (193).

11. William Veeder provides the best and most extensive analysis of Osmond and his literary roots in eighteenth- and nineteenth-century poetry and fiction. Veeder perceptively anatomizes Osmond's appearance—his face, physique, hair, and eyes—to illustrate his affinity with the Byronic male (*Henry James* 125–27), as well as with Satan (130) and other "abyss-bound villains" (131). Veeder also notes Osmond's "fundamental dualism of temperament"—"prone both to violence and to lethargy" (128)—and he links Osmond with two nineteenth-century male types, the Dandy and the Paterfamilias, while claiming that Osmond is the "most subversive Dandy in English literature because he calls into question social morality itself" (145).

12. During her fireside vigil in chapter 42 Isabel reflects that the "finest individual she had ever known was hers; the simple knowledge was a sort of act of devotion" (442). In revising the novel for the New York Edition, James placed more emphasis on Osmond's attractive manliness. Isabel thinks that the "finest—in the sense of being the subtlest—manly organism she had ever known had become her property, and the recognition of her having but to put out her hands and take it

had been originally a sort of act of devotion" (4: 194). James obviously makes Isabel and her attraction to Osmond much more physical in revision.

13. William Veeder interprets Warburton's hunting whip as proof that, despite his "liberated views, his treatment of women indicates how much the proprietary instinct endures in great radicals of the upper class" (*Henry James* 149).

14. Although neither implicates Goodwood, both Alfred Habegger and William Veeder stress triangulation in Isabel's marriage to Osmond as it affects James's own gender identity or sexual orientation. Habegger examines James's identification with Minnie Temple as part of a family romance that included Henry James Sr. and William James. "Deeply 'feminine,'" Habegger argues, "James projected himself onto his strong cousin, as onto certain heroines of fiction, but simultaneously remained in thrall to William and Henry James, Sr., two extremely vigorous and forceful men who not only insisted on reactionary views of female emancipation but specifically disapproved of Minnie's self-assertiveness" (*Henry James* 170). In Isabel's marriage, and especially in her return to Osmond at the end of the novel, Habegger says that James betrayed his cousin Minnie "in order to make her—and himself—acceptable to the patriarchy [William and Henry Sr.]" (170). Veeder, on the other hand, identifies Osmond with William James and reads the novel, particularly Isabel's marriage, as an effort on James's part to "indulge" his "homoerotic love for William" ("Feminine Orphan" 32). James was traumatized by William's own marriage in 1878, and his depiction of Osmond represents an attempt to triumph over that trauma. "As the woman scorned by William, Henry expresses through Isabel a double triumph. Her marriage with Osmond is the realization of Henry's courtship of William, while the public revelation of Osmond's marital failure constitutes Henry's revenge upon the one who had failed him by marrying another" (35).

15. Joseph Wiesenfarth, however, argues that Isabel's deathbed scene with Ralph is subtly erotic and the "greatest love scene" in the novel, a "spiritual version of the erotic maxim *post coitus tristis*—Ralph's death is mourned immediately afterwards—without any coitus," and he concludes that Ralph's adoration "ravishes" Isabel's soul (24).

16. Sara Stambaugh, like Richard Ellmann (215), argues that James based Osmond on Oscar Wilde in order to satirize the Aesthetic Movement. In her view Ralph and Osmond represent "opposing types, one an aesthete who truly appreciates the beautiful, and the other a sham bent on giving an aesthetic impression" (501). Osmond "reflects the qualities of aestheticism that James had particularly come to despise by 1880" (507).

17. William Veeder offers the most extended list of characters in *The Portrait of a Lady* with whom James identifies: Daniel and Lydia Touchett, Pansy, Osmond, as well as Ralph and Isabel ("Portrait" 104–5).

Chapter 4. Reconstructing Masculinity in The Bostonians

1. Franchot argues that "the scene outlines bitterly conflicted racial and gender identifications. If the masculine is vitiated by its identification with the white slaveholder, so is blackness contaminated by its identification with the exposed and degraded woman. To achieve 'manhood,' then, is to forsake not only the mother but her race, whereas to achieve 'blackness' is to forsake the father and his virility" (142).

2. Nina Silber has brilliantly examined many journalistic and popular culture accounts of Jefferson Davis's ignominious capture and has concluded that

"Dozens of songs, poems, cartoons, and newspaper accounts presented Davis in any and every form of womanly attire, as a feminized and feckless figure who, in his ignoble flight, affirmed the Southern system's violation of appropriate gender standards" (615).

3. Huck's cross-dressing, on the other hand, seems designed to fail, freeing him, after Judith Loftus proves that he does a girl "tolerable poor" (74), to perform various male identities through the rest of the novel. In *Pudd'nhead Wilson* (1894) Tom Driscoll (born black but switched at birth with a white baby) gets a measure of revenge for Jim and other cross-dressed black males when he dons a suit of girl's clothes, blackens his face with cork, and then stabs his white uncle, Judge Driscoll, to death (93–94).

4. Although he does not devote much attention to Ransom, David Van Leer considers him the "most sexually transgressive character in the book," and he notes that the "Southern male is always a feminised figure to Northern sensibilities" (108).

5. James subtly links Verena and her parents to race relations and abolitionism. Her mother, James notes, had once "kept a runaway slave in her house for thirty days" when Verena was a child, "but hadn't it thrown a kind of rainbow over her cradle, and wouldn't she naturally have some gift?" (60).

6. As Jonathan Dollimore points out, "by the time of Wilde, homosexuality could be regarded as rooted in a person's identity and as pathologically pervading all aspects of his being" (67). And in Ed Cohen's terms, "by the time of his conviction, not only had Wilde been confirmed as *the* sexual deviant for the late nineteenth century, but he had become the paradigmatic example for an emerging public definition of a new 'type' of male sexual actor: 'the homosexual'" (1–2).

7. Edel makes no connection between *The Bostonians* and the homosexuality and homophobia that lurks behind "The Author of Beltraffio," although he does compare the triangulated struggles in the two works in other terms—biographical terms in which James feels identified with a "powerful mother" (Olive) and at the same time with the "image of his maimed father" (Selah Tarrant) (*Henry James* 313).

8. Although he does not pursue the point, David Kramer observes that "Selah-as-angst becomes a site first of feminization, then of a homophobic version of homosexuality" (143).

9. James blurs the differences between Basil Ransom and Olive Chancellor by triangulating each with Selah and Verena. Like Ransom, Olive feels pain at the "idea" that Selah "laid his hands on" Verena to "make her speak," and like Ransom, she imagines herself taking Selah's place, mounting the platform with Verena and laying her own hands "upon her head" (133).

10. In Henry Burrage, James comes closest to depicting a truly closeted male character who seems motivated by "heterosexual compulsion" or "compulsory heterosexuality" (Sedgwick, *Epistemology* 196, 212). Burrage, James observes, is "weakly pretentious, softly original, cultivated eccentricity, patronized progress, liked to have mysteries, sudden appointments to keep, anonymous persons to visit, the air of leading a double life, of being devoted to a girl whom people didn't know, or at least didn't meet" (180). Olive theorizes, in fact, that Burrage "proposed to almost any girl who was not likely to accept him" because he was "making a collection of such episodes" (181).

11. In Dr. Mary Prance, James creates a character who resists gender classification. Although she "looked like a boy, and not even like a good boy," he also comments that "if she had been a boy she would have borne some relation to a girl, whereas Doctor Prance appeared to bear none whatever" (67). For an ingenious

examination of imperiled gender differences in *The Bostonians*, see Ian F. A. Bell. "As neither male nor indeed female, nor permitting that dissociation," Bell argues, Dr. Prance "resists standard gender-based appropriations, encouraging us to revise these absolutist categories" (37). I certainly agree, although I find such gender revisions more pervasive in the novel.

12. The "phallic critics" Fetterley cites include Charles R. Anderson, Lionel Trilling, Louis Auchincloss, and Charles T. Samuels. Anderson considers Ransom the "embodiment of the sentiment of sex, in love with the heroine Verena and determined to snatch her from the clutches" of Olive and "incipient Lesbianism" (310). Trilling calls Ransom the "only man in Boston" and the "only man in the book" (114), while Auchincloss figures the conflict in the novel as "Ransom against Boston, a real man against a city of paper men," and argues that Verena simply feels paralyzed when she meets a "real man, a warrior who has killed other men in combat and who desires her" (78). Regarding Ransom's speech about the generation being "womanized," Samuels argues, "In a novel full of 'hysterical, chattering, canting' ladies, whose other males are an androgynous prattler, a quack confidence man, and a young beau who needs his mother to propose marriage, who can doubt that these sentiments are James's?" (104).

13. Even though she finds *The Bostonians* more univocally masculinist and phallocentric than I do, Kahane points out that gender differences themselves are embattled in the novel. A "more hysterically charged issue" than the battle of the sexes, she maintains, "is the imperiled future of sexual desire and the difference on which it is based, which James saw as threatened by the woman's movement" (288–89).

14. Olive Chancellor's militant feminist rhetoric interpolates a similar bipolar extremism. Women "were her sisters, they were her own," she thinks, "and the day of their delivery had dawned. This was the only sacred cause; this was the great, the just revolution. It must triumph, it must sweep everything before it; it must exact from the other, the brutal, blood-stained, ravening race, the last particle of expiation" (64). In considering woman's rights the "only sacred cause," Olive eclipses even as she interpolates racist discourse (e.g., characterizing men as the "brutal, blood-stained, ravening race").

15. Taylor notes that the Cavalier "came to be looked upon as the characteristic expression of life in the South. Meanwhile, the acquisitive man, the man on the make, became inseparably associated with the North and especially with New England. . . . By 1850 these two types—the Cavalier and the Yankee—expressed in the popular imagination the basic cultural conflict which people felt had grown up between a decorous, agrarian South and the rootless, shifting, money-minded North" (335).

16. Silverman discusses those historical moments when the penis is not equivalent to the phallus—that is, when individual male power cannot participate in the preponderant phallic authority of the culture at large. "There is ultimately no affirmation more central to our present symbolic order," she writes, "yet at the same time more precariously maintained, than the fiction that the exemplary male subject is adequate to the paternal function" (135–36).

17. Judith Wilt attributes a "masculinist instinct" to James and argues that he "means us to feel that Verena 'consented' [to Ransom's proposal] partly because of a profound female erotic attraction 'pressed' by its male object. Her 'fall' into her sexuality is at one level as irrational, as miraculous, as is Basil's rise into his gender out of his 'womanizing' failures, and is surrounded like his rise with qualities that only highlight the miracle" (308–9).

18. Citing Ransom's comparison of his feelings as he waits in the Music Hall to

those of a "young man" who "has made up his mind, for reasons of his own, to discharge a pistol at the king or the president" (414), Joseph Litvak compares Ransom to John Wilkes Booth (227).

19. James complicates Ransom's subject position even further through the word "palpitate" by using it in another scene of desire. After Verena has moved in with Olive at the end of Book One, Olive pours forth her views of women's oppression to her "listening and responsive friend." She "presented them again and again," James observes, "and there was no light in which they did not palpitate with truth. Verena was immensely wrought upon; a subtle fire passed into her" (192). In the arguably erotic language of this scene, James subtly undercuts Ransom's later fantasy and his climactic concluding gesture; his palpitations are already—if not "always already"—implicated in a rhetoric of female homoerotic desire.

Chapter 5. Deploying Homo-Aesthetic Desire in the Tales of Writers and Artists

1. James collected these tales in volumes 15 and 16 of the New York Edition, and they became canonized as the "Stories of Writers and Artists" in F. O. Matthiessen's 1944 edition for New Directions, which included the four tales on which I shall focus, as well as "The Madonna of the Future," "Greville Fane," "The Real Thing," "The Next Time," "The Figure in the Carpet," "Broken Wings," and "The Story in It."

2. Several scholars have examined the sources for "The Author of Beltraffio," as well as the aesthetic issues the story raises. The most extensive background study is still the one by Viola Hopkins Winner, who argues that Mark Ambient represents a composite of Rossetti, Symonds, Pater, Flaubert, and James himself ("Artist" *passim.*). See also Samuel Pickering and Jonathan Freedman (144–45).

3. Leland Monk notes the prophylactic strategies of the story, "with its multiple identifications and displacements, carefully disposed within the heterosexual matrix of marriage/family/children." These allow James "both to explore intensely eroticized male bonds and to repudiate those desires as perverse and pathological" (248). The triangulation of relationships in "Beltraffio" also lends itself to the model Kaja Silverman uses in *Male Subjectivity at the Margins*, in which the doubly gendered position of the primal scene "opens onto both the positive or heterosexual, and the negative or homosexual versions of the Oedipus complex" (165).

4. As Monk observes, "The dying boy, infected with a febrile aestheticism and seemingly interchangeable with Mark Ambient's literary production, is (at least until his mother permanently removes him from that economy of exchange) the beautiful and ephemeral object of desire for this storytelling art lover [the narrator]; in every sense of the phrase, *the narrator wants to have Mark Ambient's child*" (254).

5. Shlomith Rimmon considers "Lesson" James's "first fully ambiguous story" because readers can finally make no choice between the two mutually exclusive alternatives—the "story of rivalry" and the "story of salvation" (79). Most critics, however, line up on one side or the other of the marriage question. Adeline Tintner considers St. George to be Paul's "true savior" (125) and "speaks for Henry James" (126) in valorizing a total commitment to art. Peter Barry in contrast defends Mrs. St. George and concludes that the tale does not finally oppose art and life or depict marriage negatively. Vivienne Miller claims that the story represents Paul's "permanent, total estrangement" from ordinary life, including marriage (10), and thus encourages our condemnation of St. George's advice (17). Richard Hocks reminds us of the tale's "softly humorous vein," which "includes the univer-

sal case of the rookie who is outfoxed by the veteran," but he concludes that James once again complicates the "vexing question of the mutual demands of art and life" rather than simply sets forth an "artistic dictum" through the Master (51).

6. In his brilliant Study of Herman Melville's *Pierre; or, The Ambiguities* (1852), Creech defines a textual "wink" as an encoded sign that cruises the reader. "If the object of interest does not recognize that he is the object of interest, then he is, in fact, uninteresting," Creech argues. "He is not the object which the sign is hailing" (94–95).

7. James added the observation, "It locked his guest a minute as in closed throbbing arms," when he revised the tale for the New York Edition. He obviously made the decision, in other words, to stress the physical intimacy of this conversation.

8. Sara Chapman notes that St. George's "denigration of himself both as an artist and as a man is conceived in terms of sexual impotence and reveals his perception of a complex psycho-sexual exhaustion in his failure as an artist" (41), but she ignores the important sexual and aesthetic by-play between Paul and St. George. It is not so much marriage as it is the heterosexual basis of marriage that enervates St. George.

9. The Criminal Law Amendment Act of 1885, under whose terms Oscar Wilde was prosecuted, outlawed "gross indecency" between men (Schmidgall 216–17).

10. In inscribing the heterosexual play of Dencombe's imagination, James deviated from his own source for the story—his "recollection," in Sara Chapman's words, of a trip to Bournemouth with his sister Alice and her companion, Katherine Loring, in 1885. Alice was recovering there from an illness and Miss Loring, somewhat like James's Dr. Hugh, divided her time between a demanding Alice and an equally demanding sister, Louisa Loring, who was ill in London. Henry meanwhile spent pleasant "literary hours" with his friend, Robert Louis Stevenson (136 n. 1). Although he elides the homoerotic desire of the female coupling in the tale, James does certainly foreground the homoerotic desire of his male couple. For an account of the experience Chapman cites, see Strouse (239–40).

Chapter 6. The Paradox of Masochistic Manhood in The Golden Bowl

1. Hugh Stevens has begun that process by emphasizing Maggie Verver's "masochistic fantasies, figuring herself as the abused woman in a mimetic triangle of desire," as well as Adam Verver's sadistic treatment of Charlotte (49, 55).

2. Calvin Thomas's construction and deconstruction of male identity in *Male Matters* can be helpful here. Thomas stages phallocentrism on the site of abjection, although he embraces abjection, which "de-means" phallocentrism. Thomas explores the social construction of masculinity, especially male anxiety about the body and its implication of the male subject in the messy, fluid details of embodiment. From Julia Kristeva he takes the idea of *abjection*—"what disturbs identity." One of the "most productive ways of rendering phallic idealization impossible," Thomas concludes, "would be to insist on bodily masculinity, to insist on a male body that is too disorderly to rule—that is, both too disorderly to be ruled and, more important, too disorderly to allow the easy assumption of the subject position of the one who is supposed to rule" (36).

3. For Ash, Adam's "grandiose fantasy" transforms his "somewhat crass, though rational, capitalist transaction with the Prince (an exchange wherein the Ververs acquire the Prince's social self and the Prince is paid with sufficient resources to pursue his future) into a one-sided arrangement that benefits only the Ververs" ("Narcissism" 59).

4. Ash discusses Adam's "sacrifice" as "tactical"—a ploy to encourage the illusion of an "emotional separation" between father and daughter ("Narcissism" 64). "James as implied author," she argues, "positions the reader to accept the reality of a mere appearance—the semblance of a psychic dissolution of the father-daughter bond." This appearance is "blurred and robbed of conclusiveness by this secret confirmation of Maggie's narcissistic attachment to her father" (66).

5. Seltzer observes Maggie's "domestic colonialism" by way of arguing that the "ability to put oneself in the other's skin underwrites the infiltration and displacement of the other fellow" (72). "The very ability Maggie displays—her ability to stand in two places at once—indicates the instability of her own position" (73). Prince Amerigo's desire to occupy Adam's place, not only maritally but also socially and economically, similarly destabilizes his gendered subject position.

6. Deriving the terms from Max Scheler, Kaja Silverman distinguishes between "idiopathic" and "heteropathic" identification in terms that seem useful for understanding Amerigo's relation to Adam Verver. Idiopathic identification "conforms to an incorporative model," she points out, "constituting the self at the expense of the other who is in effect 'swallowed.'" Amerigo's eating Adam "alive" seems designed on his part to constitute a male self through such an act of incorporation. Heteropathic identification, on the other hand, "subscribes to an exteriorizing logic, and locates the self at the site of the other." Vicariously, like Adam, one "lives, suffers, and experiences pleasure through the other" (205)—in Adam's case, through Amerigo and his marriage to Maggie.

7. In the famous "pagoda" passage that begins volume two, Maggie herself reviews the simple relational economy that her marriage apparently established. She "had been able to marry without breaking, as she liked to put it, with her past," James notes. "She had surrendered herself to her husband without the shadow of a reserve or a condition and yet hadn't all the while given up her father by the least little inch." Indeed, marrying Amerigo has enabled an intimate male bond to emerge, as the "two men beautifully take to each other," and "nothing in her marriage" makes her happier than "this fact of its having practically given the elder, the lonelier, a new friend" (328).

8. Kairschner refers briefly to Adam Smith's theory of the "hidden hand" to characterize the "ideological distortion" in Adam Verver's representation of his wealth. The "mere suggestion that his collection multiplies by itself [see 23:140] depends upon an ideological distortion—fundamental to finance capital—that material wealth is self-generated in some ethereal realm (guided, no doubt, by Adam Smith's 'hidden hand'), rather than in the realm of production, where it is created by human labor" (189).

9. As Bauer notes, Amerigo's perception of himself under Adam's gaze is "double-voiced." His "sideward glances at Adam's language conflict with Amerigo's own attempt to reaffirm his self, not as representative object, but as sexual subject" (61).

10. My view of male cooperation is compatible with Seltzer's observation that "every exercise of power is inevitably doubly binding. To arrange and to control is to enter into a relation with one's 'adversary,' and the bond thus formed is reciprocally coercive" (70).

11. Bauer makes a very different claim about Maggie's "carnivalization of her relations." "Because carnival celebrates the joyful relativity of all relations in lieu of hierarchy," she argues, "Maggie is able to break Adam's economic and sexual power and assert her own" (78). But it seems to me that carnivalizing Amerigo's manhood fantasmatically, as Maggie does, exaggerates it and thereby subjects it to control.

12. Boone sees ambiguity in the final scene and in its gestures, noting that if the Prince decides to "spend" himself sexually, as his holding out the money-bag to Maggie might suggest and as her obvious desire to consummate their re-marriage would encourage, he will have implicated her in an "essentially masculine 'plot' of desire whose linear trajectory must inevitably curtail the 'loosening' and 'float[ing]' tide that figures her own wished-for release" (199). Bauer sees ambiguity, too, although she sees Maggie triumphing over Adam, if not necessarily over Amerigo. "With no other interpretive model, Maggie is left to invent for herself a discourse which does not shut out Amerigo's," she argues, "but does not admit her father's selfish monolithic discourse of money and sexuality back into the picture" (88). Priscilla Walton also stresses the ambiguities in Maggie's final position—the possibility that she "dreads" both submission to the Prince and the "plurality she has promoted," because in either case she loses control over narrative closure (160). Lynda Zwinger, on the other hand, claims that Maggie normalizes relations by the end of the novel, emphasizing the way she reinforces the Father's (Adam's) power, which remains "protected in its place just beyond discourse" (91), while Seltzer claims that Maggie normalizes relations by transferring power to the Prince in this final scene. He takes literally and straightforwardly the "truth" that James attributes to Maggie's awareness—that the Prince's recovered "force" causes her "pity and dread."

13. In contrast, Adam seems to retain more power in his pocket, however much his male subject position may be constructed by Maggie. To repeat the notorious figure I cited at the beginning, James notes (from Maggie's point of view) Charlotte's final abjection as she follows Adam around Fawns: "the likeness of their connexion wouldn't have been wrongly figured if [Adam] had been thought of as holding in one of his pocketed hands the end of a long silken halter looped around her beautiful neck" (24: 287). As Boone comments, this "image of male mastery" simply "underlines the role of sexual differentiation in upholding the power structure of matrimony and patriarchal society" (193).

Works Cited

Abbott, Reginald. "The Incredible Floating Man: Henry James's Lambert Strether." *Henry James Review* 11 (Fall 1990): 176–88.
Adams, James Eli. *Dandies and Desert Saints: Styles of Victorian Manhood*. Ithaca, N.Y.: Cornell University Press, 1995.
Allen, Elizabeth. *A Woman's Place in the Novels of Henry James*. New York: St. Martin's Press, 1984.
Althusser, Louis. "Ideology and Ideological State Apparatuses." *Lenin and Philosophy and Other Essays*. Trans. Ben Brewster. New York: Monthly Review Press, 1971. 127–86.
Anderson, Charles R. "James's Portrait of the Southerner." *American Literature* 27 (1955): 309–31.
Armstrong, Paul B. *The Challenge of Bewilderment: Understanding and Representation in James, Conrad, and Ford*. Ithaca, N.Y.: Cornell University Press, 1987.
Ash, Beth Sharon. "Frail Vessels and Vast Designs: A Psychoanalytic Portrait of Isabel Archer." In *New Essays on* The Portrait of a Lady, ed. Joel Porte. New York: Cambridge University Press, 1990. 123–62.
———. "Narcissism and the Gilded Image: A Psychoanalytic Reading of *The Golden Bowl*." *Henry James Review* 15 (Winter 1994): 55–90.
Auchincloss, Louis. *Reading Henry James*. Minneapolis: University of Minnesota Press, 1975.
Banta, Martha. *Failure and Success in America: A Literary Debate*. Princeton, N.J.: Princeton University Press, 1978.
Barry, Peter. "In Fairness to the Master's Wife: A Re-interpretation of the Lesson of the Master." *Studies in Short Fiction* 15 (1978): 385–89.
Bauer, Dale M. *Feminist Dialogics: A Theory of Failed Community*. Albany: State University of New York Press, 1988.
Bell, Ian F. A. "The Curious Case of Doctor Prance." *Henry James Review* 10 (1989): 32–41.
Bergman, David. *Gaiety Transfigured: Gay Self-Representation in American Literature*. Madison: University of Wisconsin Press, 1991.
Bersani, Leo. *A Future for Astyanax: Character and Desire in Literature*. Boston: Little, Brown, 1976.
Boone, Joseph Allen. *Tradition Counter Tradition: Love and the Form of Fiction*. Chicago: University of Chicago Press, 1987.
Bordo, Susan. "Reading the Male Body." In *The Male Body: Features, Destinies, Exposures*, ed. Laurence Goldstein. Ann Arbor: University of Michigan Press, 1994. 265–306.
Bullough, Vern L., and Bonnie Bullough. *Cross Dressing, Sex, and Gender*. Philadelphia: University of Pennsylvania Press, 1993.

Butler, Judith. *Gender Trouble: Feminism and the Subversion of Identity*. New York: Routledge, 1990.
Cannon, Kelly. *Henry James and Masculinity: The Man at the Margins*. New York: St. Martin's Press, 1994.
Cargill, Oscar. *The Novels of Henry James*. New York: Macmillan, 1961.
Chapman, Sara S. *Henry James's Portrait of the Writer as Hero*. New York: St. Martin's Press,1989.
Chauncey, George. *Gay New York: Gender, Urban Culture, and the Making of the Gay Male World, 1890–1940*. New York: Basic Books, 1994.
Cohen, Ed. *Talk on the Wilde Side: Toward a Genealogy of a Discourse on Male Sexualities*. New York: Routledge, 1993.
Cooper, Michael A. "Discipl(in)ing the Master, Mastering the Discipl(in)e: Erotonomies in James' Tales of Literary Life." In *Engendering Men: The Question of Male Feminist Criticism*, ed. Jospeh A. Boone and Michael Cadden. New York: Routledge: 1990. 66–83.
Corse, Sandra. "Henry James on Eliot and Sand." *South Atlantic Review* 51 (1986): 57–68.
Creech, James. *Closet Writing/Gay Reading: The Case of Melville's* Pierre. Chicago: University of Chicago Press, 1993.
Deleuze, Gilles. *Masochism:* Coldness and Cruelty *and* Venus in Furs. Trans. Jean McNeil. New York: Zone Books, 1991.
Dellamora, Richard. *Masculine Desire: The Sexual Politics of Victorian Aestheticism*. Chapel Hill: University of North Carolina Press, 1990.
Derrick, Scott S. *Monumental Anxieties: Homoerotic Desire and Feminine Influence in 19th-Century U.S. Literature*. New Brunswick, N.J.: Rutgers University Press, 1997.
Dickinson, Emily. "My Life had stood - a Loaded Gun." *The Poems of Emily Dickinson*. Ed. R. W. Franklin. 3 vols. Cambridge, Mass.: Belknap Press of Harvard University Press, 1998. 2: 722–23.
Dixon, Thomas, Jr. *The Leopard's Spots: A Romance of the White Man's Burden, 1865–1900*. New York: Doubleday, Page, 1903.
Doane, Janice, and Devon Hodges. *Nostalgia and Sexual Difference: The Resistance to Contemporary Feminism*. New York: Methuen, 1987.
Dollimore, Jonathan. *Sexual Dissidence: Augustine to Wilde, Freud to Foucault*. New York: Oxford University Press, 1991.
Douglass, Frederick. *The Life and Writings of Frederick Douglass*. Ed. Philip S. Foner. 5 vols. New York: International Publishers, 1950–75.
———. *Narrative of the Life of Frederick Douglass, an American Slave*. Ed. Houston A. Baker, Jr. New York: Penguin, 1982.
Dwight, H. G. "Henry James—'in his own country'" (1907). In *Henry James: The Critical Heritage*, ed. Roger Gard. New York: Barnes and Noble, 1968. 432–49.
Edel, Leon. *Henry James: A Life*. New York: Harper and Row, 1985.
———. *The Master: 1901–1916*. New York: Lippincott, 1972. Vol. 5 of *The Life of Henry James*. 5 vols. 1953–72.
Ellis, Havelock. *Studies in the Psychology of Sex: Sexual Inversion* (1906). Honolulu: University Press of the Pacific, 2001.
Ellmann, Richard. "Henry James Among the Aesthetes." *Proceedings of the British Academy* 69 (1983): 209–28.
Emerick, Ronald. "The Love Rectangle in *Roderick Hudson*: Another Look at Christina Light." *Studies in the Novel* 18 (1986): 353–66.
Fetterley, Judith. *The Resisting Reader: A Feminist Approach to American Fiction*. Bloomington: Indiana University Press, 1978.

Foucault, Michel. *The History of Sexuality*. Vol. 1: *An Introduction*. Trans. Robert Hurley. New York: Vintage, 1990.
Fowler, Virginia C. *Henry James's American Girl: The Embroidery on the Canvas*. Madison: University of Wisconsin Press, 1984.
Franchot, Jenny. "The Punishment of Esther: Frederick Douglass and the Construction of the Feminine." In *Frederick Douglass: New Literary and Historical Essays*, ed. Eric J. Sundquist. New York: Cambridge University Press, 1990. 141–65.
Freedman, Jonathan. *Professions of Taste: Henry James, British Aestheticism, and Commodity Culture*. Stanford, Calif.: Stanford University Press, 1990.
Gallop, Jane. *The Daughter's Seduction*. Ithaca, N. Y.: Cornell University Press, 1982.
Gard, Roger, ed. *Henry James and the Critical Heritage*. London: Routledge, 1968.
Gifford, James. *Dayneford's Library: American Homosexual Writing, 1900–1913*. Amherst: University of Massachusetts Press, 1995.
Gilbert, Sandra M., and Susan Gubar. *The War of the Words*. Vol. 1 of *No Man's Land: The Place of the Woman Writer in the Twentieth Century*. 3 vols. New Haven, Conn: Yale University Press, 1988.
Gilmore, Michael T. "The Commodity World of *The Portrait of a Lady*." *New England Quarterly* 59 (1986): 51–74.
Graham, Wendy. *Henry James's Thwarted Love*. Stanford, Calif.: Stanford University Press, 1999.
Griffin, Susan M. "Scar Texts: Tracing the Marks of Jamesian Masculinity." *Arizona Quarterly* 53, 4 (Winter 1997): 61–82.
Habegger, Alfred. *Gender, Fantasy, and Realism in American Literature*. New York: Columbia University Press, 1982.
———. *Henry James and the "Woman Business"*. New York: Cambridge University Press, 1989.
Hall, Richard. "Leon Edel Discusses Richard Hall's Theory of Henry James and the Incest Taboo." *Advocate* (September 20, 1979): 49–53.
Halperin, David. "Sex Before Sexuality: Pederasty, Politics, and Power in Classical Athens." In *Hidden from History: Reclaiming the Gay and Lesbian Past*, ed. Martin Duberman, Martha Vicinus, and George Chauncey, Jr. New York: Meridian, 1989. 37–53.
Haralson, Eric. "James's *The American*: A (New)man Is Being Beaten." *American Literature* 64 (1992): 475–96.
———. "Lambert Strether's Excellent Adventure." *The Cambridge Companion to Henry James*, ed. Jonathan Freedman. New York: Cambridge University Press, 1998. 169–86.
Hayes, Kevin J., ed. *Henry James: The Contemporary Reviews*. New York: Cambridge University Press, 1996.
Heilbrun, Carolyn. *Writing a Woman's Life*. New York: Norton, 1988.
Henke, Richard. "The Embarrassment of Melodrama: Masculinity in the Early James." *Novel* 28 (1995): 257–83.
———. "The Man of Action: Henry James and the Performance of Gender." *Henry James Review* 16 (1995): 227–41.
Hocks, Richard A. *Henry James: A Study of the Short Fiction*. Boston: Twayne, 1990.
Holland, Laurence B. *The Expense of Vision: Essays on the Craft of Henry James*. 1964. Reprint. Baltimore: Johns Hopkins University Press, 1982.
Horvath, Brooke K. "The Life of Art, the Art of Life: The Ascetic Aesthetics of Defeat in James's *Stories of Writers and Artists*." *Modern Fiction Studies* 28 (1982): 93–107.

James, Henry. *The Ambassadors*. New York: Scribner's, 1909. Vols. 21–22 of *The Novels and Tales of Henry James*. 26 vols. 1907–17.
———. *The American*. 1879. New York: Penguin, 1981.
———. *The American*. 1907. New York: Scribner's, 1907. Vol. 2 of *The Novels and Tales of Henry James*. 26 vols. 1907–17.
———. *The American Scene. Collected Travel Writings: Great Britain and America*. New York: Library of America, 1993. 353–736.
———. *The Art of the Novel*. New York: Scribner's, 1934.
———. "The Aspern Papers." *The Aspern Papers and The Turn of the Screw*. Ed. Anthony Curtis. New York: Penguin, 1984.
———. "The Author of Beltraffio." *The Figure in the Carpet and Other Stories*. Ed. Frank Kermode. New York: Penguin, 1986. 57–112.
———. *Autobiography*. Ed. Frederick W. Dupree. Princeton, N.J.: Princeton University Press, 1983.
———. *The Bostonians*. New York: Penguin, 1984.
———. *The Complete Notebooks of Henry James*. Ed. Leon Edel and Lyall H. Powers. New York: Oxford University Press, 1987.
———. *Dearly Beloved Friends: Henry James's Letters to Younger Men*, ed. Susan E. Gunter and Steven H. Jobe. Ann Arbor: University of Michigan Press, 2001.
———. "The Death of the Lion." *The Figure in the Carpet and Other Stories*. Ed. Frank Kermode. New York: Penguin, 1986. 259–303.
———. "The Figure in the Carpet." *The Figure in the Carpet and Other Stories*. Ed. Frank Kermode. New York: Penguin, 1986. 357–400.
———. "George Sand." *Galaxy* July 1877. Reprint in *Literary Criticism: French Writers, Other European Writers, The Prefaces to the New York Edition*. Ed. Leon Edel. New York: Library of America, 1984. 708–34.
———. "George Sand: The New Life" (1902). *Literary Criticism: French Writers, Other European Writers, The Prefaces to the New York Edition*. Ed. Leon Edel. New York: Library of America, 1984. 755–775.
———. *The Golden Bowl*. New York: Scribner's, 1909. Vols. 23–24 of *The Novels and Tales of Henry James*. 26 vols. 1907–17.
———. "Guy de Maupassant." *Fortnightly Review* March 1888. Reprint in *Literary Criticism: French Writers, Other European Writers, The Prefaces to the New York Edition*. Ed. Leon Edel. New York: Library of America, 1984. 521–49.
———. *Henry James Amato Ragazzo: Lettere a Hendrik C. Andersen 1899–1915*. Ed. Rosella Mamoli Zorzi. Venice: Marsilio, 2000.
———. *Henry James Letters*. Ed. Leon Edel. 4 vols. Cambridge, Mass.: Belknap Press of Harvard University Press, 1974.
———. "Honoré de Balzac." 1875. *Literary Criticism: French Writers, Other European Writers, The Prefaces to the New York Edition*. Ed. Leon Edel. New York: Library of America, 1984. 31–68.
———. "Honoré de Balzac, 1902." *Literary Criticism: French Writers, Other European Writers, The Prefaces to the New York Edition*. Ed. Leon Edel. New York: Library of America, 1984. 90–115.
———. "Hugh Merrow." *The Complete Notebooks of Henry James*. Ed. Leon Edel and Lyall H. Powers. New York: Oxford University Press, 1987. 589–96.
———. "The Lesson of Balzac." *Literary Criticism: French Writers, Other European Writers, The Prefaces to the New York Edition*. Ed. Leon Edel. New York: Library of America, 1984. 115–139.
———. "The Lesson of the Master." 1888. Vol. 7 of *The Complete Tales of Henry James*. Ed. Leon Edel. 12 vols. New York: Lippincott, 1963. 213–84.

———. "The Lesson of the Master." 1909. New York: Scribner's, 1909. Vol. 15 of *The Novels and Tales of Henry James*. 26 vols. 1907–17. 3–96.

———. "Letter from Paris: George Sand." *New York Tribune*, 22 July 1876. *Literary Criticism: French Writers, Other European Writers, The Prefaces to the New York Edition*. Ed. Leon Edel. New York: Library of America, 1984. 702–08.

———. "The Middle Years." *The Figure in the Carpet and Other Stories*. Ed. Frank Kermode. New York: Penguin, 1986. 235–58.

———. *The Portrait of a Lady*. 1881. New York: Vintage Books/Library of America, 1992.

———. *The Portrait of a Lady*. New York: Scribner's, 1908. Vols. 3–4 of *The Novels and Tales of Henry James*. 26 vols. 1907–17.

———. *The Reverberator*. New York: Scribner's, 1909. Vol. 13 of *The Novels and Tales of Henry James*. 26 vols. 1907–17. 3–211.

———. Review of *Biographie de Alfred de Musset: Sa vie et ses oeuvres*, by Paul de Musset. 1877. *Literary Criticism: French Writers, Other European Writers, The Prefaces to the New York Edition*. Ed. Leon Edel. New York: Library of America, 1984. 596–618.

———. Review of *George Sand: Sa vie et ses oeuvres*, vol. 3, by Wladimir Karénine, 1914. *Literary Criticism: French Writers, Other European Writers, The Prefaces to the New York Edition*. Ed. Leon Edel. New York: Library of America, 1984. 775–798.

———. *Roderick Hudson*. New York: Scribner's, 1907. Vol. 1 of *The Novels and Tales of Henry James*. 26 vols. 1907–17.

———. "She and He: Recent Documents" (1897). *Literary Criticism: French Writers, Other European Writers, The Prefaces to the New York Edition*. Ed. Leon Edel. New York: Library of America, 1984. 736–755.

———. *Watch and Ward*. New York: Grove Press, 1959.

James, William. *The Correspondence of William James*. Ed. Ignas K. Skrupskelis and Elizabeth M. Berkeley. Vol. 1: *William and Henry, 1861–1884*. Charlottesville: University Press of Virginia, 1992.

Kahane, Claire. "Hysteria, Feminism, and the Case of *The Bostonians*." In *Feminism and Psychoanalysis*, ed. Richard Feldstein and Judith Roof. Ithaca, N. Y.: Cornell University Press, 1989. 280–297.

Kairschner, Mimi. "The Traces of Capitalist Patriarchy in the Silences of *The Golden Bowl*." *Henry James Review* 5 (1984): 187–92.

Kaplan, Fred. *Henry James: The Imagination of Genius*. New York: William Morrow, 1992.

Kaston, Carren. *Imagination and Desire in the Novels of Henry James*. New Brunswick, N.J.: Rutgers University Press, 1984.

Katz, Jonathan Ned. *Love Stories: Sex between Men before Homosexuality*. Chicago: University of Chicago Press, 2001.

Kennedy, Hubert C. "The 'Third Sex' Theory of Karl Heinrich Ulrichs." *Journal of Homosexuality* 6 (Fall–Winter 1980–81): 103–12.

Kimmel, Michael S. *Manhood in America: A Cultural History*. New York: Free Press, 1996.

Kramer, David. "Masculine Rivalry in *The Bostonians*: Henry James and the Rhetoric of 'Newspaper Making.'" *Henry James Review* 19 (1998): 139–47.

Lane, Christopher. "The Impossibility of Seduction in James's *Roderick Hudson* and *The Tragic Muse*." *American Literature* 68 (1996): 739–64.

———. "Jamesian Inscrutability." *Henry James Review* 20 (Fall 1999): 244–54.

Lebowitz, Naomi. *The Imagination of Loving: Henry James's Legacy to the Novel*. Detroit: Wayne State University Press, 1965.

Leverenz, David. *Manhood and the American Renaissance*. Ithaca, N.Y.: Cornell University Press, 1989.

Litvak, Joseph. *Caught in the Act: Theatricality in the Nineteenth-Century English Novel.* Berkeley: University of California Press, 1992.

Lubin, David M. *Act of Portrayal: Eakins, Sargent, James.* New Haven, Conn.: Yale University Press, 1985.

Luciano, Dana. "Invalid Relations: Queer Kinship in Henry James's *The Portrait of a Lady.*" *Henry James Review* 23 (2002): 196–217.

MacKenzie, Gordene Olga. *Transgender Nation.* Bowling Green, Oh.: Bowling Green State University Popular Press, 1994.

Mackenzie, Manfred. *Communities of Love and Honor in Henry James.* Cambridge, Mass.: Harvard University Press, 1976.

Maglin, Nan Bauer. "Fictional Feminists in *The Bostonians* and *The Odd Women.*" In *Images of Women in Literature: Feminist Perspectives*, ed. Susan Koppelman Cornillon. Bowling Green, Oh.: Bowling Green State University Popular Press, 1972.

Martin, Robert K. "Failed Heterosexuality in *The Portrait of a Lady.*" In *Henry James and Homo-Erotic Desire*, ed. John R. Bradley. New York: St. Martin's Press, 1999. 87–92.

———. *Hero, Captain, and Stranger: Male Friendship, Social Critique, and Literary Form in the Sea Novels of Herman Melville.* Chapel Hill: University of North Carolina Press, 1986.

———. "The 'High Felicity' of Comradeship: A New Reading of *Roderick Hudson.*" *American Literary Realism* 11 (1978): 100–108.

———. "Knights-Errant and Gothic Seducers: The Representation of Male Friendship in Mid-Nineteenth-Century America." In *Hidden from History: Reclaiming the Gay and Lesbian Past*, ed. Martin Duberman, Martha Vicinus, and George Chauncey, Jr. New York: Meridian, 1989. 169–82.

Mazzella, Anthony J. "The New Isabel." *The Portrait of a Lady: An Authoritative Text, Henry James and the Novel, Reviews and Criticism*, ed. Robert D. Bamberg. New York: Norton, 1975. 597–619.

McColley, Kathleen. "Claiming Center Stage: Speaking out for Homoerotic Empowerment in *The Bostonians.*" *Henry James Review* 21 (Spring 2000): 151–69.

McWhirter, David. "Restaging the Hurt: Henry James and the Artist as Masochist." *Texas Studies in Literature and Language* 33 (Winter 1991): 464–91.

Miller, Elise. "The Marriages of Henry James and Henrietta Stackpole." *Henry James Review* 10 (1989): 15–31.

Miller, Nancy K. "'I's' in Drag: The Sex of Recollection." *Eighteenth Century* 22 (1981): 47–57.

Miller, Vivienne. "Henry James and the Alienation of the Artist: 'The Lesson of the Master.'" *English Studies in Africa* 23 (1980): 9–20.

Milliman, Craig A. "The Dangers of Fiction: Henry James's 'The Lesson of the Master.'" *Studies in Short Fiction* 27 (1990): 81–88.

———. "The Fiction of Art: Roderick Hudson's Pursuit of the Ideal." *Henry James Review* 15 (1994): 231–41.

Mitchell, Lee Clark. "A Marriage of Opposites: Oxymorons, Ethics, and James's *The American.*" *Henry James Review* 19 (1998): 1–16.

Mitchell, Mark, and David Leavitt, eds. *Pages Passed from Hand to Hand: The Hidden Tradition of Homosexual Literature in English from 1748 to 1914.* Boston: Houghton Mifflin, 1997.

Monk, Leland. "A Terrible Beauty Is Born: Henry James, Asetheticism, and Homosexual Panic." In *Bodies of Writing, Bodies in Performance*, ed. Thomas Foster, Carol Siegel, and Ellen E. Berry. New York: New York University Press, 1996. 247–65.

Moon, Michael. *A Small Boy and Others: Imitation and Initiation in American Culture from Henry James to Andy Warhol.* Durham, N.C.: Duke University Press, 1998.

Morgan, Thaïs E. "Male Lesbian Bodies: The Construction of Alternative Masculinities in Courbet, Baudelaire, and Swinburne." *Genders* 15 (1992): 37–57.

Murtaugh, Daniel J. "An Emotional Reflection: Sexual Realization in Henry James's Revisions to *Roderick Hudson.*" *Henry James Review* 17 (Spring 1996): 182–203.

Neely, Mark E., Jr., Harold Holzer, and Gabor S. Boritt. *The Confederate Image: Prints of the Lost Cause.* Chapel Hill: University of North Carolina Press, 1987.

O'Connor, Dennis L. "Intimacy and Spectatorship in *The Portrait of a Lady.*" *Henry James Review* 2 (1980): 25–35.

Ozick, Cynthia. "A Master's Mind." *New York Times Magazine,* October 26, 1986, 52–54.

Pater, Walter. *The Renaissance: Studies in Art and Poetry.* London: Macmillan, 1910.

Person, Leland S. "Falling into Heterosexuality: Sculpting Male Bodies in *The Marble Faun* and *Roderick Hudson.*" *Roman Holidays: American Writers and Artists in Nineteenth-Century Italy,* ed. Robert K. Martin and Leland S. Person. Iowa City: University of Iowa Press, 2002. 107–39.

———. "Henry James, George Sand, and the Suspense of Masculinity." *PMLA* 106 (May 1991): 515–528.

Pickering, Samuel F. "The Sources of 'The Author of Beltraffio.'" *Arizona Quarterly* 29 (1973): 177–90.

Poirier, Richard. *The Comic Sense of Henry James: A Study of the Early Novels.* New York: Oxford University Press, 1967.

Porter, Carolyn. "Gender and Value in *The American.*" In *New Essays on* The American, ed. Martha Banta. New York: Cambridge University Press, 1987. 99–129.

Posnock, Ross. *The Trial of Curiosity: Henry James, William James, and the Challenge of Modernity.* New York: Oxford University Press, 1991.

Probert, K. G. "Christopher Newman and the Artistic American View of Life." *Studies in American Fiction* 11 (1983): 203–216.

Rimmon, Shlomith. *The Concept of Ambiguity—The Example of James.* Chicago: University of Chicago Press, 1977.

Rosenberg, Charles E. "Sexuality, Class and Role in 19th-Century America." *American Quarterly* 25 (1973): 131–53.

Rotundo, Anthony. *American Manhood: Transformations in Masculinity from the Revolution to the Modern Era.* New York: Basic Books, 1993.

———. "Body and Soul: Changing Ideals of American Middle-Class Manhood, 1770–1920." *Journal of Social History* 16, 4 (1983): 23–38.

———. "Learning About Manhood: Gender Ideals and the Middle-Class Family in Nineteenth-Century America." In *Manliness and Morality: Middle-Class Masculinity in Britain and America, 1800–1940,* ed. J. A. Mangan and James Walvin. Manchester: Manchester University Press, 1987. 35–51.

Rowe, John Carlos. *The Other Henry James.* Durham, N.C.: Duke University Press, 1998.

———. "The Politics of the Uncanny: Newman's Fate in *The American.*" *Henry James Review* 8 (1987): 79–90.

———. *The Theoretical Dimensions of Henry James.* Madison: University of Wisconsin Press, 1984.

Samuels, Charles Thomas. *The Ambiguity of Henry James.* Urbana: University of Illinois Press, 1971.

Sarotte, Georges-Michel. *Like a Brother, Like a Lover: Male Homosexuality in the American *Novel and Theater from Herman Melville to James Baldwin.* Trans. Richard Miller. Garden City, N.Y.: Doubleday, 1978.

Saum, Lewis O. "Henry James's Christopher Newman: 'The American' as Westerner." *Henry James Review* 15 (Winter 1994): 1–9.

Savoy, Eric. "Embarrassments: Figure in the Closet." *Henry James Review* 20 (Fall 1999): 227–36.

———. "Hypocrite Lecteur: Walter Pater, Henry James and Homotextual Politics." *Dalhousie Review* 72 (Spring 1992): 11–36.

Schmidgall, Gary. *The Stranger Wilde: Interpreting Oscar.* New York: Dutton, 1994.

Schmitz, Neil. "Mark Twain, Henry James, and Jacksonian Dreaming." *Criticism* 27 (1985): 155–73.

Secor, Robert. "Christopher Newman: How Innocent Is James's American?" *Studies in American Fiction* 1 (1973): 141–53.

Sedgwick, Eve Kosofsky. *Between Men: English Literature and Male Homosocial Desire.* New York: Columbia University Press, 1985.

———. *Epistemology of the Closet.* Berkeley: University of California Press, 1990.

———. "'Gosh Boy George, You Must Be Awfully Secure in Your Masculinity.'" In *Constructing Masculinity*, ed. Maurice Berger, Brian Willis, and Simon Watson. New York: Routledge, 1995. 11–20.

———. "Shame and Performativity: Henry James's New York Edition Prefaces." In *Henry James's New York Edition: The Construction of Authorship*, ed. David McWhirter. Stanford, Calif.: Stanford University Press, 1995. 206–39.

———. *Tendencies.* Durham, N.C.: Duke University Press, 1993.

Seltzer, Mark. *Henry James and the Art of Power.* Ithaca, N.Y.: Cornell University Press, 1984.

———. "Physical Capital: *The American* and the Realist Body." *New Essays on* The American, ed. Martha Banta. New York: Cambridge University Press, 1987. 131–67.

Sensibar, Judith L. "The Politics of Hysteria in *The Bostonians*." *South Central Review* 8, 2 (1991): 57–72.

Showalter, Elaine. "The Other Bostonians: Gender and Literary Study." *Yale Journal of Criticism* 1, 2 (1988): 179–87.

Sicker, Philip. *Love and the Quest for Identity in the Fiction of Henry James.* Princeton, N.J.: Princeton University Press, 1980.

Silber, Nina. "Intemperate Men, Spiteful Women, and Jefferson Davis: Northern Views of the Defeated South." *American Quarterly* 41 (1989): 614–35.

Silverman, Kaja. *Male Subjectivity at the Margins.* New York: Routledge, 1992.

Smith, Stephanie A. "The Delicate Organisms and Theoretic Tricks of Henry James." *American Literature* 62 (1990): 583–605.

Sofer, Nomi Z. "Why 'different vibrations . . . walk hand in hand': Homosocial Bonds in *Roderick Hudson*." *Henry James Review* 20 (Spring 1999): 185–205.

Stambaugh, Sara. "The Aesthetic Movement and *The Portrait of a Lady*." *Nineteenth-Century Fiction* 30 (1976): 495–510.

Stevens, Hugh. *Henry James and Sexuality.* New York: Cambridge University Press, 1998.

Strouse, Jean. *Alice James: A Biography.* Boston: Houghton Mifflin, 1980.

Sundquist, Eric J. *To Wake the Nations: Race in the Making of American Literature.* Cambridge, Mass.: Harvard University Press, 1993.

Symonds, John Addington. "A Problem in Modern Ethics." *Sexual Inversion.* 1928. New York: Bell, 1984.

Taylor, William R. *Cavalier and Yankee: The Old South and American National Character.* Garden City, N.Y.: Doubleday, 1963.

Thomas, Calvin. *Male Matters: Masculinity, Anxiety, and the Male Body on the Line.* Urbana: University of Illinois Press, 1996.
Thomas, Brook. "The Construction of Privacy in and around *The Bostonians.*" *American Literature* 64 (1992): 719–47.
Thomson, Patricia. *George Sand and the Victorians: Her Influence and Reputation in Nineteenth-Century England.* London: Macmillan, 1977.
Tintner, Adeline R. "Iconic Analogy in 'The Lesson of the Master': Henry James's Legend of St. George and the Dragon." *Journal of Narrative Technique* 5 (1975): 116–27.
Torsney, Cheryl. "Henry James, Charles Sanders Peirce, and the Fat Capon: Homoerotic Desire in *The American.*" *Henry James Review* 14 (1993): 166–78.
———. "Specula(riza)tion in *The Golden Bowl.*" *Henry James Review* 12 (1991): 141–46.
———. "Translation and Transubstantiation in *The American.*" *Henry James Review* 17 (1996): 40–51.
Trilling, Lionel. *The Opposing Self: Nine Essays in Criticism.* New York: Viking, 1955. 104–17.
Twain, Mark. *Adventures of Huckleberry Finn.* Ed. Walter Blair and Victor Fischer. Berkeley: University of California Press, 1985.
———. *Pudd'nhead Wilson* and *Those Extraordinary Twins.* Ed. Sidney E. Berger. New York: Norton, 1980.
Van Ghent, Dorothy. *The English Novel: Form and Function* (1953). New York: Harper & Row, 1967.
Van Leer, David. "A World of Female Friendship: *The Bostonians.*" In *Henry James and Homo-Erotic Desire*, ed. John R. Bradley. New York: St. Martin's Press, 1999. 93–109.
Veeder, William. "The Feminine Orphan and the Emergent Master: Self-Realization in Henry James." *Henry James Review* 12 (1991): 20–54.
———. *Henry James—The Lessons of the Master: Popular Fiction and Personal Style in the Nineteenth Century.* Chicago: University of Chicago Press, 1975.
———. "The Portrait of a Lack." In *New Essays on* The Portrait of a Lady, ed. Joel Porte. New York: Cambridge University Press, 1990. 95–121.
Walton, Priscilla L. *The Disruption of the Feminine in Henry James.* Toronto: University of Toronto Press, 1992.
Wardley, Lynn. "Woman's Voice, Democracy's Body, and *The Bostonians.*" *ELH* 56 (1989): 639–665.
Warren, Joyce W. *The American Narcissus: Individualism and Women in Nineteenth-Century American Fiction.* New Brunswick, N.J.: Rutgers University Press, 1984.
Warren, Kenneth. *Black and White Strangers: Race and American Literary Realism.* Chicago: University of Chicago Press, 1993.
Weeks, Jeffrey. "Inverts, Perverts, and Mary-Annes: Male Prostitution and the Regulation of Homosexuality in England in the Nineteenth and Early Twentieth Centuries." In *Hidden from History: Reclaiming the Gay and Lesbian Past*, ed. Martin Duberman, Martha Vicinus, and George Chauncey, Jr. New York: Meridian, 1989. 195–211.
Weisbuch, Robert. *Atlantic Double-Cross: American Literature and British Influence in the Age of Emerson.* Chicago: University of Chicago Press, 1986.
White, Robert. "Love, Marriage, and Divorce: The Matter of Sexuality in *The Portrait of a Lady.*" *Henry James Review* 7, 2–3 (1986): 59–71.
Whitman, Walt. "Song of Myself" (1855). *Leaves of Grass.* Ed. Malcolm Cowley. New York: Penguin, 1959.

Wiesenfarth, Joseph. "A Woman in *The Portrait of a Lady.*" *Henry James Review* 7, 2–3 (1986): 18–28.
Wilde, Oscar. *The Picture of Dorian Gray* (1891). Ed. Norman Page. Peterborough: Broadview Press, 1998.
Williamson, Joel. *New People: Miscegenation and Mulattos in the United States.* New York: Free Press, 1980.
Wilson, James D. "The Gospel According to Christopher Newman." *Studies in American Fiction* 3 (1975): 83–88.
Wilson, R. B. J. *Henry James's Ultimate Narrative:* The Golden Bowl. St. Lucia: University of Queensland Press, 1981.
Wilt, Judith. "Desperately Seeking Verena: A Resistant Reading of *The Bostonians.*" *Feminist Studies* 13 (1987): 293–316.
Winner, Viola Hopkins. "The Artist and the Man in 'The Author of Beltraffio.'" *PMLA* 83 (1968): 102–8.
Woods, Gregory. "The Art of Friendship in *Roderick Hudson.*" In *Henry James and Homo-Erotic Desire*, ed. John R. Bradley. New York: St. Martin's Press, 1999. 69–77.
Wyatt-Brown, Bertram. *Southern Honor: Ethics and Behavior in the Old South.* New York: Oxford University Press, 1982.
Zwinger, Lynda. "The Sentimental Gilt of Heterosexuality: James's *The Golden Bowl.*" *Raritan* 7 (1987): 70–92.

Index

Boldface indicates primary discussions.

Abbott, Reginald, 177–78 n. 20
Adams, James Eli, 36, 93, 183 n. 3, 184 n. 10
Allen, Elizabeth, 5, 93–94, 157
Althusser, Louis, 106–7
Andersen, Hendrik, 10, 12–13, 48, 57, 135, 156, 179 n. 11, 180 n. 20
Anderson, Charles R., 187 n. 12
Armstrong, Paul B., 27
Ash, Beth Sharon, 9, 95, 151, 153, 189 n. 3, 190 n. 4
Auchincloss, Louis, 187 n. 12

Balzac, Honoré de, 2, 21–24, 25, 32, 33, 34, 113–14, 115, 145, 177 n. 13
Banta, Martha, 84, 181 n. 3, 182 n. 14, 183 n. 18
Barry, Peter, 144, 188 n. 5
Bauer, Dale, 157, 159, 161, 190 nn. 9, 11, 191 n. 12
Bell, Ian F. A., 186 n. 11
Bergman, David, 144
Bersani, Leo, 2
Boone, Joseph Allen, 172, 191 nn. 12, 13
Bordo, Susan, 180 n. 18
Bullough, Bonnie, 106
Bullough, Vern, 106
Butler, Judith, 8, 9, 16, 175 n. 5

Cannon, Kelly, 9–10, 28, 43
Cargill, Oscar, 42, 60
Chapman, Sara, 139, 141, 189 nn. 8, 9
Chauncey, George, 158, 171, 172, 177 nn. 15, 19
Cooper, Michael, 133, 135
Corse, Sandra, 19
Creech, James, 133, 189 n. 6
Cross-dressing, male, 106

Custer, George Armstrong, 69

Davis, Jefferson, 35, 117, 123, 185 n. 2
Deleuze, Gilles, 149, 155
Dellamora, Richard, 125
Derrick, Scott, 57
Dickinson, Emily, 162; "My Life had stood—a Loaded Gun," 162
Dixon, Thomas, 35, 105–6, 107, 111, 121–22; *The Leopard's Spots*, 35, 105–6, 107, 111, 121–22
Dollimore, Jonathan, 127, 130, 144, 147, 186 n. 6
Douglass, Frederick, 105, 107, 108, 111, 112, 118–19, 122; "Letter to Thomas Auld," 108, 111, 122; *Narrative of the Life of Frederick Douglass*, 105, 107, 108, 118–19
Dwight, H. G., 6

Edel, Leon, 1, 5, 10, 42, 88, 109, 132, 178 n. 2, 186 n. 7
Ellis, Havelock, 14–15
Ellman, Richard, 47, 179 n. 3
Emerick, Ronald, 42, 180 n. 16

Feminism, 19, 23, 32, 106, 110, 117, 119, 120, 187 n. 14
Feminist criticism, 4, 8, 110
Fetterley, Judith, 4, 110, 187 n. 12
Foucault, Michel, 8, 125, 175 n. 5
Fowler, Virginia, 78, 93
Franchot, Jenny, 105, 185 n. 1
Freedman, Jonathan, 44, 94, 184 n. 6, 188 n. 2
Freud, Sigmund, 6, 28, 83, 102, 149, 155, 175 n. 3
Fullerton, Morton, 10

204   Index

Gallop, Jane, 95, 181 n. 8
Gifford, James, 16, 33, 176 n. 11
Gilbert, Sandra, 4, 175 n. 1
Gilmore, Michael T., 95, 100
Gosse, Edmund, 127
Graham, Wendy, 9, 11, 45, 49, 176 n. 7, 179 nn. 4, 5
Griffin, Susan M., 180 n. 17
Gubar, Susan, 4, 175 n. 1
Gunter, Susan, 12

Habegger, Alfred, 5, 183 n. 4, 185 n. 14
Hall, Richard, 5
Halperin, David, 6–7
Haralson, Eric, 9, 25–26, 68, 69, 80, 177–78 n. 20
Henke, Richard, 9, 10, 65, 77, 178 nn. 21, 1
Hickok, Wild Bill, 69
Hocks, Richard, 141, 188 n. 5
Holland, Laurence B., 24
Horvath, Brooke, 126

James, Henry, and masculinity. *See* Masculinity
James, Henry, works
 The Ambassadors, 21, **24–34**, 53, 114, 152
 The American, 3–4, 35, **65–85**, 86, 87, 88, 89, 90, 91, 92, 93, 94, 95, 96, 100, 110, 117, 152, 156, 161, 163, 165
 The American Scene, 69
 "The Aspern Papers," 24, 63, 125–26
 "The Author of Beltraffio," 36, 109, 124, 126, **127–32**, 134, 136, 141, 143, 144, 146, 147
 "The Beast in the Jungle," 10, 30, 33, 44, 122, 131
 The Bostonians, 23, 35, 68, 70, 101, **105–23**, 152, 163, 164, 168
 "Daisy Miller," 58, 65
 "The Death of the Lion," 36, 38, 124, 136, **143–48**
 "The Figure in the Carpet," 37, 126–27
 The Golden Bowl, 36, 55, **149–74**, 181 n. 2
 "Hugh Merrow," 1, 2, 4, 16–17, 24, 33–34, 39, 52, 128, 140
 "The Lesson of the Master," 36, 124, **132–39**
 Madame de Mauves, 65
 "The Middle Years," 36, 124, **139–43**, 145
 "A Passionate Pilgrim," 65
 The Princess Casamassima, 92, 100, 101
 "The Pupil," 11

Notes of a Son and Brother, 4, 7–8, 36–37, 66
The Portrait of a Lady, 23, 35, 66, 80, 81, **86–104**, 110, 117, 151, 152, 154, 156, 158, 159, 161, 163, 164, 166, 168, 169, 172
The Reverberator, 66, 179 n. 7
Roderick Hudson, 35, **39–64**, 65, 69, 70, 78, 80, 86, 89, 90, 136, 150, 152
A Small Boy and Others, 11, 181 n. 1
Washington Square, 89
Watch and Ward, 23, 39, 184 n.7
The Wings of the Dove, 89, 104, 168
James, Henry, Sr. (father of Henry James), 36, 185 n. 14
James, William, 5, 36, 52, 176 n. 10, 185 n. 14
Jobe, Steven, 12

Kahane, Claire, 108, 187 n. 13
Kairschner, Mimi, 158, 171, 190 n. 8
Kaplan, Fred, 10, 48, 135, 179 n. 11
Kaston, Carren, 5, 88, 100
Katz, Jonathan Ned, 11–12
Kennedy, Hubert, 14
Kimmel Michael, 110
Kingsley, Charles, 69
Krafft-Ebing, Richard von, 14
Kramer, David, 186 n. 8

Lacan, Jacques, 181 n. 8
Lane, Christopher, 176 n. 6, 180 n. 19
Leavitt, David, 27
Leverenz, David, 112
Litvak, Joseph, 187 n. 18
Lubin, David, 183 n. 2
Luciano, Dana, 183 nn. 1, 4

MacKenzie, Gordene Olga, 17
Mackenzie, Manfred, 178 n. 2
Maglin, Nan Bauer, 4
Martin, Robert K., 40, 42–43, 47, 52, 57, 90, 176 n. 12, 182 n. 11, 183 n. 2
Masculinity: and androgyny, 10, 17, 20, 34, 51, 73, 166; and business model of manhood, 5, 20, 25, 36–37, 44–45, 46, 49, 51, 65, 66, 69–70, 72, 78, 88–89, 90, 112, 113, 114, 137, 151, 157–58, 159; and camp, 8–9, 13, 28, 29, 37–38, 145; and Christian Gentleman stereotype, 50, 66, 69, 74, 93, 100; and Civil War, 46, 49, 69–70, 88, 106, 113, 115, 116, 119; experiments in constructing, 7, 9, 29, 35,

42, 43, 68; and feminization, 4, 5–6, 16, 18, 21, 22, 23–24, 26, 56, 72, 73, 79, 82, 84–85, 86, 88, 91, 95, 98, 102, 106, 108, 109, 110, 111, 112, 113, 114, 115, 149–50, 151, 156, 157, 167, 168, 171; and gender indeterminacy, 18, 31, 82–83, 109, 113, 120, 122–23; and heterosexual compulsion, 10–11, 29, 30, 40, 50, 54, 55, 75, 122, 125, 131, 143, 164; and heterosexuality, 9–10, 18, 27–28, 29, 31, 32, 33, 34, 41, 50, 53–56, 67, 74, 76–77, 81–82, 85, 91, 95, 108, 109, 114–15, 119, 122, 130, 132, 133, 139, 147, 161, 163, 168, 169–70, 171; and homosexuality, 6, 7–8, 10–15, 18, 27, 28, 29–30, 31, 33, 34, 35, 40–41, 42, 43, 45, 47, 57–58, 74, 75–77, 79, 91, 95, 102, 108, 109, 113, 114–15, 122, 124–48 passim, 158, 168, 169–70; and homosocial desire, 49, 51, 72, 74, 75, 78, 81, 85, 93, 109, 112, 113, 118, 122, 129, 142, 157–58, 159, 164, 169; and inversion, gender and sexual, 6, 14–15, 28, 29, 30, 31, 32, 34, 37, 42, 56, 79, 83, 84, 86, 95, 105, 106, 108–9, 111, 115, 117, 122–23, 124, 130–31, 133–34, 147, 165, 166, 172; and lesbianism, 109–10, 113, 142; and Masculine Achiever stereotype, 50, 63, 66, 69, 74–75, 87, 93, 95, 100; and pedophilia, 131; and phallocentrism, 7, 22–23, 53, 77, 79, 80–81, 83–84, 86, 88–89, 91, 92, 95–100, 103, 107, 110–11, 115–16, 117, 118–20, 126, 130, 140, 144, 146, 150, 151, 152–53, 156, 162, 165, 166, 168–69, 172, 173; pluralization, 4, 6, 7–8, 20, 22, 24, 28, 29, 31, 34, 38, 59. 86, 88, 144, 150; and queer theory, 10–11; and sadism, 55, 105, 150, 154, 155–56, 162, 163–64, 168–69, 174; and spermatic economy, 71, 82, 84, 92, 97–98, 103–4, 130, 141–42, 144, 151–52, 159, 160, 173; and transsexuality, 16, 17, 19–20, 23, 30, 31, 91–92, 106, 122, 171. *See also* Masochism, male

Masochism: male, 26, 28, 32, 36, 43, 45, 149–50, 153, 154, 155–56, 162, 163–64, 165, 168–69, 173, 174, feminine, 150

Maupassant, Guy de, 177 n. 18

Mazella, Anthony, 88

McWhirter, David, 36, 175 n. 3

Melville, Herman, 41, 74, 96, 142, 165, 182 n. 11; "Benito Cereno," 165; *Moby-Dick*, 41, 74, 96, 142, 182 n. 11; *Pierre; or, The Ambiguities*, 189 n. 6

Mérimée, Prosper, 31

Miller, Elise, 183 n. 2

Miller, Nancy K., 119–20

Miller, Vivienne, 188 n. 5

Milliman, Craig, 134, 179 n. 12

Misogyny, 93, 105, 110, 112, 113, 115, 117

Mitchell, Lee Clark, 182 n. 15

Mitchell, Mark, 27

Monk, Leland, 188 nn. 3, 4

Moon, Michael, 9, 11, 179 n. 10

Morgan, Thaïs, 109–10

Murtaugh, Daniel, 179 n. 11

Musset, Alfred de, 22, 24, 26, 28, 30–31

O'Connor, Dennis, 94

Ozick, Cynthia, 177 n. 14

Pater, Walter, 47–48, 179 n. 3

Paulding, James Kirke, 69; *The Lion of the West*, 69

Pedophilia, 131

Peirce, Charles Sanders, 75

Perry, Thomas Sargeant, 67

Persse, Jocelyn, 10, 12, 14

Pickering, Samuel, 188 n. 2

Poe, Edgar Allan, 134, 182 n. 17; "The Purloined Letter," 134

Poirier, Richard, 44

Porter, Carolyn, 68, 70, 84, 182 n. 9

Posnock, Ross, 8–9

Probert, K. G., 181 n. 7

Proust, Marcel, 110

Queer theory, 8, 9, 11, 17–18

Reik, Theodore, 149

Rimmon, Shlomith, 188 n. 5

Rosenberg, Charles E., 41, 66, 88, 97

Rotundo, Anthony, 69, 112, 118

Rowe, John Carlos, 4, 9, 10, 121, 182 n. 12

Samuels, Charles T., 187 n. 12

Sand, George, 2, 3, 4, 16, 17, 18–25, 26, 28, 30, 32, 33, 34, 53, 59, 109, 113–14, 115, 145, 147

Sarotte, Georges-Michel, 5, 178 n. 22

Saum, Lewis O., 181 n. 4

Savoy, Eric, 36, 37–38, 129, 137, 140

Schmitz, Neil, 46, 179 n. 6

Secor, Robert, 182 n. 17

Sedgwick, Eve Kosofsky, 9, 10–11, 17, 18, 30, 37, 50, 74, 76, 81, 122, 131, 167–68, 175 n. 4, 176 n. 10, 186 n. 10
Seltzer, Mark, 150, 151, 152, 163, 171, 173, 181 n. 5, 190 nn. 5, 10, 191 n. 12
Sensibar, Judith, 117
Showalter, Elaine, 110
Sicker, Philip, 61
Silber, Nina, 114, 117, 185 n. 2
Silverman, Kaja, 6, 16, 28, 65, 99, 108, 110, 149–50, 155, 168, 187 n. 16, 188 n. 3, 190 n. 6
Smith, Stephanie, 102, 184 n. 8
Sofer, Nomi, 40–41, 63, 179 n. 13, 182 n. 13
Stambaugh, Sara, 185 n. 16
Stevens, Hugh, 9, 11, 26, 36, 43, 165, 168, 177 n. 16, 189 n. 1
Stowe, Harriet Beecher, 105; *Uncle Tom's Cabin*, 105
Sturges, Jonathan, 10
Sturgis, Howard, 10, 12, 13
Sundquist, Eric, 105, 108
Symonds, John Addington, 10, 11, 13, 14, 15, 124, 125, 126, 176 n. 9

Taylor, William, 112, 187 n. 15
Thomas, Brook, 35
Thomas, Calvin, 189 n. 2
Thompson, Patricia, 25
Tintner, Adeline, 188 n. 5
Torsney, Cheryl B., 75, 76, 77, 157, 158, 181 n. 7
Twain, Mark, 35, 105–6, 107, 186 n. 3; *Adventures of Huckleberry Finn*, 35, 105–6, 107, 186 n. 3; *Pudd'nhead Wilson*, 186 n. 3
Tyler, Royall, 69; *The Contrast*, 69

Ulrichs, Karl, 14, 15

Van Ghent, Dorothy, 94
Van Leer, David, 186 n. 4

Veeder, William, 5, 86, 87, 175 n. 2, 180 n. 15, 183 n. 1, 184 n. 11, 185 nn. 13, 14, 17
Walker, Peter, 176 n. 8
Walpole, Hugh, 12, 13–14
Walton, Priscilla L., 86, 130, 142, 165, 191 n. 12
Wardley, Lynn, 112
Warren, Joyce W., 5
Warren, Kenneth, 105, 107
Weeks, Jeffrey, 177 n. 19
Weisbuch, Robert, 94
White, Robert, 93, 184 n. 9
Whitman, Walt, 8, 41, 47, 52, 57, 67, 78, 81
Wiesenfarth, Joseph, 185 n. 15
Wilde, Oscar, 8, 11, 109, 125, 127, 128, 147, 185 n. 16, 186 n. 6, 189 n. 9; *The Picture of Dorian Gray*, 128, 142
Williamson, Joel, 107
Wilson, James D., 69
Wilson, R. B. J., 156
Wilt, Judith, 187 n. 17
Winckelmann, Johann, 47–48
Winner, Viola Hopkins, 188 n. 2
Woods, Gregory, 179 n. 8, 180 n. 14
Wyatt-Brown, Bertram, 107, 112

Zacharias, Greg, 176 n. 8
Zorzi, Rosella Mamoli, 12
Zwinger, Lynda, 156, 158, 159, 191 n. 12

Acknowledgments

Earlier versions of several parts of this book have been published previously, and I am grateful for the permission to reprint them in revised form. For the introduction I have drawn upon "Henry James, George Sand, and the Suspense of Masculinity," *PMLA* 106 (1991): 515–28, and have enjoyed the opportunity to revise and update that essay here. A much shorter version of Chapter 4 appeared as "In the Closet with Frederick Douglass: Reconstructing Masculinity in *The Bostonians,*" *Henry James Review* 16 (Fall 1995): 292–98. Part of Chapter 5 was published as "James's Homo-Aesthetics: Deploying Desire in the Tales of Writers and Artists" in the *Henry James Review* 14 (1993): 188–203, and the rest as "Reading Sexuality: The Object Lesson of James's Master" in the *Arizona Quarterly* 53, 4 (Winter 1997): 23–37. A slightly different version of Chapter 6 appeared as "Jamesian Sadomasochism: The Invisible (Third) Hand of Manhood in *The Golden Bowl,*" *Questioning the Master: Gender and Sexuality in Henry James's Writings*, ed. Peggy McCormack (Newark: University of Delaware Press, 2000), 149–75.

I feel fortunate to have participated in conversations, conferences, and writing projects with so many excellent James scholars. I want to thank Beth Sharon Ash, Martha Banta, Daniel Mark Fogel, Wendy Graham, Susan M. Griffin, Eric Haralson, David Leverenz, David McWhirter, Robert K. Martin, Julie Rivkin, John Carlos Rowe, Eric Savoy, Cheryl Torsney, Peter Walker, Priscilla Walton, and Lynda Zwinger for helping me at various stages of this project.